The Quest For The Eastern Cougar

Extinction Or Survival?

Robert Tougias

iUniverse, Inc.
Bloomington

The Quest For The Eastern Cougar
Extinction Or Survival?

iUniverse books may be ordered through booksellers or by contacting:

iUniverse
1663 Liberty Drive
Bloomington, IN 47403
www.iuniverse.com
1-800-Authors (1-800-288-4677)

ISBN: 978-1-4620-1057-8 (sc)
ISBN: 978-1-4620-1058-5 (ebk)

Printed in the United States of America

iUniverse rev. date: 08/08/2011

CONTENTS

IN MEMORY OF
MRS. ARTHUR TOUGIAS AND JOYCE FULLER WILAND

ACKNOWLEDGEMENTS

The idea of a book on cougars began many years ago with the publication of my first article in the *Daily Hampshire Gazette* of Northampton, Massachusetts. Had it not been for the enthusiasm of their editor Larry Parness, I might not have made it this far. Since that small but informative piece came two nature books and several more magazine articles.

With each cougar article came increasing knowledge that would not have been realized had it not been for the generosity of two eastern cougar experts: Dr. Jay Tischendorf and Helen McGinnis. Dr. Tischendorf and I spent countless hours analyzing all aspects of the topic. There was not one angle or piece of evidence that was not thoroughly discussed. Thank you, Jay. I could not have written this without you. Thank you for your contributing chapter on field study. Thank you for being available at each phase of this project.

In the last few months of this endeavor it was Helen McGinnis who made it all possible. Helen fine-tuned the manuscript by providing important pieces of information upon a moment's notice. Helen answered a wide variety of emails and double-checked on facts for me. She researched citations and sent many of them to me. Helen was very helpful in putting together the sections on cougar sightings. Those in the field of wildlife biology know of Helen's limitless giving. Thank you.

I sincerely acknowledge the late Dr. David Maehr who took time out of his busy schedule to review two chapters and respond with a line by line personal critique. I am grateful to Melanie Culver and Holly

Earnest for their information and answers. Dave Denoma contributed his photography of the cougars.

I really enjoyed talking with Jim Halfpenny, who provided several references and insights. I enjoyed sharing wildlife stories with Sue Morse, who loves the Vermont woods as I do. Dr. Pat Rusz also provided information from his neck of the woods. Bob Downing offered material and insights on cougars. A special thanks to Virginia Fifield for her work in the Quabbin Reservoir and for sharing it with me.

The late Ted Reed is another person who provided me with information. His words have echoed in my mind throughout this entire process, as he helped lift the bias from my view and revealed the facts about cougars in the East. I believe it was Ted who truly introduced me to the actual issue as it was in 1992.

Jim Cardoza, Tony Gola, Eric Orff, and Wally Jakubus are among many state wildlife biologists who answered phone calls, emails, and sent documents out as requested. To all of you a sincere thank you. Our state wildlife biologists never get the acknowledgement they deserve for protecting and managing our precious wildlife. On that same note, I would like to express my appreciation to Rainer Brocke and Fred Van Dyke for providing information in the early years. Rainer's contribution to the eastern cougar body-of-knowledge seems to have been taken for granted.

Mark Dowling, founder of the Cougar Network, has also been very helpful. Gilbert Allardyce responded upon a moment's notice and provided a much-needed photograph. Claudia Becker was particularly helpful with the many crude drafts, offering improvements. Dr. Nancy Eaton sacrificed many hours proof-reading in the final stages. Valerie Vaughan was equally helpful in applying her knowledge as an editor. Many agencies provided photographs and historical documents for which I am appreciative.

I greatly acknowledge the assistance of all those others who spent their time, shared their knowledge, and provided needed materials. In this book I was enriched by other people's published experiences, experiments and opinions, and an understanding of my indebtedness can be seen in the endnotes which are numbered in the text and listed by chapter at the back of the book.

Finally, to my daughter who politely waited on many occasions to share my work area. I hope the witnessing of this and previous books will instill in you the love of learning, reading, and writing.

INTRODUCTION

From his perch in a tree stand, Walter Patenaude heard the sound of a large animal moving upwind. He turned, ready to take aim on a buck but instead saw a large cat leap eight feet onto a rock ledge about thirty yards away. He lowered his rifle and observed the majestic sight that held his wonder. "It was long -- bigger than a deer or dog, and it trailed a large tail. I was able to see every move it made as I watched with my binoculars to bring it even closer," Patenaude reported.[1]

Patenaude's claimed sighting of a cougar is just one of thousands fueling a long debate that has captured the curiosity and imagination of sport hunters, nature enthusiasts, biologists, and the general public alike. The eastern mountain lion has long been declared extinct, yet each year otherwise credible individuals report seeing this legendary cat.

But despite the huge number of sightings and the steady accumulation of more tangible evidence, the overwhelming majority of biologists who staff fish and game agencies throughout the eastern states question the claims of cougars inhabiting their assigned jurisdictions. Consequently, the issue drums up great controversy and heated debates throughout the length of the Appalachian Mountains. While many of the believers are lay people and individuals having allegedly seen an eastern cougar, many have been wildlife biologists themselves. The book discusses the many reasons for believing in the "Ghost Cat" or "Spirit Cat" and the other equally convincing arguments that contradict the reality of eastern cougar populations.

For example, scientists who believe that cougars are present have tried to demonstrate that few game biologists east of the Mississippi River have enough familiarity with the animal's field sign to recognize whether they are present. Skeptics, on the other hand, do not believe that the huge numbers of sightings constitute evidence. They cite the countless reports investigated by state wildlife authorities that turn out to be cases of misidentification. What is it people are seeing? If the cougars were eliminated decades ago, then why do so many people continue to report them? What about the physical evidence -- the videos, tracks, scat, fur, and confirmed mountain lion DNA? If the last officially confirmed cougars in the East were killed in the late 1800s and early 1900s, why is it that cougars are still occasionally being killed or otherwise documented? Is it really so hard to imagine that one of nature's most adaptable predators could have survived the tempest of European settlement and still prowl the woodlands of its ancestors?

The cougar, after all, is successful in a wide variety of environments. It is found in habitats of every kind, from the most southern reaches of South America or Pantogonia to the Yukon Territory in northern Canada.[2] It is because of this large geographic range that the species has so many different names, a convincing indication of its superior survival skills. The mountain lion, panther, puma, and cougar are all names given the same species. In this book, it will be consistently referred to as the cougar, with exceptions where appropriate.

In the colonial Northeast, the settlers called it "cat of the mountain," and this was later abbreviated to "catamount." The colonists in the Massachusetts Bay knew it as "painter cat", and further south along the Carolina Coast it was known as the lion or "leone;" the settlers there believed it was the same animal they knew in Africa. In the Southwest it was referred to as a puma, while in the Southeast it is called a panther. The eastern Native American nations spoke of the cougar's silent and mysterious ways and called it a "Phantom" or "Ghost Cat." In the Southeast the Creeks called the cougar "Katalger," or "Great Wild Hunter," and to the nearby Cherokees it was known as "Klandagi," meaning "Lord of the Forest." In the north country along the St. John River, this elusive cat was called "Pi-Twal," or "The Long-tailed One." The cat was revered in the East as it was in the West, and some even referred to it as "The Spirit

Cat." Native Americans in northern Maine called the mountain lion "The Devil Cat" or "Lunk Soos." There are no fewer than forty names that have been used to describe this one species.[3]

Eventually the cougar was studied by scientists and given a Latin name *Felis concolor*, which was changed in 1998 to its present and correct scientific name *Puma concolor*.[4] While the puma does share many characteristics with the smaller North American felines, molecular studies show the cat is unique and not closely related to other purring cats. The name Puma was chosen as this cat's apropos moniker because unlike mountain lion the name does not imply a specific habitat. This name (*Puma concolor*) means the cat of one color, but it is truly the cat of many names.

The confusion arising from these many names is typical of most aspects of the large carnivore's story. Colorful characters fill the story, such as the young woman who spent a night in a secluded forest near a Massachusetts reservoir to observe what was anticipated to be a cougar returning to its deer kill. There are pages filled with such exciting individual investigations, none of which were so scientifically and patiently conducted as that of the federal researcher who hiked miles in an Appalachian snowstorm on the trail of what was verified as a large cougar sized cat. Large interest groups organized themselves and also found the cat elusive, but nevertheless continue to plead for its protection. One would think that if most authorities dismiss its existence then the species would have been listed as extinct, but instead it is merely considered extinct while paradoxically it is legally listed as endangered in many states. It wasn't until the spring of 2011 that the federal government via the United States Fish and Wildlife Service officially declared the species extinct in the East.

In a world where the human population is exploding and the extinction of wildlife species occurs yearly, it is hard to believe that some species are thriving. The fact that there are more deer in North America today than at any other time in history is encouraging. This is especially significant for this very rare predator, if it indeed survives, for its chief prey is deer. The increase in deer has created an increase in western cougars; these abundant cougar populations in the West have allowed for many cases of emigration eastward. Is the East ready for this large powerful carnivore? This book -- The Quest For The

Eastern Cougar: Extinction or Survival? -- fully explores this question, including the possibility that this unobtrusive species may have in fact never vanished but rather held on in low numbers, hidden in the quiet corners of the eastern United States.

PART ONE:

THE HISTORY AND THOSE WHO SEARCH

The author does not make a personal claim about the present day status of *Puma concolor* east of the Mississippi and north of Florida -- rather he presents the facts, long awaited information and evidence necessary for the reader to make their own conclusion. It isn't until the end that in summarizing the information a conclusion points much more strongly in one direction.

Puma concolor: known as cougar, panther, mountain lion and many other local names.

CHAPTER ONE

CARNAGE AND CLEARING

In January 2004, Debbie Nichols fought to save the life of her dear friend, Anne Hjelle, from the blood-stained jaws of a full-grown cougar. This well-publicized news story of a cougar attack in California re-invoked fear of an animal that has killed fewer than twenty people in four hundred years. The event helps us understand the early settler's attitudes toward such powerful creatures as the cougar, wolf, and grizzly bear. Fear defined the settlers' relationship to all predators.

The courage of the early European settlers to endure the grueling voyage across the Atlantic and their willingness to meet the challenges of survival in a strange, savage world were rewarded when they arrived on the North American continent. It was a wilderness seemingly as vast as the constellations. They found towering forests filled with a multitude of species, islands covered with beautiful birds, as well as lakes, rivers, and tidal bays teaming with fish. Their new home had an astounding diversity of wildlife that could hardly be imagined and that will never be known again. Yet they feared this wilderness and yearned to conquer and subdue it. The settlers' nights were filled with fright, as unclaimed animal voices echoed hauntingly throughout the darkness. Large carnivores such as the cougar, bear or wolf could carry off children into the forest to be eaten.

When Europeans arrived the Northeast was cloaked with mature trees, occasionally broken up by swamps and natural meadows. There were indigenous people who had an influence upon the land, as they would burn areas to improve forage, both for their prey and for themselves as hunter/gatherers.[1] Although some agricultural planting took place, these Native Americans lived in relative harmony with the land, without destructively altering the natural environment.

In the centuries since the arrival of European settlers, however, human activity has drastically altered this landscape. The tree species that once dominated were American beeches, maples, birches, eastern hemlocks, and a variety of spruces. Further west, in the Ohio River Valley, tremendous chestnuts, oaks, and hickories grew. It is estimated that forest covered 85-90% of the landscape east of the Ohio River. However, by early 1800, only 30 % of the land remained forested, everything else had been logged or cleared for farming.[2]

The process of ecological destruction began soon after the Europeans set foot in New England in 1620. By 1675, the Native American population and way of life had changed drastically; the clearing of the land was already well underway. Expansive growths of virgin white pines were abundant in the Northeast, and the timber fell quickly. Deforestation spread into the interior Northeast and along the coast.[3]

By 1890, agricultural clearing had made its way to southern coastal Maine. Interestingly, northern Maine was never farmed; the settlers began to move west before deforestation reached that far. Northern Maine stood as the last piece of wilderness in New England.[4] Although most of the tree-cutting was for agricultural purposes, many parts of northern New England, especially Maine, were logged for wood. Land logged for timber was not cleared; it was cut and then ignored. Land that was put into agriculture, on the other hand, was stripped of everything. The settlers cut every tree, uprooted every stump, removed every rock, and then tilled the soil thoroughly. Remnant virgin forests stand as testimonials to what was lost, and their scarcity is a sobering indication of how extensive the clearing really was.

Modern biogeography has accurately demonstrated the patterns of human deforestation in the Northeast, a clear correlation with topography and water exists; many of our current old growth forests are consequently found in regions that could not be easily accessed. Such areas include swamps and mountainous terrain, but hollows or basins without rivers were also spared because of the absence of a waterway for transporting logs.

With the destruction of the forest came the decline of many winged species such as the wild turkey. Once fairly common throughout mid- and southern New England, the turkey quickly became scarce. It was extirpated in southern Vermont, New Hampshire, Maine, and Massachusetts.[5] Fortunately, some populations held out in other states, including Pennsylvania and New York.

Native populations of elk and woodland buffalo were among other species that suffered. Today it seems odd that these hoofed creatures once lived in the East, but buffalo did roam as far east as the Berkshires in western Massachusetts and the western edges of the Adirondacks in New York. Buffalo remains have even been found further east on Cape Cod. Elk roamed Pennsylvania until 1877 when the last bull was shot. Currently, an imported free-ranging herd survives there. Buffalo persisted in the Northeast until the last one was shot in 1810. Other species that became extinct, and which are now remembered only by historical accounts, included the stately heath hen, great auk, sea mink, Labrador duck, gray whale, eastern wolverine and passenger pigeon.

Beaver were also extirpated in most of the East. Ironically, wildlife initiated the rapid spread of settlement beginning about 1640. Canada's late historian Harold Innis recognized the beaver as "the central figure in the exploration and conquest of the North American continent."[6] The beaver, *Castor canadensis*, lured Europeans in search of the animal's fur. As is commonly known, it was the fashion for every man to wear a beaver skin cap. The era began with simple trade between Native Americans and Europeans, then advanced to large trading posts supplied by efficient slaughtering.[7] Three centuries of exploitation ended with the use of steel traps and the depletion of the species as a resource. By 1843 the beaver era was completely over.[8]

The decline of the passenger pigeon had little effect on the cougar, and the disappearance of the beaver alone had limited effect on the larger carnivores.[9] But beaver, turkey, and other small mammals were good substitute prey for cougars looking in vain for deer, which had nearly been wiped out. An animal of great importance to Native Americans as well as to the cougar, the deer had existed in significant numbers within the forest, the burned areas and wetlands. Europeans also saw value in them, however, and they were hunted to depletion for commercial meat markets.

The decline of one species often impacts another. Some species decline together while others have an inverse relationship. Deer and cougar are inextricably interconnected in a relationship created through evolution. When deer are few, so too are the cougar. This once abundant resource was reduced with amazing speed. Fortunately, conservation efforts were initiated soon enough to save the white-tailed deer. The deer's situation was one of the first indications that people could and would make changes in order to save a wild animal.

Very early in New England's history, laws were constructed to protect the deer. In 1741 the first laws were made and implemented by the New Hampshire Grants. Although a few deer survived in isolated pockets throughout the East, they had disappeared in most places. They were so scarce that the first laws had little effect, and stricter laws were implemented in the late eighteenth century. But by 1850, deer were exceptionally rare.[10] Eventually some regions rebounded, and these deer were transferred to bolster populations elsewhere.

Once harmed by humans, deer were now given an advantage. Better soil, plowing improvements, and the opening of the Erie Canal allowed for westward migration of humans. By 1890, old farmland began to grow back to a wild state, and the Northeast was on its way to becoming 70% forested - - almost a complete reversal from 1810. The abandoned farmland was overtaken by a succession or young forest that provided ideal browse and cover. At the start of the twentieth century, the New England landscape was again undergoing a drastic change, and with growing industrialization, human populations were concentrating in and around cities. Soon the hills and valleys were alive again with wildlife, and the Northeast states began receiving complaints of nuisance deer.[11] Nevertheless, it appears this rebound came too late for the cougar, which had almost exclusively relied on deer as its primary food source.

If any cougars survived in the East, they would have had to supplement their diet with alternative prey -- difficult to do without beaver or turkey. It is possible that the cougar might have dispersed with the wolf into Quebec and northern Maine where forests remained and woodland caribou were the prey. Wolf howls can still be heard today north of the St. Lawrence River, as they have for thousands of years.

For thousands of years, Native American cultures lived in balance with nature. The animals were a part of their lives, and they understood the cycles and interconnections between all creatures. Predators, especially wolves and eagles, were admired for their stealth and spirit. In fact, among all carnivorous predators, the cougar was most respected and revered.

In the West, evidence that the cougar or puma stood for fierce skill and strength is found among many tribes. The Apache dangled cougar paws above the bed of their sick while other tribes scratched the chest of the sick with cougar claws, believing in the cougar's healing powers. In New Mexico the Cochetee Indians erected a shrine in honor of the great cat.[12] Other North American tribes bestowed supernatural powers upon the cougar and invoked the animal's fighting spirit before going to battle. This kind of reverence is seen throughout native cultures, with the exception of the Inca. Who regularly hunted it to limit its impact on the vicuna, a close cousin to the llama, and a Inca food source.

Every three years, the Inca gathered in tremendous numbers to hunt vicuna. Groups of over twenty thousand would organize a circular hunt. Half would drive game from the left and half from the right, caught in the middle was an assortment of animals. Hoofed animals were harvested in the thousands, along with the cougar, sometimes as many as fifty at a time.[13]

Although the Inca considered the cougar a food competitor, they nonetheless incorporated it into their culture and artwork. Archaeologists have found numerous inscriptions on rocks portraying the cat in dignified postures. High in the Andes, several gold cougar sculptures and small figurines were discovered, reflecting the animal's persistent presence in Native American life. Perhaps the most significant expression of the cougar's importance can be found in the ancient city of Cuzco, where the entire city is laid out in the shape of the cougar.[14]

Compared with western tribes, the eastern Native Americans did not leave mark of the cougar's role in their society with such grand expression. Instead, more benign expressions are found. Tecumseh, the great Shawnee chief who lived in the Ohio area, was a leader whose name means "panther in the sky" or "panther passing through." Tecumseh was a fearless warrior who led a resistance against the Europeans.

Europeans, on the other hand, feared the animal and their attitude toward the cougar ran in direct contrast with those of the natives. Many immigrants arrived from European regions that no longer had predators, and so they aimed their muskets without hesitation at the great cat of the Americas. In colonial Vermont, for instance, the cougar played a significant role in local folklore and history. Cougar killers basked in the limelight along with wolf and bear hunters. They were heroes in their own time, and villagers gathered to glorify men returning home with dead cougars. The settlers were on a cultural mission, much like the modern quest to explore space and conquer disease. America's wilderness needed to be conquered. The cougar, in particular, represented all that was feared about the vast frontier. Their fear is understandable, considering that they did not know cougars don't typically kill humans, very little was known about the ecological value of wildlife and their habits. They did not have the luxury of appreciating wildlife from the security of civilization. And so today, history is filled with the stories of brave men returning to the villages with the carcass of a cougar draped across their shoulders. The early legends are exciting, describing the uncertainty of having a large carnivore lurking at the edge of a settlement.

In 1779, the Vermont legislature offered a monetary reward for the carcass of what it called a catamount. The bounty was eight pounds for an adult and four pounds for a kitten. It was later reduced to three pounds for an adult then raised up again to six pounds. In the nineteenth century, the bounty remained at twenty dollars until the animal's assumed disappearance.[15]

The bounty exemplified public feelings for a predator at a time when it was generally believed that nature was to be tamed and early accounts of the cougar offer little insight into the biology or habits of the species. There are a few mounted specimens to tell us something of their general appearance. Postured in ferocious contortions, these mounts show us the excitement value of eighteenth and early nineteenth century cougar encounters.

One of the earliest descriptions of a cougar encounter was chronicled in 1793 in Dr. Samuel Williams' Natural and Civil History of Vermont:

> This seems to be the most fierce and ravenous of any animal which we have in Vermont. Some years ago, one animal was killed in Bennington. It took a large calf out of a pen, where the fence was four feet high, and carried it off upon its back. With this load, it ascended a ledge of rocks, where one of the leaps was fifteen feet in height. Two hunters found the cat on a high tree. Discharging his musket, one of them wounded it in the leg. It descended with the greatest agility and fury; did not attack the men but seized

their dog by one of his ribs, broke it off, and instantly leaped into the tree again with astonishing swiftness and dexterity. The other hunter shot him through the head, but his fury did not cease, but with all the last remains of his life. These animals have often been seen in Vermont but were never numerous, or easily taken. Of their fecundity, I have no particular information. On account of their fierceness, activity, and carnivourous disposition, the hunter esteemed them to be the most dangerous of any animal.[16]

Another well-known story involved the prominent Benjamin Bellows, who ventured upon a large cougar near Rockingham, Vermont. Bellows, a respected colonel, had just shot a bear, but then found himself face-to-face with an angry cougar. Writing of Bellow's encounter, historian Thomas Altherr researched his account as follows:

A rustling in the bushes nearby attracted his attention immediately, and he saw the round eyeballs of a large catamount glaring at him above the brakes. He knew instinctively his new customer was a different class of animal to deal with than the clumsy bear, from which there was no great danger. Fearing the savage disposition of this last animal if wounded and not killed, he brought up his gun with much trepidation, and aiming at the eyes, fired. All was silent. Not caring to investigate, Bellows beat a hasty retreat home, returning at once with his men. They found the cougar dead, the ball having struck squarely between the eyes.[17]

The Wardsboro Panther shot in 1875 measured
over six feet and weighed 105 pounds.
Courtesy Museum of Science Boston

Hunters in Wardsboro, Vermont, became the focus of much attention when they tracked down a lone catamount, killed it, and returned home as heroes on November 1, 1875. In 1867 near Wethersfield, Vermont, a similar event took place and was recorded in the words of Charles Aldrich: "Yesterday there was great excitement in consequence of a hunt for an animal which proved to be a panther. He was driven into a cave and shot." [18] Aldrich wrote that the panther stretched seven feet long. The cat was displayed at a local hotel bar for many years and is now being kept at the Dan Foster House in cooperation with the Wethersfield Historical Society.

In 1809, Abel Smith, a cattle farmer in Eden, Vermont, was bringing his cattle home when he heard a sound that " made his hair stand on end." Smith reached into his food sack and threw down a piece of meat to divert the pursuing cougar. Hemenway wrote in the *Vermont Historical Gazeteer* that, "Smith hustled his cattle homewards, and the catamount, giving a few screams to denote his dissapprobation of the means to cheat him of his prey, turned off another way." [19]

During a similar incident in 1818, a panther followed the grandfather of Evelyn Fletcher Townsend. She recalled that he was trailed "by this most dreaded wild beast." The grandfather diverted the catamount's plans by throwing it a piece of pork. Further documentation of the nineteenth century attitude concerning the waning cougar are found in Samuel Hall's "The Geography and History of Vermont." It reads as follows: "Catamount is a fierce and terrible animal. It destroys other animals much larger than itself, and is capable of leaping to great distances to seize its prey." [20]

Eventually, by 1840, human encounters with catamounts had begun to decline. In an interesting selection from Henry David Thoreau's diary, a paragraph on a cougar appears in September of 1856. Thoreau was a visitor to Brattleboro that fall, and he entered these words in his journal: "The most interesting sight I saw in Brattleboro was a skin and skull of a panther, Felis concolor, which was killed, according to written notice attached, on the 15 th of June by the Sarnac Club of Brattleboro, six young men on a fishing and hunting excursion." The animal's wild eyes and size made a deep impression upon Thoreau's inquisitive mind. He went on describing the sight: " I was surprised at its great size and apparent strength. It gave one a new idea of our American forest and vigor of nature here. It was evident that it could level a platoon of men with a stroke of its paw." The experience occurred just days after Thoreau had expressed remorse about living in what he was beginning to feel a "tamed and emasculated country." He soon realized that the woods beyond Concord still held adventure and mystery.[21]

In 1881 Alexander Crowell shot what was assumed to be the last catamount to prowl Vermont.[22] However, reports of the animal continued after that time, leaving it a matter of opinion for the next hundred years. Today, the taxidermy catamount that Crowell shot can be seen at the entrance of the Vermont Historical Society Museum in Montpelier.

The famous Barnard Panther supposedly the last cougar shot
in Vermont. It was killed by Alexander Crowell, seen here,
in 1881 and is now on display in the Vermont Historical
Museum Library. *Courtesy Vermont Historical Society*

In New Hampshire, it is believed that the last mountain lion was
taken in 1853. Connecticut allegedly lost cougars in 1835, but there
is no certainty as to when the last specimen was shot.[23] Research has
uncovered similar dates for other Northeast states, and the general
consensus puts cougars extinct in the East by 1890.[24] However, reports
continued to come in from remote areas. Amazingly, in Maine a cougar
was taken as late as 1938 at Little Saint John Lake.[25]

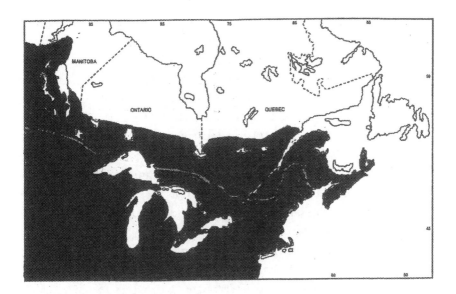

The former range of *Puma concolor* before European settlement
included all of North America to the northern limit shown here.

As defined in the hallmark book <u>The Puma, Mysterious American
Cat</u> by Stanley P. Young and Edward A. Goldman, the cougar's former
range in the East extended from south Florida and east of the Mississippi
River to the southern shores of the Saint Lawrence River.[26] According to
Young and Goldman, the cat was never easy to see, but in some regions
such as the southern Catskills and northern Adirondacks, cougars
were more evident. Both Virginia and the Berkshire Hills region of
Massachusetts had many cats in very early times (before 1750).[27]

From Young and Goldman, a commentator named Emmons
speculated, "The puma is not found at present in the Massachusetts
state (1840). It has, however, been seen in the western part of the state
since its settlement." [28] Could it be Emmons was wrong? After all,
one was shot in 1858, supposedly on top of Mount Tom, in Holyoke,
Massachusetts. This region was extensively cleared by then, and any
lion taken in this region must have represented a surviving population
from somewhere outside the Connecticut River Valley.[29] This specimen
is on display at the Massachusetts Audubon Society's Arcadia Wildlife
Education Center, in Easthampton.[30] Another report by Young and
Goldman cites the case, presumably a sighting, of a lion as late as 1929

in Massachusetts.[31] Obviously, this would push the last account of the cougar in that state up from 1840. If the Mount Tom specimen represents the last individual, how can the 1929 report be explained?

And so a mystery actually begins around the dates when the kills cease but the sightings persist. A review of the evidence together shows that the lion must have been nearly extinct, if present at all, by 1900. But with lingering reports and isolated rumors of cougars being shot decades later, it is not unreasonable to assume that perhaps in some areas of the East the absence of confirmed kills and carcasses may not necessarily have meant extinction. Is it not possible that an animal as unobtrusive as the cougar may have held out undetected in some rugged, impenetrable terrain?

This question can only begin to be answered by speculation and an examination of historical accounts of cougars that were recorded after the alleged time of regional extinction or extirpation. Such research shows that at no time has there been an absence of reported sightings.[32] In fact, there has never been a time since the first settlers arrived that these long-tailed cats did not turn up somewhere. Rather, the reports continue to this day.

Therefore, the question must be asked, were the animals observed in the early twentieth century really cougars, or are these early sightings merely cases of mistaken identity? Would it not make sense that those early sightings were surviving stragglers? If that were true, then would it not follow that those which are seen today are descended from these survivors? Does the absence of kills constitute the extinction of an animal, or does it simply mean that the animal has become scarce or has moved into regions infrequently hunted? Who declared the eastern mountain lion extinct, and when did they conclude this? Was extinction fact or was it just assumed? [33]

If these creatures did survive, they had to take advantage of the remaining deer or other larger prey. Since deer were nearly destroyed, it is tantalizing to speculate where these predators may have held out. Clearly humans could not have destroyed all available deer habitat at once. It took decades. While some regions were denuded, surely others were still untouched, and simultaneously some places would have begun to regenerate. Swamps or rugged mountain tops could have harbored such relic cougar populations.

As mentioned earlier, northern Maine escaped the axe, as did those specific places where access was difficult. Few peaks above 3,500 hundred feet were visited by loggers. Some peaks were set on fire to eradicate predators, but many were not burned over. In New York State's Adirondack Park 50,000 contiguous acres of virgin forest remain. A recent estimate utilizing new standards for the six million-acre park's total old growth or virgin forest is at a half million acres.[34] This suggests that a few possible hideouts did exist for black bears, wild turkey, and a few other species. Therefore, relic cougar populations might still exist somewhere.

The decades from 1620 to 1900 were dark years for the nation's natural resources. Lured by the pelts of beavers, Europeans explored and mapped the North American Continent. The wilderness was subdued, and the cougar, among the many other vital components of the ecosystem, was destroyed due to persecution and habitat loss. Or was it?

We are left only with specimens that document the last of these great cats from their respective regions. These lifeless forms seem to tell us that the cougar is extinct - end of story. This is what we have been assuming. But over one hundred years later, sightings continue. What are the explanations? Has anybody bothered to search for proof, and if so what have they discovered?

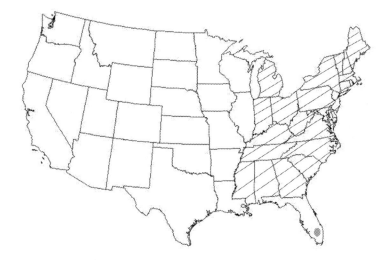

The area in question. Includes all states east of the Mississippi except Florida where shaded area shows range of Florida panther (approximated). The primary focus in this discussion centers mostly on Appalachia and the Northeast.

CURRENT RANGE

The present range of *Puma concolor.*

CHAPTER TWO

GHOST OF QUABBIN-PHANTOM OF APPALACHIA

Active interest in the cougar's possible existence east of the Mississippi River was actually begun by a little known man from Vermont, who in 1938 organized a group of people claiming cougar sightings. Reverend William Ballou did not keep records of sightings, nor did he engage in critical thinking, but instead left it all to faith.[1] The real research began with Bruce S. Wright in New Brunswick, Canada. Wright is the person who started asking the questions and publishing professional ideas about surviving pre-settlement cougars.[2] Courageous as a person and scientist, he was not forever alone in his pursuit, as across the border Hal Hitchcock would continue the quest at the end of Wright's career. Hitchcock, like Ballou, was a Vermonter, and they have become two of many in history who have been compelled by the belief in surviving cougars.[3]

Intrigued by the large number of people in Vermont who had said they encountered a cougar or catamount, the Reverend Ballou shared stories of the cougars he had seen out west in Wyoming as a child. After talking with several witnesses claiming to have seen the long-tailed cat, Ballou believed there must be cougars living in the Vermont mountains that at the time were returning to forest. Then, on a cold December day in 1934, the Reverend made a startling discovery. He cast-molded the large feline-looking track that lay before his path in Chester. Immediately, the Reverend formed a group of believers known as the pantherites. Theirs was the beginning of a long-standing preoccupation with catamounts in Vermont. Sightings must have continued there and all across the Northeast long after the group had faded, because in Canada Bruce Wright became the next person to carry the torch.[4]

Wright was an exceptionally talented man of many interests and accomplishments. He was born in Quebec City, Canada in 1912, but grew up in England. He moved back to his native Canada as a young adult, where he soon entered the armed forces. While in the Navy Wright invented the idea of using divers in covert missions; he created the frogman commando concept, an innovation that found a way into the military's strategic methods. History will always be indebted to him for his idea, which led to the creation of the Allied Sea Reconnaissance Unit. This unit was partly responsible for the success of the battle of Burma.[5]

Upon his release from the Navy, Wright studied wildlife biology and continued to show promise as an innovator. He was a student of Aldo Leopold, the great pioneer conservationist and author of <u>A Sand County Almanac</u>. Leopold was perhaps the deepest thinker that the wildlife field had yet produced.[6] This was one of many important experiences that allowed Bruce Wright to have a fascinating and productive life. Eventually, he settled in New Brunswick, and it was there that he became the director of the Northeast Wildlife Station. One day while he was at work fighting a forest fire, a co-worker saw a cougar running from flames, and it was then his fascination with the eastern cougar began.[7]

He quickly investigated the presence of cougars in that district. Cougars were called panthers in that region and had been so for some time. Wright had been under the assumption that there were no panthers in the East. He was amazed when his colleague told him about the sighting. The colleague also told Wright that he used to see them as a youth, back home in upper Maine near Ashland, and Wright's fascination with the animal burned brighter.

Bruce Wright spent the better part of his life researching wildlife.
Here he is displaying what he believed was evidence of a panther
in New Brunswick. The track was discovered in 1948. It has
recently been determined to have been made by a wolf.
Courtesy UNB archives

According to the locals in Maine and in New Brunswick, the cougar
was alive. There weren't many of them, but everybody knew they were
there. However, it was an idea that had not gained official acceptance.
Undeterred, Wright set out to learn more. In 1948 he found three sets of
tracks, which he thought came from a group of panthers.[8] One set has
since been identified with better methods and now appears to have been
made by a wolf. He researched the history of the species in the East,
especially in Eastern Canada, and he struggled over whether he should
disclose his suspicions regarding their continued existence. Within his
notes on the cougar are several quotes detailing his personal thoughts.

Eventually Wright contacted his former professor, Aldo Leopold,
who responded with caution. Wright records Leopold's correspondence
as follows:

When I first told my then teacher and good friend the late Aldo Leopold, that there were still panthers in the forests of New Brunswick, he was as incredulous as everyone else eventually proved to be. Later, after we had examined the evidence, his first words were: 'we must not tell anyone.' He feared that the knowledge of the animal's presence would bring about its demise. He felt someone would shoot one just to boast their skills and to prove its existence.[9]

Wright's secret investigations apparently appeared bizarre to his peers, as he reflected in 1972, "This problem of keeping quiet, and at the same time asking the Game Department to help, was to cause me much trouble, as for some time my actions were regarded with deep suspicion by certain officials."[10] Wright's covert activities soon ended, as local newspapers had started to consistently report panther sightings. He could not contain his secret or his excitement any longer, and he knew it was futile, as the press was running away with it. By 1948 Wright published his first work on the eastern cougar. This was soon followed by an article in the September 1948 issue of *Field and Stream*, entitled "The Fundy Lions." Later on he wrote a book known as, The Ghost of North America (1959).[11]

Help from professional peers was not quick to follow. Nevertheless, he was now able to pursue his work publicly. Soon the public began to send their reports to him, enabling Wright to investigate fresh sightings. He was able to show a loose correlation between the recovering deer populations and the frequency of cougar sightings in certain regions.

In 1966 Wright was successful in changing the status of the panther by persuading the IUCN (International Union for the Conservation of Nature) to list it not as "extinct" but as "rare and endangered."[12] His next major work, written in the 1970s and currently out of print, was appropriately called The Eastern Panther and was largely a concentration of the best anecdotal accounts. The book features a photograph of a track that Wright was certain came from a panther, but has been determined today to be most certainly canine. This one error prompted Dr. Stan Van Zyll de Jong of the Canadian Museum of Nature to discount all of Wright's work and to theorize alternative explanations for the 300 sightings he had collected. Van Zyll de Jong was not as convincing, and Wright's work remains in high regard. Perhaps, Wright's greatest contribution was his careful documentation of sightings, which are too numerous to list. Two are provided here and read as follows:

> In 1932 a deer hunter was hunting on Little River and was walking along an old woods road. He was just about to cross a ten-foot wide stream when he heard heavy breathing coming toward him. He stepped off into the bushes and a buck deer running full out came down the road, with a large tawny cat with a long tail held straight out behind running just after it. The cat was about eight feet from tip to tip.[13]

By the 1940's, many decades since their assumed extirpation, forest conditions had improved and deer were numerous. In 1955 Wright shared a typical panther report along a roadway:

> At last on July 15, 1955, a man and his wife were rounding a bend on the same road when they saw a panther standing in the road ahead. It stepped off as they came on and they stopped where it had entered the ditch. The man got out and gathered stones to throw into the bush to make it show itself. Suddenly, the wife saw the panther lying in the bush only five feet away from her husband. He hurriedly re-entered the car, and they both watched as it got up and walked slowly away with frequent glances back at them. When the man discovered it at such close quarters, it snarled at them and lashed its tail, but as soon as he retreated it showed no aggression.[14]

On September 28th of 1966, Wright, himself, saw a cougar.[15] This was significant because few trained wildlife biologists have disclosed personal sightings. A few years later another biologist admitted a sighting, offering greater credibility as to the identity of these sightings. On May 25, 1970, Dr. Uno Paim, Professor of Biology of the University of New Brunswick, witnessed a panther cross in front of his car on the Harvey-McAdam road near Magaguadavic Bridge. He stopped his car and followed the animal into the woods. He was about ten paces from it before he saw it again. The movement of the black tip of the tail caught his eye. "It was a heavy-set, gray-brown animal with a black tip to its long tail. It was gone in a flash."[16]

Meanwhile, as Bruce Wright was aging and losing his steam for the quest, a biologist in Vermont was gaining momentum in his interest. Harold Hitchcock, a renowned biologist at Middleburry College, had earned a reputation for his interest in the alleged Vermont panthers.[17] Cougar sightings and rumors had become far too popular for this Vermont professor to ignore, and he began to investigate the situation. But for Hitchcock, a reputable scientist, an interest in cougars that most authorities denounced would put a lot at stake. Ignoring these reports, however, seemed irresponsible, and as a member of the local scientific community, Hitchcock embarked on the journey. In retrospect it proved a worthwhile venture for him, as he gained the respect of his fellow Vermonters and managed to escape ridicule by his scientific peers.

Harold Hitchcock graduated from Harvard in 1938 and then taught at the University of Ontario until 1943, when he settled in Vermont.[18] From 1943 until 1968 Harold, or Hal for short, taught at Middlebury College.[19] It was here where he began to make a name for himself in the area of mammalian research. He had developed a keen interest in bat biology while a graduate student at Harvard and had focused this interest in Vermont with extensive studies of the Nickwacket Caves. Before his second decade at Middlebury College he had begun to establish himself as an authority on bat migration and population.[20]

Like Bruce Wright, Hitchcock was an innovative, intelligent, well-educated man, and was likewise compelled by the thought of the majestic cougar roaming through his neck of the woods. Shortly before Wright's death in 1975, Hitchcock started his compilation of data on Vermont cougar sightings, and his research reached maturity a few years later.[21]

However, well before this time, Hitchcock's assumed role as the Vermont cougar man had already begun informally. Beginning in the 1940s he had saved letters documenting sightings. One in particular is of human interest. Buried deep in his files there is a letter from a 92-year-old woman who had taken the time and effort to write a detailed and delightfully descriptive account of a cougar sighting near Springfield, Vermont.[22]

According to her account, this old woman had happened upon a cougar while out walking up a hill behind her home. She had gone out on a beautiful spring day to enjoy the weather and the view of the village of Springfield. While on the crest of this hill, she sighted a lion of tremendous proportions heading her way. To get a better look, the women raised her binoculars, but as she focused in on the cat, the sun was reflected off the lenses, evidently startling the cougar. The cat turned to run, leaping several feet over a clump of spruce. Fearlessly, she reached the spot where it stood and with a wide view of the surrounding slope, she saw that the animal was already down the other side.[23]

Hitchcock continued his interest with cougars right up to his last days. He was able to see attitudes changing in Vermont to the point where wildlife agents were becoming more open about cougars. He was a leader in a conference at St. Johnsbury, which gathered together local wildlife experts and some of Hitchcock's followers to discuss evidence. The conference was audiotapped and is available for all to hear at the Vermont Historical Library in Montpelier.

Hal died in 1995, a respected and admired scientist and community leader.[24] He had remained active after his retirement at the college, helping graduate students and giving lectures. Even years after his death, Hitchcock's bat migration research remained at the forefront of its field. Hitchcock had banded more bats than any other researcher of his kind. Above all else, Hitchcock's overall credibility was high enough to sustain his unconventional interest in the eastern cougar, and when he died he left his community with a deep interest in his belief that there were indeed wild cougars still alive in Vermont.

Bruce Wright and Harold Hitchcock were both accomplished men, but they never convinced their academic peers about the existence of the cougar in the East. Instead, they left a contribution to us all. They gave us the appreciation of this amazing predator's legacy and the knowledge and methods to preserve this legend for our future. The story of the cougar cannot be told without mention of these two great men, who loved and cherished all that is wild and free.

Bruce Wright and Hal Hitchcock pioneered cougar research in the Northeastern United States using sightings. However, it was not until

1972, when a young Massachusetts woman learned of cougar sightings within a reservoir area near her home, that a field investigation took place in the Northeast.[25] Virginia Fifield's search for cougars is little known but significant. She focused on nothing but looking for sign, and did so with credibility still respected to this day by local wildlife officials.

Originally from Wisconsin, Fifield lived near the cultural mecca of Amherst/Northampton, Massachusetts, where stories flourished about people seeing cougars in the nearby Quabbin Reservoir's protected 80,000-acre watershed. After hearing of sightings near her house at the Quabbin, Fifield was quick to investigate. She responded to these rumors and found out that there had actually been a state game biologist who claimed he saw a cougar there. With a little bit of asking around and checking of old newspaper articles, Fifield learned of the "cougar mystery."

Fifield happened to know cougars intimately. The daughter of an attorney with connections at the local zoo, she was lucky enough to have the experience of raising a cougar at her home. Her pre-existing fascination soon reignited and took her further into the world of cougars.[26] At first, her investigation involved long hikes into the quiet forests of the Quabbin. Hiking through areas she felt were potential habitats that a mountain lion might prefer, Fifield looked for evidence of these secretive cats. At other times, she would respond to recent sightings or rumors of lions. Eventually, her interest matured, and she organized an all-out quest for the elusive feline. In 1972 she founded the Eastern Cougar Survey Team. With funding from the Worcester Science Institute, the first formal search for *Puma concolor* in the Northeast had begun.[27]

Initially, Fifield was alone. Soon, however, she had the co-operation of state fish and game officials who were willing to relay cougar sightings directly to her. Later, she gained more support, until a network of interested people and qualified experts were at her disposal. Up to this point, reports had been going to the state biologists, who were dismissing them. It would be safe to say that prior to 1972, almost none of these earlier sightings had ever been followed up with an on-site investigation. Fifield, young and dedicated, was about to be the first to take on this challenge.[28]

She circulated posters with pictures of dog and cougar tracks, side by side, for comparison. A small picture of a cougar appeared on these flyers, along with some brief information and her phone number. What happened next was a revelation into human psychology. Everyone started seeing cougars. The frequency of reports increased dramatically, but almost none of the reports described a convincing sighting. They were all obvious cases of mistaken identity.[29]

Finally, the rash of sightings declined, and at the same time word circulated of her research independently of the flyers. As time went on, the situation became more focused. Fifield could efficiently discriminate between the reports that seemed legitimate and those that did not. Eventually she was also able to see that the sightings formed a pattern. Some reports were coming in simultaneously from two different specific areas, indicating that people might be seeing two different animals repeatedly.

Not surprisingly, one area of concentrated cougar reports was the Quabbin Reservoir. Fifield was now able to arrive quickly at the precise location of each report. On some occasions tracks were found. None of the tracks from the Quabbin would cast clearly enough to be used as evidence. However, in her travels through some of the Quabbin's most remote parts, she happened upon a deer kill that bore the marks of a cougar.[30]

There before her, in the isolated region of the Quabbin known as the Prescott Peninsula, were the mutilated remains of a half-eaten white-tailed deer. The kill had been covered in typical, distinctive cougar fashion. To Fifield the significance of this cache was exhilarating. Because the kill was so fresh, Fifield knew a cougar would almost certainly return to feed.

Now, the moment of truth was at hand. Fifield needed only to find a concealed location from which to sit and wait for night-fall and the silent return of the eastern cougar. Equally probable, the cougar might be some place close by, resting before nightfall. Fifield reflects: "I was really excited about my quest at that moment. I had surveyed the kill closely. It was highly indicative of a cougar kill. Sitting there quietly in the wilds of the Quabbin, I felt sure the big breakthrough was about to happen."[31] After sitting patiently and overwhelmed with excitement in the middle of the pitch-black Quabbin night, the curtains opened on the drama taking place before her. The outline of a large cat emerged from the dark depths of the still forest; but as it slinked closer, Fifield could see that this cache belonged to the large bobcat now feeding in front of her.[32]

Fortunately, it was not long before she received word of another sighting from a young man in the Berkshires, the other concentrated area of reports. The Berkshires is a mountainous area in the far western part of Massachusetts. His call re-invigorated her mission. In the Berkshires there are miles of forests heavily populated with deer. In the bucolic valleys, farming hangs on as a way of life, but the majority of this region is quiet and picturesque. It is largely a forgotten land, except during the fall foliage tourist frenzy and the deer hunting season.

This part of the state produces the majority of the cougar reports.[33] Fifield was anxious to explore the possibility of cougars in this heavily forested region. As it turned out, the youth who had claimed to have located an active den site, never revealed the den. Just as she was preparing to make the journey in and behold a den of cougars, the deal fell through. Terrified that the publicity would endanger these young kittens, the young man decided to keep the location secret and to continue to view the marvel in solitude.

He did provide Fifield with a plaster cast taken near the site.[34] What seemed like viable evidence to the enthused youth was unacceptable to Fifield, who thought the casting lacked definition. Nevertheless, she explored the case further by hiking the wooded area of this region herself. After much searching, Fifield did uncover some evidence from the small village of Peru. She yielded a perfectly formed plaster cast of what she knew was a cougar track. Later, in Ashfield, in the same northwestern part of the state, she secured one more plaster cast of what she also believed was a cougar track.[35]

The state wildlife biologists did not agree on the track from Peru; they dismissed the tracks as indeterminate and remained unconvinced. The track from Ashfield was a close fit, but it also failed to convince them. Jim Cardoza, a state biologist studying black bear in this same region, has little confidence in the possibility of cougars holding out or passing through the Berkshires.

Cardoza believed that the question of cougars existing in the Berkshires was foolish. "For years people have been reporting them and have not been able to provide a den site or a dead animal, not even a road kill." Completely unconvinced about the cougar's presence, Cardoza went on even further: "People ask me all the time, and for a century they have been looking for that ghost of a cat." Cardoza says, "I have never seen any sign of them. They do not have a viable presence. Until someone can come up with a carcass, I couldn't accept this as fact."[36]

Thomas French, another wildlife biologist and colleague of Mr. Cardoza, disagrees on a few points: " I am open minded to the existence of cougars here in Massachusetts and even more so up north." He believes it is possible for cougars to survive in remote areas to the north in Vermont or western Maine, undetected and quietly co-existing with man.[37]

In the end, after uncovering very little in the way of hard evidence, Ms. Fifield concluded her work with this discouraging statement:

> I am sorry to say, after all our investigations, that there simply is no scientific conclusion to substantiate the presence of *Felis concolor* in Massachusetts. In areas where lions are scarce, there can still be found some concrete signs of their activities, and here in Massachusetts that is not the case.[38]

The survey team was disbanded in 1985, and Fifield returned to her native Wisconsin in 1992.[39] She did, however, remain open minded "off the record" and encouraged others to continue with that attitude.

Fifield was not the only women to have investigated the cougar in the East. Further south, Nicole Culbertson searched the Great Smoky Mountains National Park for positive sign of cougars. Her work was published in 1976 within the Great Smoky Mountains Management Report. This investigation received little publicity but had actually found convincing reports, leading her to believe there were as many as seven cougars and possibly more inhabiting the park and adjacent private land.[40]

In the Nantahala National Forest, cougar sightings occur just as often as in Massachusetts, and by the 1960s reports had really begun to increase and gain attention. Further adding fuel to the fire, the issue came to a head in 1977 when several cougars had been seen in an area scheduled for logging.[41] Fearing loss of the cougar and their supposed habitat, local garden clubs became alarmed when they learned of the Forest Service's plans to start cutting in the Nantahala National Forest. The federal government was entered into a suit to halt the proposed logging project.[42]

Robert Downing, a U.S. Fish and Wildlife biologist, investigated those reports. He was the first person to perform a professionally planned and scientifically executed cougar field search on foot in the Southeast followed by published material. Downing was from Texas, had developed his career with the U.S. Fish and Wildlife Service in the Southwest, and was familiar with western Texas cougar populations.[43] He was selected to search the Appalachian Region and make proof positive sure that no cougars were presently there and had been overlooked. Throughout the course of his study, Downing, indefatigable hiked countless miles in these mountains but only found a few answers.

He wrote in his summary report, which appeared in the *Proceedings of the 1981 Non Game and Endangered Wildlife Symposium*, that no subject has been more controversial among professional wildlife managers and researchers in the East than the cougar.[44] Over the past ninety years twelve cougar kills were documented from the study area in North Carolina, but none of the specimens were authenticated. Supposedly a 1965 kill was taken to Louisiana and mounted.[45]

A few deer kills found during his search raised his suspicions. One was very compelling, replete with long scratch marks where the animal had extended its front leg in order to cover the kill. The reach was beyond that which one would suspect from a large bobcat. Downing stayed with that site for many days and found nothing but bobcat tracks in the immediate area. He logically concluded it must have been a bobcat's kill.[46]

The other intriguing kill site was also scrutinized closely and perceived as the work of a bobcat by tracks and disturbance in the snow a considerable distance from the kill. A skilled woodsmen and tracker, Downing's investigation of the site revealed a large tuft of cat fur where the bobcat had been injured by the defending deer. Tracks in the snow suggested the bobcat had ridden the deer for some distance before the deer succumbed to its prolonged biting. A cougar, on the other hand, typically kills swiftly with a powerful bite and twist to the neck.[47]

Another kill was discovered in Shenandoah National Park, covered with leaves and sticks in classic cougar fashion; the cache was visited by an internationally known cat expert, Dr. Paul Leyhausen, who observed the kill and examined it closely.[48] He saw mortal wounds in the form of puncture marks on the neck just below the base of the head.[49] The wide spacing of these puncture marks ruled out bobcat. Bobcats often go for the throat or as mentioned bite repeatedly in hopes of overwhelming the victim.[50] He noted that a bear had disturbed the cache, but he concluded confidently that the kill was the work of a cougar-sized cat.[51] Downing was invigorated and called attention to the discovery, hoping to get more people involved in the search for cougar sign around Shenandoah.

Downing set out in his quest as a tracker but soon realized that few roads in the area of his research had good tracking medium.[52] He solved the problem by doing extensive tracking in winter. But even that was a challenge because often only the mountain peaks would experience snow. He felt that cougars, like the bobcats, might wait out the snows or travel to lower elevations with the deer. Deer tended to feed during snowstorms or shortly after their conclusion, and so Downing did not lose all hope.[53]

Eventually, on a cold and windy day not far from the Blue Ridge Parkway, he came upon a set of indistinguishable tracks. Ignoring the wind and biting cold, Downing followed the tracks to the satisfaction of an inner voice begging him to continue. He recognized something in the trail that made him trudge ahead through the maelstrom of blowing snow.[54]

He noted the distance between tracks and the places where the animal chose to go over obstacles instead of under, and all these things began to speak in concert with his inner self. Soon he followed the trail to a log where the animal had chosen to walk along the top of the log, which was a feline behavior. The stride was on average 45 cm -- a little long for a bobcat. His exhilaration began to escalate.[55]

Next he found places where the cat had jumped and he measured these with astonishment as he rolled out the measuring tape further than it had ever been before. This was a monster size cat, he thought and now these measurements put the creature well beyond the known capacity of a bobcat. His inner voice had served him well, and he documented the trail carefully.[56]

He never casted tracks, explaining that the conditions in these forests are poor for tracking. "The leaf litter is very thick here, and as one steps on the forest floor they literally bounce back up."[57] Downing had never found good substrate to walk along and search mile end to mile end. The tracking was done in the snow, and when there was none, he would investigate past sightings. When asked about the reports received of cougars in these remote parts, Downing answers that these are, for the most part, cases of mistaken identity. "I would say ninety percent of these sightings are false, but there has to be something to the other ten percent. Many of these sightings are coming from experienced biologists and sport hunters."[58]

Downing laughs about making any comments on whether he feels they exist or as to the identity of these sightings:

> It sure is a perplexing case study, and indeed the cougar is most secretive. I really do not know what to make of it. We will have to wait and see. There is no logical reason why they could not have survived. Game officials must become further involved and accept the present evidence. I would look to the north for the answer. It seems more possible up there.[59]

Downing believes the deer herds in the East were available for the cougar, contrasting to some degree what is popularly thought and stressed as the limiting factor for the cougar. Concrete evidence shows that cougars did survive into the 1890s, possibly the early 1900s, and by 1914 The Weeks Act had begun bolstering the return of the deer.[40] His study area was appropriately in one of the few places where both shelter and deer remained over time. He mentions the 100,000 acres of virgin forest found in North Carolina and the George Vanderbilt land that protected the last remaining deer in the region. These are large enough areas for the cougar to have hidden and survive on deer that were known to have endured.[60]

Downing finished up his cougar research in 1983 and said the following: "I was unable to prove that a viable population existed."[61]

Dutifully, he wrote the mandated recovery plan for the return of the cougar in the East. Recovery plans are always written but often left as mere ideas on pages and not activated with a recovery team, such was the case for the cougar in the Appalachians.[62]

CHAPTER THREE

ON COMMON GROUND

From the early inquiries of Reverend Ballou, Bruce Wright, and Hal Hitchcock to the research of Nicole Culbertson, Robert Downing, and Virginia Fifield, cougar sightings increased steadily. And while their efforts failed to prove the cougar in the central Appalachians or the Northeast, they did generate further interest. Fifield collected tracks that she alone felt were good. Culbertson was convinced there were a few cougars living in and near the Smoky Mountains, but lack of physical evidence left her report largely ignored. Downing's work is thought to have come up dry; but he did have the tracks in snow and the deer kill to think about. The fact that three investigations could not produce anything more substantial suggests that cougars were either too scarce or completely absent. All of these investigators remained open-minded and encouraged others to keep looking.

Not surprisingly, shortly after Fifield's small survey team disbanded, two larger groups formed. These groups were primarily interested in convincing state wildlife authorities that the cougar still held out. Unfortunately, as mentioned, agencies were often unwilling and financially unable to consider the existence of this species. Their focus was on game species prior to 1970, and their budgets were as tight then as they are today. Seldom had a sighting been investigated, and in those rare instances when they had been, the investigation typically took place many days too late for biologists to find quality evidence. In most cases, it was not until the mid-1980s, after Fifield's work in Massachusetts, that calls from the public were given attention. Whether in Maine, Maryland or South Carolina, the reception for anyone reporting a cougar had been a unified statement of disbelief and cynicism. Nevertheless, sighting reports continued to filter into the various state game agencies, and in 1974 a man named Ted Reed reported a cougar. Prior to this sighting, Reed had no knowledge of the cougar east of the Mississippi. The experience was to affect him deeply.

> In late May of 1974, I encountered a panther in Digby County, Nova Scotia. I had a clear broadside view of the animal straight ahead of me at a distance of less than fifty feet. It was a full-grown adult of the classic tawny color, and I estimated its weight to be at least 150 lbs. I could see it was a wild creature. The way it moved, the way it leapt, the way it looked, the way it carried its tail, all spoke of an animal in the prime of its life and powers and in superb condition. It was the most exciting wildlife experience I ever had, and its image was burned into my consciousness for good. I wish I could better express the impression this experience had upon me.[1]

Reed reported his experience to the authorities and found that his zeal was not matched or welcomed. He was assured there were no panthers. Convinced beyond all doubt of the identity of what he had just seen, Reed set out to investigate. It did not take him long to discover that cougars once roamed the East. He learned how they had supposedly become extirpated many decades ago. After additional research into the cat's extirpation, he was further convinced that what he saw was a wild cougar and that this animal must have struggled on undetected over the decades. He knew that what he saw was a glimpse of history and a piece of the past.

A graduate of Harvard and a successful businessman, Reed became forever changed by the experience and made the decision to use his skills as an accomplished academic scholar to research the history behind the animal's current status of alleged extinction. He found accounts of cougars dating back to the 1890s that occurred simultaneously while the animal was rumored to be extinct. In Reed's words, "There is this most shy creature that has never left us. The research all points in that direction. The animal never became extinct." He went on to show that sightings and occasional tracks, while not evidence, do suggest survival. "If they were killed off, why would rumors, sightings, and tracks continue to appear?"[2] Reed also demonstrated to the authorities that the evidence failed to show the creature's exact date of extinction. "There is no formal research that confirms extinction in any region. Upon what evidence did they establish this fact?"[3]

Theodore B. (Ted) Reed, founder of Friends of the Eastern Panther (FOTEP), inspects a set of tracks in the New Brunswick snow, 1992. *Photo by Jay Tischendorf*

Upon his retirement in 1989, Reed established an organization called Friends of the Eastern Panther (FOTEP). The group was formed with two simple and clearly defined objectives. First, the organization would provide the political pressure to force the state and federal authorities into taking cougar sighting reports seriously. Without question, this had been the most challenging barrier in proving or disproving the animal's existence. Second, the organization would attempt to gain the resources necessary to conduct a full search for the animal, and if this proved unfeasible initially, then the first objective might make it possible. Reed also acted as an educator. Several FOTEP sponsored lectures were conducted across New England and in New Brunswick; topics included identification, cougar biology, and tracking methods.[4]

In 1990 Reed was notified of a significant sighting in Waasis, New Brunswick, Canada, where film footage of an alleged cougar kitten had been taken. Reed knew the sighting and the accompanying piece of evidence could help FOTEP move toward its goal of gaining the authorities' attention and a serious commitment to the investigation of cougars in eastern states.[5]

Reed contacted Jay Tischendorf, a young biologist whose extensive experience with fieldwork and carnivores, including tracking and tagging cougars in Yellowstone National Park, made him a likely candidate to review the video for authenticity. Donna and Roger Noble of Waasis, New Brunswick, made the video on May 15, 1990.[6] This unsuspecting couple could not have anticipated the degree of attention that Reed was able to give their most credible sighting. Their quaint farm and workshop received considerable attention, but the video attracted even more attention. In September, 1990, the New Brunswick Department of Natural Resources and Energy (DNRE), offered an official press release highlighting the exciting moment and all the work put into the validation of its subject. Copies of the video were provided to the public at the DNRE office in Fredricton, New Brunswick. The Nobles retained the original video and authorized rights to numerous publications and newsrooms.

Tischendorf described his impression of the video as believable. Furthermore, based on his experience he suspected that the kitten was about 8 to 12 months old. He was unable to determine the size of the cougar. In addition, the Royal Canadian Mounted Police crime lab had been contacted and had aided in the analysis of the film. The lab concluded that the feline in the film was 25 inches high at the top of its head. They based this statement on their painstaking scrutiny of the animal in the film and a series of measured reference posts placed in a re-reenactment film created by the area game biologist in cooperation with the crime lab.

Tischendorf narrated the film's actual contents in the following statement:

> Filmed in the late afternoon along the mixed forest border of a south-central New Brunswick farm field, the work was hardly a masterpiece. Roger Noble filmed while his sister-in-law shouted instructions from afar. His unfamiliarity with the device is apparent as was his breathlessness from seeing the cat and running for the

camera. Replete with nervous wavering, long distance shots, poor resolution, and irrelevant aiming, the video reminded me of the famous Patterson Sasquatch film.

Nonetheless, there are several clear sequences of the animal performing various behaviors. The cat's build, particularly the shoulders, was impressive, its sinewy muscles rippling through its immaculate coat as the animal walked the edge of the grassy field. It was initially unconcerned, apparently, by the people nearby; the distance from the cat to the witnesses ranged from about 100 feet to 500 feet. The cat's relative proportion was best seen when it stepped out onto a dirt road. It paused, looking at the camera with its body at an angle.[7]

Others reviewing the film and the site where it was filmed included Gary Moore, a regional wildlife biologist, and David Cartwright. All agreed, including Ted Reed, that the animal seen in the video was indeed a young, healthy cougar.

The cougar had been filmed in an area that Bruce Wright had cited years ago as being an active breeding habitat for cougars. Wright had an even greater feeling, based on his research and field observations, that a region further to the southeast and far more rugged was likely to contain a remnant population. He believed, that this area, known as the Fundy Coast, was a home for the eastern cougar, and that many of the sightings originated as transients from this location. With deep respect and admiration for this incredibly accomplished man, Reed put together a mission to explore this remote and rugged coastal forest.

In 1992 his mission was realized. Reed immediately selected Jay Tischendorf, a proven friend by this time, and then later he chose a renowned naturalist named Sue Morse. With the help of Tischendorf and Morse, Reed set out for the Fundy Coastal area. Searching on snowshoes and snowmobiles, the FOTEP team found it difficult terrain. Morse noted that the region had sustained some heavy logging and that the forest was mostly boreal with very few hardwoods. Intuitively, she sensed that the area, although hidden and remote, was not productive habitat for cougars and their primary prey - white-tailed deer.[8]

The group managed to hire a pilot who flew them over the forest several times. Morse commented that, "It was a beautiful and wild country, but it had been logged and the habitat was not conducive to cougars in my opinion, nor did we find any evidence of them there."[9]

She pointed out that the region to the northwest was a mixed hardwood forest, and it was there she felt a population of cougars would more likely survive.

Although, nothing in the way of evidence came from their excursion, it gave them a first hand bird's eye view of the habitat there and their opinions were presented to the Canadian biologists; FOTEP, had, nonetheless, inspired sincere respect from these previously disinterested agency personnel. Reed saw success in this realm -- major changes in attitude from key people working on wildlife issues in the East. These changed attitudes were a result of the group's hard work. Gary Donovan, Chief of Maine Inland Fish and Game Division said, "We are now taking the eastern panther sightings seriously, in that there may be a small population."[10] Alan Graham, New Brunswick's Minister of Natural Resources said, "There are definitely cougars in New Brunswick, not many mind you, but they are there."[11] David Cartwright, tragically killed in an automobile accident shortly after the Waasis video evaluation, said before his untimely death, "We can no longer ignore the evidence."[12] Dan Tourtelotte, Warden of Greenville, Maine admitted, "We are keeping a positive attitude on eastern cougars."[13] Cedric Alexander of the Vermont Fish and Game commented, "We are actively pursuing reports."[14] Soon afterward, the New Brunswick Panther Research Team was formed with this great momentum.

While FOTEP explored the evidence at hand in the Northeast, another group did much the same in the mid-Atlantic states. John Lutz, founder of The Eastern Puma Research Network (EPRN) successfully gathered reports that he felt were credible from every state east of the Mississippi except Rhode Island. Their criteria for a credible report include the following requirements: multiple witnesses, experienced observer, extended time of sighting, and some evidence such as hair, tracks, a photograph or video. EPRN collected 2,200 sightings between July 1, 1983, and January 1, 1994, that met these criteria. An additional 3,900 reports were received that did not meet these criteria. The following ten years produced similar figures.[15]

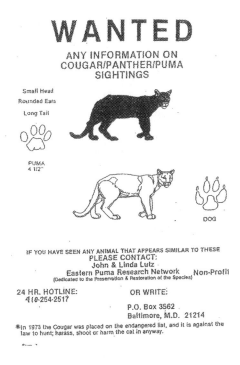

WANTED

ANY INFORMATION ON
COUGAR/PANTHER/PUMA
SIGHTINGS

Small Head

Rounded Ears

Long Tail

PUMA
4 1/2"

DOG

IF YOU HAVE SEEN ANY ANIMAL THAT APPEARS SIMILAR TO THESE
PLEASE CONTACT:
John & Linda Lutz
Eastern Puma Research Network   Non-Profit
(Dedicated to the Preservation & Restoration of the Species)

24 HR. HOTLINE: OR WRITE:
410-254-2517
P.O. Box 3562
Baltimore, M.D. 21214

*In 1973 the Cougar was placed on the endangered list, and it is against the
law to hunt; harass, shoot or harm the cat in anyway.

The EPRN circulated posters and flyers

Members of EPRN and FOTEP range from outdoor enthusiasts such as anglers, hikers, hunters, and campers to the anthropomorphizing animal rights activists and radical environmentalists. Often the most active members of these groups were people who felt they had seen a cougar. In most cases, those having claimed a sighting were ordinary homeowners living in rural areas, but more often than that cougars were seen from motor vehicles on remote or rural roads. In other words, most of these witnesses had no previous interest in wildlife, and the others were not pursuing wildlife or outdoor recreation.

FOTEP and EPRN have given continuity to the cougar question, by recording the sightings and gathering related information. Reed had an extensive file of cougar-related news clippings, peer-reviewed articles, and correspondences in his Exeter, New Hampshire office. His most precious collection was the research file of Bruce Wright, given to him personally by Wright's widow. EPRN has also amassed an extensive clearinghouse of cougar reports, plaster track casts, and even videotapes. The work of these groups has contributed to speculations made by many professionals who have tried to grapple with the issue. Reed passed away in 2001, and his extensive collection of data remained with his widow until Tischendorf, in collaboration with her, had it transferred to the University of New Brunswick, where it is now a contribution to cougar history and science.[16]

These groups had gathered the resources to effectively argue their case. The result is that today a larger number of reported cougar sightings are recorded by state biologists, and channels are open to receive and analyze any evidence. Reed's organization FOTEP disbanded in 1994.[17] The Eastern Puma Research Network has continued, and in 2009 gathered over 700 reports.[18]

EPRN was informally conceived in 1965 by John Lutz, a reporter for WFBR Radio in Baltimore, Maryland. Lutz describes his first introduction to the eastern cougar as follows:

> When walking into the newsroom on the fateful day of June 5, 1965, the first thing my mentor and boss, Louis Corbin, said to me was, 'I have just the story for you, John' -- It turned out some wild animal was causing a great deal of panic and commotion, and I was assigned to check it out. The wild animal we eventually discovered causing 'farmyard and domestic deaths' was a puma as described by the late Dr. Roth, who checked into the incidents. I then wrote my first article about this story, and it was called 'Phantom Cat.' My love affair with the mysterious cat had begun.[19]

In the 1960s and 1970s Lutz gathered reports from all of Maryland, which is where his EPRN is located. Slowly he expanded and began investigating the status of cougars throughout the Mid-Atlantic region. In the beginning the bulk of his reports came from southern Pennsylvania and Virginia. From 1965 through 1979 Lutz had received over 500 sighting reports, and people were beginning to ask about membership. His experience with the media allowed him to promote his interest. It was not until 1983, however, that the group was formally established as EPRN. Dr. Pennington Smith, a wildlife biologist, and Roth, a zoologist, helped to get the group going. Smith resigned after a short time.[20]

Compared to EPRN, FOTEP probably accomplished more in the way of establishing credible pieces of evidence and affecting change in the response of agencies. FOTEP gained a tremendous respect and cooperation from the Canadians in New Brunswick, and was instrumental in having the Waasis video professionally evaluated.[21] On the other hand, EPRN has amassed data invaluable for the present and future understanding of the sightings mystery. Lutz, who has no formal scientific or biological training, unfortunately, has also alienated state agencies, as he is a zealot-like believer and suspects a cover-up has been orchestrated not only on the state level but federal as well. He also opines covert release of cougars by state and federal agents.

Lutz's sometimes "far out" approach has served to stigmatize the notion of surviving cougars and has done little to separate the search from those of Bigfoot and the Loch Ness Monster. Lutz's own introduction to the cougar question came from that end of the spectrum. With Louis Corbin as mentor, could it have started any other way? United States Army Lieutenant Colonel Corbin was a former Blue Booker. Having worked on project Blue Book, the classified army study of UFOs, Corbin gravitated toward strange phenomena. In addition to his experience in the study of UFOs, he studied spontaneous human combustion.

At the time, government agencies were viewed with suspicion. The rise of the EPRN group in the 1980s helped fuel such suspicions with the notion that there was a cover-up concerning cougars. It was popular in the entertainment culture during the 1980s to foster belief in government secrets, and the public was receptive. Logical explanations do exist for some of these suspicions, but this does not imply that there are or were cover-ups. It means that there are reasons why some may believe a cover-up exists. First, consider the policy ramifications under the Endangered Species Act that would impact land use should this wide-ranging carnivore be discovered. Second, consider the fear that might follow if cougars were officially discovered and disclosed near human habitation. Third, there are liability issues when talking about large powerful carnivorous predators. Some have claimed that a cover up exists in the Smoky Mountains. There are documents acknowledging cougar sightings in the park and park staff who have commented on their disbelief regarding a resident cougar population -- but there is no evidence of park professionals hiding anything.[22]

Such suspicions eventually lend themselves to creating more controversy. They help to cause communication problems between agencies and witnesses, as the witnesses have what they believe is proof and the biologist has the burden to prove it. The inability to prove it is seen as denial by witnesses, who are sure of their experience or findings, and the doubt, an appropriate attitude for the scientist, is later misconstrued as a wish to cover-up. From the professional biologists' point of view, the noble efforts and conclusions of groups such as FOTEP and EPRN may actually discredit any existing evidence by masquerading it under the scientifically unsound methods employed in obtaining it.[23] This view does not take away from the contributions of independent researchers or interest groups; without their data and observations, the whole cougar question would remain adrift. Their work was done outside of scientific communities, and yet it was the wish of these groups that the scientific community would get involved or meet them half way. Perhaps, this is why FOTEP with the cooperation of Tischendorf and Morse had better credibility.

As Wright influenced Reed, so too did Reed influence Tischendorf, and in doing so, the scientific community did finally meet the issue half way. Initial contact with the scientific community began with Steve Ropski. Having wanted for several years to hold a symposium focused on cougars in the East, Tischendorf, through a referral from another scientist, contacted Ropski, an enthusiastic biology professor at Gannon University, in Eerie Pennsylvania. Tischendorf and Ropski went on to organize the first Eastern Cougar Conference at Gannon, which assembled the first meeting of scientists and lay persons to discuss and account for the evidence of eastern cougars. From this conference a tremendous amount of information was processed and made available; the meeting put substance behind the issue and provided historical perspective and an overview. The Eastern Cougar Conference of 1994 opened the door for scientific involvement at last.

The conference of 1994 cleared the way for new cougar groups to form. These two new groups pursued cougars with the help of highly qualified biologists. Unlike older cougar groups, the recently organized Cougar Network and the Eastern Cougar Foundation employ the Internet as their marketing or recruiting vehicle. Each group was formed to document the presence of cougars in the East. The Cougar Network is new to the scene and a spin off from the Eastern Cougar Foundation, that has been active since 1999. Because of its well-organized approach and focus on presenting existing evidence rather than searching for new, the Cougar Network has been very influential.

With the help of Jim Close, Ken Miller, and Bob Wilson, Mark Dowling formed what was then called the Eastern Cougar Network in July of 2002. Dr. Clay Nielsen joined as Director of Scientific Research in the summer of 2003, and then Harley Shaw was eagerly made their general Director in 2005.[24] In their effort to document the cougar, they petitioned the help of a wide number of federal, state, provincial, and nationally known wildlife biologists. By working with these professionals, the Network is able to obtain moment to moment cougar-related information. Furthermore, the information that is received can then be reviewed by the group's consultants, qualified biologists or forensic experts. Until recently, the Cougar Network did not consist of members, but rather, was a nonprofit organization that accepted contributions for its own research. Basically the Cougar Network was a website sustained by its dynamic networking ability to present and evaluate up-to-date cougar evidence. Since 2004 the Cougar Network began to accept members and became rapidly active in acquiring donations to channel into research.

In contrast to the Cougar Network, the Eastern Cougar Foundation, while maintaining a website, was always largely supported by members.[25] Its mission was originally to prove the presence of the eastern cougar and protect it. This is a far more pro-active approach than the Cougar Network's news postings. Like the Cougar Network, the Eastern Cougar Foundation has at its side the input and guidance of trained professionals, and these people make up the Board of Directors. Together their combined knowledge and enthusiasm for the intriguing topic acts to steer the organization toward reaching its objectives and goals, which were clearly stated by its founder and first president Todd Lester.

Lester aimed to document the cougar in areas of highly credible sightings, and he remains acutely interested in locating any possible breeding populations. Also, he intends to promote legal protection of all cougars in the East, regardless of debatable origin or genetic history. Finally, he believes that education will lead the way for the cougar to find a future and return safely to its former eastern forests.[26]

Mark Dowling, an attendee at the 1994 conference, had originally decided to investigate the real story that sustains the cougar controversy when he visited an Internet discussion board on cougars and sightings. Turned off by the "fanatics" he encountered on the Internet's discussion boards, chat-rooms and list-serves, Dowling set out to mitigate the "nonsense." As he learned more about the cougar, his interest grew and he was inspired to offer an objective approach to the issue. In doing so he created an invaluable tool, upon which observers can clearly see patterns in cougar activity. Dowling's "on the wall for you to see" approach to the issue has, without persuasion or direct selling, convincingly changed the views of many.[27]

Lester's quest for the cougar was born in the early dawn one day when he was out hunting and saw a cougar make its way down a hillside. This 1983 encounter with a cougar in West Virginia's Wyoming County made a lasting impression on him. In contrast, Mark Dowling of Newton, Connecticut, does not believe the great cat still roams free. "If Lester saw a cougar then it must have been an escaped pet or a western cougar marching east," Dowling explains.[28]

But Lester, while open minded and fully aware of the improbability of what he saw, instinctively believes that the cougar he saw was of pre-settlement origin. Since his 1983 sighting Lester has gone on to educate himself on the ways of the cougar. Lester, a former military man, was once stationed in south Florida at Homestead Air Force Base, where he took full advantage of the presence of the Florida panther and perfected his tracking skills gained from running the ridges of his native West Virginia. He took this skill back with him to West Virginia, where he earned a reputation as a woodsman and expert houndsman.[29]

Lester recalls the day when he announced his sighting to the game biologists in West Virginia -- he was impolitely dismissed. They had no interest, but Lester, like Ted Reed, never doubted his experience. Lester then went on to form a well-equipped organization complete with non-profit status. The ECF was an organization more closely reminiscent of those bygone ones such as FOTEP, in that it sought to vindicate believers who were, as Lester has been, sometimes dismissed by wildlife authorities.

Meanwhile, Dowling's success with the Cougar Network can be credited to the excellent cooperation from the very same agency personnel that once rejected Lester. While the Cougar Network simply requests for agencies to relay their cougar confirmations, Lester's group asked the agencies to recognize that these confirmations meant something. Thus, the two different approaches elicit two different results for cougar enthusiasts.[30]

Lester was not an extremist; and denies believing in a cover-up, but he himself once pursued the Great Smokey Mountains Park Administration using the Freedom of Information Act to obtain additional documentation. Lester, who is a coal miner by profession, seeks more acknowledgment regarding cougar encounters. He feels the need to at least gain protection for the cougar, even if it is only symbolic protection. Having seen a cougar in the wild, there is more than just a sense of responsibility that drives Lester; there is emotion.

As mentioned, one of the group's objectives was to seek formal legal protection for the cougars that might exist or arrive in the East anyway it could. Looking to Florida, it found the "Similarity of Appearance Clause," which Lester used to appeal to the then Secretary of the Interior Bruce Babbit. The "Similarity of Appearance Clause" states that all cougars regardless of subspecies or origin are protected, based on outward similarities to the endangered subspecies. In other words, all panthers roaming free in Florida can be assumed to be Florida panthers *Puma concolor coryi*, which are endangered and under full protection. Likewise, if granted to cover the eastern cougar, this would mean any cougar found in the East, north of Florida, is considered the endangered eastern cougar *Puma concolor couguar* (*couguar* noting subspecies-spelled couguar not cougar) and given full protection.

The hopes of Lester's group were high, and with the blessings of his supportive wife who has a legal background, Lester carefully addressed Secretary Babbit. The answer: the U. S. Fish and Wildlife could not consider the Clause to afford the cougar protection until there was absolute, unquestionable proof of a wild breeding, self-sustaining population. Lester has been looking ever since, and in March of 2004, the Eastern Cougar Foundation placed 20 motion-sensitive cameras in West Virginia's Monongahela National Forest.[31] The cameras were obtained with grants from two wildlife foundations, and the remote camera survey was conducted in wonderful cooperation with the U.S. Fish and Wildlife Service, the U.S. Forest Service and the state Division of Natural Resources. Using a grid system, as recommended by his Board of Directors, Lester systematically bracketed his study area, setting up the auto cameras in hopes of catching the elusive cougar by surprise some dark night. Lester, a skilled outdoors person, confessed, "I would have rather set these cameras randomly on instinct rather than in quadrants."[32]

Deer, coyotes, bears, bobcats and raccoons were the most
common species to appear on the camera traps set by
the ECF. There were no cougars photographed.
Courtesy Cougar Rewilding Foundation

The first to come aboard his fledgling organization was a woman from his own neck of the woods. Chris Bolgiano, a librarian and assistant professor from rural Appalachia, had written several articles on cougars and was eager to give Lester assistance. Before long Lester had managed, in spite of his quiet disposition, to gain the assistance of Bob Downing, now retired from the USFWS and Helen McGinnis. Helen McGinnis is currently an independent wildlife researcher, a wildlife author and a former paleontologist scholar. She has done extensive research on cougars in Pennsylvania and Mississippi. Lester's completed Board of Directors eventually included a variety of knowledgeable, highly accomplished, wildlife experts to act as a "think tank." Most of the key players in the hunt for and discussion of the eastern cougar were placed on board, which gave his organization a great deal of credibility. In 2007 Lester resigned and Jay Tischendorf assumed the vacancy. Tischendorf saw the need to begin looking forward, and changed the organization's objective. The goal of the ECF is now to facilitate the recovery of the cougar in all suitable habitats and so it voted to change its name in 2010 to the Cougar Rewilding Foundation. The same year that conservationist Mark Spatz took over as the present day president. Spatz, is sharp witted, well educated and an enthusiastic rock climber.

The Cougar Network's Mark Dowling also constructed an impressive coalition of reputable scientists for his cause. Most prominent among them is Harley Shaw, a renowned cougar biologist with 27 years of experience under his belt. Being a successful business employee for General Electric, Dowling used his people skills to bring together those involved or interested in the eastern cougar. This spirit is reflected in the comments of Adrian Wydeven, a Wisconsin wildlife biologist, on the positive role of the Cougar Network:

> Coordination of cougar reporting in the eastern and mid-western U.S. is critical for documenting the presence and possible colonization of this large predator back into its former range in the Midwest and East. An objective, scientific based approach for reporting, discussing, examining and reviewing of information on 'eastern' cougars will be extremely useful in establishing their presence. The Cougar Network will be extremely helpful in determining the changing status of cougars in this portion of the U.S.[33]

In May of 2004 a second conference took place in Morgantown, West Virginia. The conference was set up by Helen McGinnis and Jay Tischendorf, who with other members of the ECF or Cougar Rewilding Foundation, gathered a diverse set of speakers. Like Wydeven, Tischendorf appreciated the contribution from various individuals, agencies and interest groups in determining the future status of the cougar in the East.

Dr. Jay Tischendorf, initiated the 1994 and 2004 Eastern
Cougar Conferences. He is one of the leading authorities
on the subject and is seen here standing behind a discussion
panel at the conference. *Photo by Dave Denoma*

A very big part of the eastern cougar story is the appreciation of a
wide variety of eccentric and creative characters it has attracted; but
equally important has been the tremendous patience, devotion, and
wisdom of those courageous scientists and organizers from the days
of Bruce Wright and Hal Hitchcock, to those active today, such as
Jay Tischendorf, Helen McGinnis, and Mark Dowling. So often in
the beginning of understanding, there are those who are perceived as
with incredulity. Almost always, they are scoffed at, but then one day
the tide of new information brings the consensus to accept the new
and radical thought as truth. Without the volunteer non profit work
of the private Cougar Rewilding Foundation and Cougar Network,
the scientific community would be at a great loss for explanations and
insights regarding this most intriguing and perplexing phenomena.
Such researchers and all those mentioned in the previous chapter will
bring us to the objective thinking that will allow opinions and beliefs
to mature.

PART TWO:

THE EVIDENCE

CHAPTER FOUR

EVIDENCE IN THE NORTHEAST

Though the evidence produced from Bruce Wright, Virginia Fifield, Robert Downing, Nicole Culbertson, Hal Hitchcock, and those noble cougar organizations were all a part of the dialogue at the cougar conferences, many more sightings accumulate via the state wildlife agencies. These important pieces of the puzzle were not neglected by the enthusiasts, but so much of what is reported to these entities is flimsy. Nevertheless, they comprise the bulk of the cougar question. Largely consisting of sightings without documentation, exciting reports of the long tailed carnivore at close proximity make for serious consideration because some of the evidence presented is very convincing. In fact, in some regions the appearance of a cougar is irrefutable.

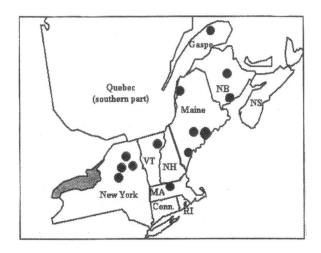

The Northeast has many good sightings. The circles
represent credible reports with evidence. Each year there
are hundreds of reports that cannot be confirmed.
Courtesy Cougar Network

In the next two chapters the evidence is presented state by state,
each beginning with some historical appreciation. There were certain
regions that held more cougars than others and a brief mention of their
previous status or presence is therefore given. The significant sightings
and pieces of evidence from each state are provided, and the conclusions
made by the respective agencies are mentioned, too.

DELAWARE

Few accounts of the cougar came from this state during its early years
of settlement, but given the wealth of deer that once thrived there, it is
likely cougar could have been found.[1]

Today, they claim cougars slink about at night, slipping quietly
through backyards and school playgrounds, roaming hungry, searching
widely. These large flesh eating carnivores leave little proof of their
presence. Yet according to the Delaware Division of Fish and Wildlife,
that presence, confirmed by their biologists, however small, was proof
enough for them to disclose that cougars were living in the state in
2006. It is ironic that such a highly developed region would bring
forth such news, but state authorities believed that there were at least
two cougars roaming free in New Castle County along the northern

border. But despite, a publicly confirmed presence, there is no evidence of sustained residency, and reports have long since dwindled. It is rumored that the sighted animals escaped from a small enclosure in Coatsville, Pennsylvania. Scats have not been obtained and origins remain unknown.

Sightings have come from a variety of sources, including state environmental police and conservation officers.[2] Butch LeFebvre, a law enforcement officer, attempted to capture one of these big cats. In previous attempts almost every method had been tried except for the most promising - hounds. Houndsmen had been called in to help but were ultimately not used because of the suburban setting. The cougars were chased on foot by environmental police carrying tranquilizer guns and night vision goggles. Not surprisingly, they were unsuccessful.[3]

Biologists say they have found proof that the cats are killing Canada geese and frequenting residential areas. New Castle County is highly suburbanized, but there is a large state park surrounded by estates with significant woodlands in private ownership. A few sightings come from White Clay Creek State Park, and also from outside of New Castle County along Route 40, between Route 1 and Route 896.[4] Normally, you have agency personnel discrediting sightings, but in this bizarre situation, they are openly confirming that there are cougars without sharing any proof. They seem confident the animals are escapees.

CONNECTICUT

Although Connecticut is heavily developed, the white-tailed deer numbers have reached record highs; virtually everywhere, these herbivores push the carrying capacity and are forced to inhabit suburban yards. There is an estimated 50,000 deer in this tiny industrial state.[5] Unlike many parts of the United States, Connecticut's suburban sprawl is interwoven with undeveloped land. The trees are often left standing in subdivisions, and sections of yards and towns retain small woodlots. Viewed from afar, the state would appear to be rather well forested. Small woodlots work to the advantage of deer because the human proximity eliminates hunting due to safety concerns. While Connecticut is a poor candidate for relic populations, it is conceivable that cougars could travel corridors into the deer-rich state from the north and northwest. The question is, could they remain long enough to take advantage of the available prey before human interference would occur?

Hundreds of years ago, the rich deciduous hills and fertile valleys must have made Connecticut a hospitable environment for large carnivores dependent on herbivores. In the northwestern corner of the state, steep hills covered in giant hemlocks provided suitable habitat for the cougar, who may have used the land to retreat for raising young and to surprise occasional prey. Oaks, hickories, laurels and hemlocks constituted the Connecticut landscape, along with towering white pines and black, yellow, and white birch.

The cougar was believed to have once been common in Connecticut. Goodwin said in his 1935 publication *The Mammals of Connecticut*, the cougar is "not uncommon in the mountainous country of Litchfield County."[6] This state has produced many cougar reports, but few of them have been established as credible. Here, as in other New England states, there is a great deal of interest in the topic. It was always a good issue for sportsmen to debate, but ever since the full-page picture of a cougar adorned the pages of *The Hartford Courant's Northeast Magazine* in April 2003, everyone has been talking about cougars.[7]

Most of the talk is just that -- and there has been very little in the way of good evidence until just recently. But when calls are received, they come from the "right" places -- the regions that offer cover, isolation, and prey. Cougars are seen in the northwest part of the state in the Litchfield Hills, the wooded areas around Barkhamsted, and of course along the Massachusetts border, near Burlington and beyond.

Frequently heard rumors consist of cougars being released by a breeder just over the state line in South Egremont, Massachusetts. However, investigations there turned up negative in the way of captive cougars or breeding licenses. In 2003, Tony Gola, a Massachusetts game biologist, received numerous reports of a cougar that was allegedly sunning itself regularly at the edge of a golf course in that same county. Barkhamsted has had some interesting sightings over the decades, but what is striking is the story of an intentional release. Apparently, a story surfaced of a wealthy outdoorsman who enjoyed running dogs on cougars out west and wanted to do the same in Connecticut. Since there were no cougars near his home in Barkhamsted, he would run the dogs on bobcats and then let the cats go free. He soon tired of this and traveled west to keep his hobby active and the dogs in practice. He then concocted a scheme to bring back a few mountain lions from Colorado.

He told the story to local columnist, Dave Sampson of the *Norwich Bulletin*, and confessed of illegally importing cats purchased in Colorado. The cats were set free with the hope of establishing a breeding population in western Connecticut. The release seemed to produce only one sighting, a week later in the same town, but there were no reports anywhere after that. They were never accounted for again.[8]

Sampson has often wondered if cougars allegedly seen in Pachaug Forest in Voluntown, Connecticut that same year may have been one of the released cats. Pachaug has since had a small cluster of sightings, as has nearby Stonington, Connecticut. Even though Stonington is wooded, it is an island in a sea of development, and an unlikely site for a cougar. A released pet cougar could hide in the area, but this is another unlikely possibility. Pachaug, however, does have some proximity to the Quabbin, connected by a corridor of green.

Paul Rego is the wildlife biologist who handles cougar sightings and information. Rego is absolutely convinced there is no such animal lurking in his state. Rego receives close to one hundred cougar calls a year, and he handles each one responsibly. He records all the details regardless of how ridiculous some of the reports may seem. There is no cluster area, and although many come from west of the Connecticut River, many others are spread throughout wooded parts of the state. Although Rego does follow up on reports more than most other state biologists in New England or elsewhere, he has never found any credible evidence. "Many reports sound credible over the phone, but there are always these limiting factors like the short duration of the sighting and the distance from the viewer. Each time I visit a site, the witness is excited and convinced, but the evidence is not convincing."[9]

Rego believes that there are so many people in Connecticut that if cougars were there, someone would have at least brought him some tracks or scat -- something to suggest a presence. He believes Connecticut may have some suitable habitat to lure a cougar in from surrounding areas if any did exist, but they do not -- according to him. In the eastern part of the state, there is the 23,000-acre Pachaug State Forest, and in the western part, contiguous woodlands can be found around the Barkhamsted Reservoir and its adjacent 9,000-acre Tunxis State Forest.[10] Is it possible these wooded regions may have enticed a cougar in from its travels through the region? Because in June of 2011 residents in Greenwich began reporting a large cougar roaming across their lawns and woodlots. The state biologists believed it to be a bobcat but were proven wrong when a week later a 140 pound male cougar was struck and killed on the Wilbur Cross Highway. The animal showed no signs of having been in captivity and the state was very thorough in their necropsy. The DNA findings and other tests will be mentioned later in this book.

VERMONT

In the deep forests of the Green Mountains, where thrush sing into the dark and the fawns lay silent in the sun-dappled, fern-covered wooded glades, people in the small villages of Vermont think often of the "Great Spirit Cat," or as they esteem him -- the catamount. With their deep connection to the beast, Vermonters cannot help but believe that somewhere above the farms on some distant hill, the great predator has been watching them all along. Thus, they continue to talk of him, and the newspapers continue to respond. Throughout the decades, the articles appeared, giving the catamount a level of media attention not seen anywhere else except Pennsylvania.

Such interest was so great that for many years, a column ran in a local newspaper, written by a person who went by the pen-name Panther Pete. The entire column was devoted to alleged panther sightings, but it was all about poking fun at those who claimed to see one. Panther Pete used every name imaginable to ridicule those who witnessed a panther. According to Panther Pete, there were believers and non-believers; believers were deemed "pantherites." He tried to portray them as impressionable people. During the 1960s the air finally cleared, and it was safe to publicly report a sighting. Panther Pete's readership had eventually faded with time like the yellowing pages of his original newspaper columns now preserved in the Vermont History Museum. About that same time cougar reports began to increase and one wonders just how severely the slanderous satire of Panther Pete stifled the forthcoming of witnesses? Whatever the case, the encounters increased steadily into the 1990s.[11]

In Vermont, like nowhere else, there is documentation of a constant flow of cougar sightings and evidence, beginning with Alexander Crowell's 19th century trophy and continuing to this very day. Osgood wrote in 1938 that "there have been repeated reports of panthers seen and heard in various parts of the state, but to date none has been captured to secure a reward of $100 offered by a local paper for a Vermont panther dead or alive."[12] Spargo, a well-known local author, opined in 1950 that although the last physical proof of a cougar in Vermont was 1881 in Barnard -- he would not be surprised if cougars still lurked in the hidden shadows of the Green Mountains. "Never common in the Green Mountains, cougar kills in the state were less than 200." However, Spargo believed that for every one killed there were another 500 to 1,000 allegedly sighted.[13]

There are just a few kills available for documentation from the 19th century; kills occurred in 1870, 1875, and 1881. In the early part of the next century two unauthenticated reports of specimens killed come from 1914 and 1923. The 1914 kill was thought to occur in Lamoille County at Belvedre Basin Hollow and was noted by Vermont's cougar man Hal Hitchcock in 1986. The 1923 cat was allegedly shot by a deer hunter in East Orange and was judged to weigh about 120 pounds.[14]

The next incident occurred in 1934 at Grafton Gulf near Chester in Windsor County. A track was casted by the aforementioned Reverend William Ballou and verified by Goldman at the American Museum of Natural History as mountain lion. The cast is now located in the Bennington Museum, in Bennington, Vermont, and is currently considered to have been incorrectly identified.[15] In 1941 another cast of tracks was taken, this time from Orange County in the town of Randolph. These were also taken to the American Natural History Museum and verified as mountain lion. These are now with the Barnard specimen in the Vermont Museum. In 1989 a claw, considered to be from a large cat, was shown by a student refusing to part with the item. He claims to have found it on Camels Hump in Addison County.[16]

Ironically, with so many sightings and the consistent nature of them over this long period of time, a pattern or cluster was not seen until a year before a well publicized report, that will be mentioned later, occurred in Craftsbury. Since then, sightings cluster in that area as well as in Chittenden County. Sightings from 1999 to 2000 resulted in many calls coming from the town of Fletcher. A total of eighteen credible reports were taken in that time frame. The total credible and noncredible for that span was 308 cougar sightings.[17] Many have guessed that cougars would have retreated to the highest peaks, and that this is where evidence might be found. Surprisingly, few sightings are reported from Vermont's summits, instead most come from the hills. This may be because there are few people on the summits, but state records show cougar reports occurring at lower elevations between the years 2000 and 2004.[18]

Unfortunately, Susan Morse's group Keeping Track, with its trained volunteers monitoring large carnivores, has not come across anything on high ground or low that may have been left by a catamount. The group finds plenty of tracks of bear, coyote, and bobcat, but never anything suggesting the haunts of a catamount. Cautiously, Morse has said that there is a recent case of a trained cougar hound picking up a trail in the Northeast Kingdom region. The general consensus among state wildlife biologists is that cougars may be present within the state at certain times, but they are probably the result of intentional release or escape. Vermont biologists have an open mind regarding the high number of alleged encounters and do not rule out naturally occurring transients.[19] Following the Craftsbury event in 1994, they proclaimed the existence of cougars in the state, but have retreated on this issue since that time.

PENNSYLVANIA

If you travel this state's highways, you will eventually see a deer. You may have to brake for one, too. They are everywhere, in high numbers, throughout the landscape. High deer densities and miles of lush deciduous forests are everywhere in northern and central Pennsylvania. Bobcats abound also, and in good health they travel unmolested across woodlands and pasture. Sometimes an indicator of good cougar habitat, the bobcat is on a strong comeback. Could it be that the cougar may also return to the areas with an abundance of its prey and plenty of cover?

The first settler to mention the existence of cougars in print was William Penn, in August 1683.[20] Philip Tome, who roamed the wilderness of north-central and northwestern Pennsylvania between 1789 and 1823, estimated he saw "some thirty" in his lifetime, an impressive total for this region.[21] Meshach Browning (1781-1859), a farmer in western Maryland who evidently took advantage of every opportunity to track down and kill cougars in Pennsylvania, claimed he killed "at least fifty" in his lifetime.[22]

Shoemaker (1917) claimed considerably higher kills for Pennsylvania hunters, but his figures are based on hearsay and exaggerated second- and third-hand accounts. For example, he quoted Tome's relatives as saying he killed hundreds of panthers during his lifetime.[23] Shoemaker was a Pennsylvanian historian with a gift for storytelling. He chronicled the gradual elimination of the cougar, beginning with the earlier settled and more densely populated southeastern portion east of the Blue Ridge Mountains. By 1895 he speculated that the cats survived only in the Havice and Treaster Valley of Mifflin County, although sight reports suggest they may have survived in a few other areas. At this time, uncontrolled hunting was bringing the cougar's principal prey, the white-tailed deer, to the verge of extirpation. Like the cougar, white-tails persisted mainly in remote areas.

During the mid-1800s, E. N. Woodcock spent more than fifty years hunting and trapping in north central Pennsylvania and the watershed of the Allegheny River. Apparently he knew of only one panther kill in that region during his lifetime, in southeastern Potter County. By 1903 he was convinced that none survived in the areas with which he was familiar. However, Woodcock did not range into southern Clinton County and northeastern Clearfield County, where the cougar apparently did persist.[24]

Most authorities assume the cougar had been extirpated by 1900. It is uncertain when or if the last individual was killed because so few alleged reports have been backed up with physical evidence. The last substantiated kill that author and naturalist Samuel Rhoads documented occurred in 1871, although he said that two may have been taken in 1891.[25] The last that Shoemaker was certain of were two litters of kittens taken from the same "nest" in Mifflin County in 1892 and 1893, but he believed that a few still survived in the state into1943. Young maintained that the cougar was extinct in Pennsylvania, but accepted a report from the 1920s from the northeastern part of the state. Doutt maintained that cougars still survived in 1910.[26]

At least four specimens killed in the 1800s have been preserved -- a skull collected at Wolflick Run, Elk County, in 1847 (USNM 260574 in the Smithsonian Institution's mammal collection), plus three mounted skins. The "Brush Panther", now at Pennsylvania State University in

State College, was killed around 1859 by Samuel Brush in eastern Susquehanna County.[27] The "Lycoming Panther" was presumably killed near the Loyalsock River near the turn of the century; it is now in the Lycoming County Historical Museum in Williamsport.[28] The "Dorman Panther," possibly killed by a Mr. Motx in Penn's Valley east of Aaronsburg in 1868, is now at Albright College in Reading. In addition, the Carnegie Museum of Natural History has fragmentary upper and lower jaws with teeth plus various isolated teeth that have been recovered from archeological sites and cave deposits.[29]

Believed to have been shot near the Loyalsock River, north of Williamsport, Pennsylvania, this Lycoming County specimen is accepted as an "eastern" cougar. The faded mount is on display at the Lycoming County Historical Society and has never been assigned a specific date. The steep forested hills of north-western Pennsylvania may still harbor this cat's descendents.
Lycoming Historical Society

Shoemaker was one of the first cougar enthusiasts to collect sightings; he listed other possible kills of cougars in the early 20th century :

> 1901: "Delbert Reynolds tells of seeing a panther caught in a trap and shot at Brookfield in northern Tioga County; it had been after cattle for several weeks."

1902: "A giant panther comes on roof of Simcox lumber camp, on Scootac, to get at hams hanging from rafters; it was shot; was very grey, and few teeth left, indicating advanced age."

1903: "Captain Moore sees carcass of panther on 'bar room floor of "Fallon House,' Lock Haven, surrounded by huge crowds. Killed on Scootac by Earl Monaghan."

1914: "Aaron Hall finds three panther cubs in a nest on Rock Run, Centre County; his sons gave the pelts to the writer of this article, 1914."[30]

In the late 1970s and early 1980s, McGinnis collected published reports and solicited additional reports from Game Protectors and the public. The localities of sightings and alleged kills from 1890 to 1982 were plotted on maps and compared with deer population density and road density. Since deer were abundant throughout the state, no correlation to deer density was found. However, the sightings tended to come from areas with few roads and sparse human populations.[31]

The only confirmation of a free-ranging cougar during the 20th century was the carcass of a 48-lb. female shot near Edinboro, northern Crawford County, on October 28, 1967. McGinnis interviewed the hunter and other people who were present. She also examined the mounted skin, skull, and partial skeleton. Details of the hunt and her conclusions on the possible origin of the specimen have been published. Her conclusions:

> (1) the cougar was a subadult or young adult, not "a little less than half grown" as Doutt had assumed; (2) two cougars escaped from the farm of a former circus performer near Pierpoint, Ohio -- about 40 miles west of Edinboro -- a 1-1/2-year-old male that escaped on 29 October 1966 and was killed near the farm the next day, and a three-month-old kitten of unspecified sex that escaped in early May 1967 and was not recovered; (3) the Crawford County cougar could not have been either of these escapees; (4) the Crawford County cougar was accompanied by a larger individual, seen by five witnesses, that was slightly wounded but escaped; and (5) abnormalities in the

postcranial skeleton indicate the cougar had been reared in captivity. Its coloration and unusually small size suggest it was derived from Central or South American stock.[32]

Since the late 1960s, John Lutz, you will recall he is founder of the Eastern Puma Research Network, has solicited and collected alleged sightings of evidence of cougars and has also searched for evidence. In the January 2003 issue of the organization's newsletter, The Eastern Puma Network News, Lutz totaled the number of reports received by the state since 1983. There were almost twice as many reports from Pennsylvania during this time (1,020) as from any other eastern state. The large number of reports is partially explained by the fact that Lutz has several Pennsylvania associates who help him collect reports. Also, he lived in Baltimore during most of the twenty-year period and then moved to northern West Virginia; it is to be expected that more reports would come from nearby areas.[33] What is amazing is that despite all these reports, some of which are highly credible, the only undoubted evidence is the 1967 Crawford County kill.

Proud of his kill, John Gallant admires the female cougar he shot in 1967 while in Crawford County, Pennsylvania. The origin was never proven but best evidence suggests it was not a native wild cougar.
ECF

Pennsylvania has more than enough deer to support a substantial cougar population. In fact, overabundant deer are identified as a major threat to biodiversity in the state. Hunters, especially deer hunters, are also very abundant. One would think that hunters, hikers and rural dwellers would stumble upon characteristic big cat deer kills from time to time, but none have been documented even though in the late 1970s McGinnis went to considerable effort to locate people and publications with credible cougar sightings. Today, it is rare to be with any group of outdoor or rural people without at least one person in the group claiming to have seen a cougar or knowing someone who has.[34]

RHODE ISLAND

Hidden deep within a great and impassable swamp, Native American warrior King Philip addressed his people in 1675 about the need to suppress the Europeans. They were driven into the swamp to escape the settlers who had left them with virtually no land. Metacomet, or King Philip as he is popularly known, led his followers out from the Great Swamp and proceeded to attack. We know the event as the King Philip's War, which was the Native American's final effort to defend southern New England. Like the Native American, the cougar is thought to have retreated into the impassable swamp, where it is believed by die-hard enthusiasts to be living today. Yet Rhode Island has never produced a credible track or scat and has remained one of the least active places for cougar sightings. Until recently, this state was the only place where sightings were never reported to the EPRN, but now calls come in a few times a year.

Although never common in Rhode Island, the cougar undoubtedly once hunted there. Young and Goldman are quoted: "Records of the puma in this state are exceedingly rare". The early naturalists listed it among the mammals living in Rhode Island. The last cougar kill took place in West Greenwich during the year 1847; that specimen is now archived at the Museum of Comparative Zoology at Harvard in Boston, Massachusetts. It stands 29.5 inches high at the shoulder and is 7.5 feet long, a large specimen. It seems unlikely that it could have lived in Rhode Island at that time, since the wolf had already vanished and deer were rare. Since then, very few reports came from this coastal region, which is sandwiched between Boston and New London, Connecticut.[35]

The capital, Providence, and its junior cities such as Warwick offer the imagination very little in the way of possible sightings. Nevertheless, during 2004 the state has had an increase in reports. Rhode Island wildlife biologists Charles Brown says that he received about six calls in 2004:

"I frequently get calls now from people inquiring about cougars and sometimes receive reports of large cats or strange looking felines. These are not specific calls to announce a mountain lion sighting but instead are reported as large cats. I have never obtained tracks or scat or anything even remotely suggestive of a cougar's trail."[36]

Interestingly, there are large wooded areas in this little industrialized state. The Arcadia Wildlife Management Area encompasses 16,000 acres of well-managed forest. The historic Great Swamp, where King Philip gathered his warriors, is 3,500 acres. One of the state's strongest believers is Bill Betty, who claims to have seen cougars there on several occasions. Betty has been outspoken on his seeing cougars in Rhode Island and has been interviewed on National Public Radio. He claims to have encountered a cougar while it was visiting a deer kill, but strangely has no documentation. Betty, a self-educated "eastern" cougar expert, does have many intriguing ideas about their presence in the East. He asserts that Rhode Island has all that a cougar would want - wooded cover and many, many deer. Betty says he sees cougars because he hikes at sunset.

NEW HAMPSHIRE

The craggy cliffs of the White Mountains in New Hampshire seem a fitting place for modern day cougar investigations, but surprisingly there is little mention of the famed cat here. The exception, a video taken in 1998, will be discussed later. Some state wildlife biologists are rather reluctant to talk about catamounts or perhaps their focus on assigned game species has been seen as a lack of enthusiasm. Either way, public dialogue appears suppressed in New Hampshire.

In the 1927 *Journal of Mammalogy* there appeared a paper written by Ned Dearborn describing the last killing of a cougar in the state:

> About the year 1900, I heard of a mountain lion that had been killed, years before, in southeastern New Hampshire by William F. Chapman, who was then

living in New Market, New Hampshire. As it was the only instance of the actual killing of this animal within the limits of the state that had, or has come to my attention, I visited Mr. Chapman to learn the particulars. He showed me the 14-gauge double, muzzle loading gun with which he turned the trick.

Mr. Chapman was an enthusiastic fox hunter. On the morning of November 2, 1853, he started out with his hounds after foxes. In the township of Lee, Rockingham County, his dogs gave voice, and before long were evidently close to something either treed or held in a growth of young pines among which were several wide spreading trees. Swaying its tail from side to side, it was giving its entire attention to the dogs. Bringing his gun to his shoulder, the hunter approached slowly and silently till within a few feet of the lion. Suddenly the lion looked down at the man, and at an instant a number four shot passed through the lion's eye and entered its brain. For a bit, it hung by one foot, then it dropped and proceeded to tear up the ground as head-wounded animals often do. It weighed 198 pounds and measured 8 feet and 4 inches from tip to tip.[37]

Young and Goldman wrote that "records seem to indicate that the puma was not of great abundance in this state." Goodwin added in a 1936 *Journal of Mammalogy* article that "a few remained in northern Vermont and New Hampshire until about 1888." Others were less generous, putting extirpation at 1852. One author stated in 1902, "But there are still rumors from time to time of them having been seen in the northern part of the state, especially since deer have become more common."[38] Rumors persisted the longest in the remote and boggy region of Lake Umbagog. Talk of a pair of cougars can be documented as recently as 1920: "a pair of cougars existed...in the early 1920's, along the east side of the Adroscoggin River in the town of Cambridge to the southern shores of Lake Umbagog."[39]

Throughout the century catamounts were seen in various locations, and a number of them have been recorded in a variety of sources. Bruce Wright, for example, mentioned a sighting on August 27, 1948, along the Swift River, which was followed up a few days later with additional appearances. According to Wright, sightings continued throughout the Granite State and the catamount was eventually given legal protection;

because sightings continued to appear in the press, New Hampshire signed a bill into law in 1967 which provided protection for cougars. Thus, New Hampshire was actually the first state to formally protect the big cat. Republican Representative George Kopperel sponsored the historic bill into action. Unfortunately, this enthusiasm was not championed for very long, and those in the state government, including the game biologists, never took any further initiative with the issue.[40]

Today, Eric Orff is the wildlife specialist who handles most of the cougar encounters, and he has shown the public cooperation and interest. He receives cougar sightings almost weekly and says the state has retained much of them dating back to 1950. While Eric is interested in these sightings, he has not been able to obtain any hard evidence. He wrote the following:

> I have been keeping record of these sightings for two decades. I get calls nearly weekly but none have ever turned out to be mountain lion. Each regional office captures the sightings reports on a New Hampshire Mountain Lion Sighting Report Form. I have dozens in a file. I did enter numbers in a data base to see if any cluster groups would show and nothing did - they were scattered evenly all over the state. Staff members have responded to several perceived cougar encounters soon enough, even immediately, upon receipt but no evidence has been found by any staff.[41]

The official word on New Hampshire from all counties, north and south, up and down the breadth and width of the mountainous state, is that there is no breeding population. Fortunately, Eric Orff has maintained an open mind and has not been jaded by the countless hundreds of unconfirmed reports:

> My biological opinion is that there are no resident mountain lions in New Hampshire. There have been no confirmed sightings in New Hampshire in over one hundred years. If mountain lions do occur in the state then they are transient individuals. However, the

New Hampshire Fish and Game Department will continue to monitor 'sighting reports' and will continue to investigate any potential sightings that could lead to confirmation. As experienced biologists we realize that wildlife is dynamic; although the possibilities of a resident population becoming established is small, we remain committed to collecting scientific data that would corroborate their existence.[42]

MASSACHUSETTS

Gentle, rolling hills spread west from the rocky coastline in Massachusetts. Across the Connecticut River these hills increase, and join the Appalachian Range. The Harvard Forest, parts of Mount Greylock, and the Dunbar Brook Preserve are all that remain of what this land once looked like when cougars roamed wild. These sites are the last significant stands of virgin or old growth forests.

During the exploration and settlement of this state, the panther, called "painter cat" in the early colonies, was considered common. It was less so to the north and south, but continued to persist in Massachusetts even during the clearing for widespread farms in the late 1700s and early 1800s. Shortly afterward, the occurrence of this great cat eventually began to subside. It is believed that the last one was shot in 1860. Young and Goldman describe its persecution in Massachusetts.

> During the early colonization period, the puma was known to range the greater portion of this State. It was early outlawed, however, and persistent warfare on the part of everyone who carried a musket, dug pits, or set traps, gradually brought about its complete extinction, so that by the middle of the 19th century it was doubtful that a single individual remained.[43]

As is the case elsewhere within its original eastern range, reports continue, especially west of the Connecticut River, where mountains and some woods lay intact. Young and Goldman quote an early naturalist as follows: "It has, however, been seen in the western portion since its settlement." Another documentation of its existence suggests the possibility of the cougar being extant. Joycelyn Crane, an early nature writer, wrote in 1931 of an occurrence as late as January 18, 1926. Sightings continued to increase very slowly from this decade on and reach a high in the late 1970s.[44] A sampling of the more memorable ones demonstrates the continuous presence of the cougar in the local culture.

Reasonably good documentation and a variety of newspaper stories have followed the cougar encounters to our present day. In 1953 there were several cougar sightings in Massachusetts that ushered in an era of increasing cougar activity. That year, untrained dogs trailed two cougars that were seen on the New Boston Road. The dogs were eventually foiled, as one member of their pack was mauled, and they gave up the chase.

Bruce Wright also recorded a 1960 sighting by a trained wildlife officer:

> Along the New Hampshire border, Conservation Officer Roland D. Gaudette of Mountain Lakes followed tracks on February 13, 1960. The tracks of two cougars trailed through snow revealed a hunting route through old camps, open fields and into brush under cover. Around this time several sightings from the region were called in. Gaudette estimated at least 20 reports. Residents talked of noises in the night. They said their "dogs were going crazy" and "awful noises were heard."[45]

On November 15, 1960, a cougar was hit on the Massachusetts Turnpike, but the body was never recovered. In the words of the driver, the incident went down as follows:

> An animal which I feel I must call a mountain lion, came down the embankment and out onto the pavement. I hit it dead center. It is my opinion that no animal struck in this manner could have survived. This occurred at 7:45 p.m. and was reported to the attendant at the tollbooth. I must call it a mountain lion, for the following reasons. I spent two years in Arizona and saw three mountain lions there, two alive, and one I shot myself.[46]

On October 12, 1968, a well-known and very credible event took place in the quiet forest of the Quabbin Reservoir. A wildlife biologist/ photographer, then employed by the Fish and Game Department, saw a cougar cross before him while he was slowly driving out of the Reservoir area on a narrow service road. Jack Swedberg was returning from a day of photography in the Quabbin when he saw the seven-foot tawny feline.[47]

The next year another sighting was acknowledged from the Quabbin. Harry Hodgdon had an experience he would treasure for some time on August 25, 1969. The University of Massachusetts wildlife graduate student recorded his experience on tape. This is what Hodgdon says:

> I just saw an animal out here that I am still not sure whether to believe or not. As I drove in Gate 17, I rounded a small curve, and there in the road about two hundred feet ahead of me was this animal walking toward the truck, down the middle of it between the wheel tracks. It spotted me about the time I spotted it, because it stopped, still facing me with the rest of its body still behind, directly away from me. It was a cat... definitely cat. It turned around broadside, then it started walking back up the road, going directly away from me. I still don't believe it. It was light tan, long deep bodied -- back to stomach; big -- biggest cat I have ever seen, and had a long tail. Mountain lions are not suppose to be around here, but that sure wasn't any bobcat. That was one big cat -- it's a cat, no question in my mind, and must be close to eighty to ninety pounds, maybe more, but I sort of doubt that because it was low to the ground.[48]

The believers now abound in the state of Massachusetts. "There have been excellent sightings" acknowledged Mike Ciberowski, wildlife biologist in the Connecticut River Valley District. During a *Springfield Union News* interview, Ciberowski stated, "I've spoken to people who say they've seen them -- experienced observers who know what to look for and who take a rather disciplined approach to observing." Ciberowski's agency collected 40 sightings in four counties between 1991 and 1995.[49]

Virginia Ottis, a resident of Goshen, Massachusetts and a former nature writer for the *Daily Hampshire Gazette* of Northampton, receives many of the public's thrilling accounts of the big cat. She says, "I'm absolutely sure there is a viable population of mountain lion around here."[50] Many Massachusetts residents have an open and enthusiastic attitude towards these mystical visitors, but Ciberowski sums up the state's professional stance, "Our position is that a sighting is a sighting and not a documented report."[51] Wildlife biologist James Cardoza is the leading cougar expert in Massachusetts. He takes sightings very seriously but cautions their scientific use.

Sightings continue to come on a regular basis from the forested acreage protecting the watershed, making the deer-dense Quabbin a cluster area. In the fall of 2002, a mountain lion cranium was reportedly discovered along the western shoreline of the Quabbin. The site of the skull was between Gates 8 and 9, a few miles from Route 202. Two hikers from nearby Pelham noticed the skull still attached to some decomposed tissue beneath the detritus. They collected the cranium from the tissue and because of its odor, immersed it in household cleaning bleach. Unfortunately, doing this may have destroyed any DNA. In August of 2003, they gave it to Tom Abruzese from Londonderry, New Hampshire. One month later, Mr. Abruzese drove to the Quabbin and investigated the site where he was told the cranium had been found. Upon investigating the area very thoroughly, Abruzese found additional bones. He collected what was confirmed as an ulna, metatarsal, and two ribs. Abruzese offered the bones to the Museum of Comparative Zoology at Harvard University in Cambridge, Massachusetts.[52]

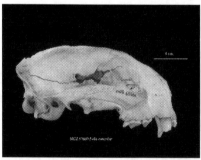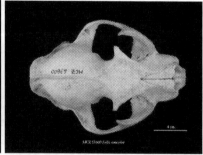

A lateral and dorsal view of the cougar skull found in the fall
of 2002 at Quabbin Reservoir not far from Gate 8.
Harvard Museum of Comparative Zoology

Does this skull represent the first skeletal remains of a free-ranging cougar in the Northeast in over 100 years? Had the skull not been donated to Harvard, we could not have had this debate. Under the care and supervision of Judith Chupasko in the Mammal Department at Harvard Museum, the skull has been analyzed for initial understanding. Among some of the basic questions are subspecies, sex and age.

Chupasko and other scientists have determined that the skull does in fact come from a cougar and not a similar species. One very important question was whether the bones all came from the same animal. Chupasko discovered that they did not. The Quabbin skull did not match the sizes of the other bones. The skull was not in proper proportion to the ulna and metatarsal. The skull size was compared to another skull of a cougar and its corresponding ulna bone. While the Quabbin skull was much smaller, the ulna bone was much bigger than the comparison. A similar discomparison was discovered with the metatarsal bone.[53]

Chupasko compared the Quabbin skull and bones with other skeletal specimens to give her some reference on size and stature and to see if some indication of subspecies could be made. Measurements and photographic images have been used on an ongoing basis to compare the specimen with other cougars from the region and across North America. Chupasko took fifteen measurements from all specimens in the Harvard collection and compared them to the Quabbin skull. These measurements were then compared to historic measurements of cougar as noted in Young and Goldman. In addition to cranium measurements, others were made of nasal bone shape and presence of palentine foramen. Further testing will be made using DNA to determine the animal's origins. Publicity has been restrained in order to give the Harvard Museum enough time to conduct all the studies and tests necessary.[54]

Although it may seem that the bones indicate the death of either a transient or resident cougar in the Quabbin, the fact that the bones represent more than one animal is suspicious. Is it possible Mr. Abruzese did not locate the exact site of the first find and subsequently discovered an additional scene of evidence? Could one specimen be a kitten or immature? Did it stay with its mother out of dependency and die? The answer to the first question might never be known, but Chupasko is certain the bones are not juvenile. One possibility is that the animals were traveling together and were both illegally shot. Another possibility is that these cougars were brought to the Quabbin and dispatched, or that their carcasses were taken in and planted. Some observed the lack of weathering, decay, and animal damage that is usually present in bones found on the forest detritus.

The Quabbin skull does have brain case damage, which appears very much like a fracture caused by the penetration of a bullet. The site was checked for that evidence but nothing was found. From the angle of the fracture, it would seem the bullet might have traveled into the vertebrae or out of the foramen. For many months the hole in the skull was thought to represent such an event, but by spring of 2004 the theories had changed. Today, it remains unclear what might have caused the hole.[55]

Not all the reports of cougar in Massachusetts come from the Quabbin; the Berkshire Hills and areas to the north of Quabbin also produce sightings. Sometimes claims come from populated regions such as the one made by Robert Whelihan. Whelihan claims to have chased a cougar off the property of his Hadley home. Whelihan was suited for the task, being the Animal Control officer for that town; he once had to remove a black bear from the town village.

In Holyoke a cougar was reported but descriptions were so inconsistent with cougar sizes and behavior that it was written off as a clear case of mistaken identity. At twenty pounds this cat would have been too small even for a cougar kitten.[56] Sightings from places like rural West Granville, Massachusetts, go down as more believable. Cobble Mountain Reservoir is just south east of the Berkshires and has many sightings worth mentioning. This is a wooded region and has steep rocky hills. Dorothy Smith saw a cougar on Wildcat Road in Granville on March 13, 1997. It was loping across the road in front of her. Tan with a long tail, it looked larger than a fox and longer than a dog. "It was a mountain lion -- like the one that appeared on the front cover of the newspaper not too long ago." In Montgomery, Matthew Couture reported in 1996 that a "cougar was walking along the edge of my fishing pond. I was fishing alone and looked up after baiting my hook and saw this very large cat."[57]

In November of 1995, Mike Adams saw a cougar in Wilbraham on the way to work one morning and was impressed at the cat's ability to jump. "Its first leap took it clear to the center of Wilbraham Road. At this point in time it was no more than 30 feet in front of me in the high beams. This animal was no immature cat. I estimate it weighed between 90 and 100 pounds, and it was a little longer from nose to tail than my 1989 Chrysler LaBaron is wide."[58]

With reports coming in from all across the Berkshires and its surrounding hill towns, Todd Doiron was not too hesitant to report his 2002 sighting. Doiron, of Westfield, was driving east on Route 20 after an early morning fall turkey hunt. It was a beautiful October day about noon-time when the huge carnivore slipped gently down an embankment hidden partially by leaves and then out into the open roadside. Doiron talked of the event with great excitement, "I thought it was a deer at first but as it glided down the hill, its catlike movements were distinct. The minute it came to the blacktop at the edge of the road, it wheeled around, and the long rope-like tail could be clearly seen. The tail was as long as the cat. I could not get over the size of the animal and the strength it seemed to contain. It was so wild."[59]

In the town of Heath, there was questionable but compelling evidence that was presented in the form of bite marks on a 150-pound calf. The bite marks were consistent with cougar attacks only in that they were found on the neck at the base of the skull. There were no claw marks, which suggests that, had it been a cougar, it might have been a de-clawed former pet. The incident appeared in an outdoor column from the *Springfield Sunday Republican* with no further details.[60]

While the previously mentioned sightings indicate steady reports throughout the years, a recent report joins many made during 2009. "I was fishing the Hubbards River, and saw a cougar on a log that had fallen across the water. I saw the cougar just standing there for several minutes, and it never saw me. It yawned, white teeth caught the sun," said Faye Becklowski of nearby Springfield about her June 2009 encounter.[61]

All of these sightings do count for something, but they really don't establish that the cougar is extant. There is, however, a piece of tangible evidence that goes way beyond a sighting as an indication of cougars living in Massachusetts. It was a scat that was found in the Quabbin woods by an experienced tracker. It was tested in a laboratory and confirmed to have originated from a North American cougar. It will be discussed in detail in another chapter. This piece of evidence does give more weight to the sightings and the bones found at Quabbin. The fact there have been credible sightings and two pieces of physical evidence from that one area does warrant some consideration of a self-sustaining cougar population. It just seems that if it were true -- the Quabbin is frequented enough -- that more definitive proof would be readily available. Enthusiasts will, however, continue to talk of the cougars supposedly holding out here.

MAINE

In the vast fir and spruce lands of Maine, there is much optimism for the existence of the reclusive cougar. During the years of European settlement the caribou that were so successful here began to shift north and the white-tailed deer filled in behind them, which made the region more suitable for the cougar. This occurred as forests were being cleared to the south.

Maine covers a large land area that includes coastland, low lying hills, and high Appalachian peaks. Down East, there are barren lands where the blueberries stretch to the horizon. In the north, there are vast expanses of forest and large uninhabited regions, where only lumbering and outdoor recreational activities account for human presence. This is the land of endless logging roads, where the song of the white-throated sparrow rings out from the fir, a place where every stream and river has native trout, and evening grosbeaks flash their yellow and black feathers from the very tops of tall spruce. It is hoped by conservationists that in these forests the cougar still lives.

Bruce Wright wrote about this land and the encounters that men had with its wildest inhabitant. The most encouraging cougar incident he knew of took place in 1965 when Charles Wilcox was driving to Lincoln and caught five cougar kittens in his headlights playing on the highway. The story is one of only a few coming from this region that historically was better suited for the wolf. Wolf packs were more capable of grounding the larger woodland caribou and moose than could the sleek solitary cougar.[62]

Because deer were few in Maine, it is not surprising that Young and Goldman believed that the cougar was never common there. In fact, Arthur H. Norton, a noted naturalist, said, "rare, and probably never more than a straggler."[63] Most of the early naturalists listed the cougar among the mammals living there, as did Norton, but only Norton made mention of their numbers. Documentation of a cougar kill near Lake Sebago in 1845 was considered the last wild ranging cougar to exist in Maine. However, the killing of a cougar in 1938, nearly one hundred years later, leaves reason to believe there were more.

This well documented specimen was taken near Little Saint John Lake in Somerset County, at the very far northern tip of the state. The site of the kill is not far from Ashland, where Wright was told that it was common knowledge that cougars still lived free. The specimen was acquired from a trapper, Rosarie Morin of Saint Zacharie, Quebec, which is not far from the site. It has been generally accepted that this 1938 cougar is of pre-settlement origin, and it has come to represent the last eastern cougar known to man. Later the mounted specimen was sold to Bruce Wright, who studied it in great detail. For many, the fact that a cougar was taken at such a late date is proof that they did survive. By that time deer had fully rebounded, and the sporadic small patchy clearings made by the first loggers had regrown. Still, the skeptics point out that traveling circuses were popular at that time, implying this was just another escapee.[64]

The first modern-day confirmed sighting of a cougar in Maine came from a populated region just outside of Portland. Rosemary Townsend reported seeing the animal while walking in an undeveloped area in the southern part of Cape Elizabeth on March 11, 1995. Game wardens who investigated found hairs that were tested and proven to be those of a cougar. Townsend said she was out on a morning walk when she saw "this yellow Lab-looking animal slip out from the bushes; it stopped to drink from a pond and when it looked up at me I could see it was no dog -- it was a lion." The Maine Inland Fisheries and Wildlife biologists reacted with great skepticism because of the suburban location of the sighting. They believe the confirmed sighting represents an escaped pet.[65]

Further north, however, opinions change a little, as several probable cougar encounters have occurred in wilder settings. In northern Maine along the Quebec border, a man reported seeing a cougar through his telescopic lens on February 4, 1994. His experience was investigated by two game wardens, who found tracks and photographed them. State biologist Ken Elowe identified the tracks in the photos as those of a cougar. Elowe finds the sighting of great interest because of the wild location and because of the presence of what the witness said were kittens.[66]

There was a great deal of excitement when a photograph of a cougar was presented to state officials only two days after Elowe's finding of a track in northern Maine. The sighting was claimed to have occurred in Cartunk, Maine, and appeared in an outdoors column of the Maine Sunday Telegram on February 6, 1994. After much initial excitement, discussion, and media attention, the photograph was eventually scrutinized a bit closer and determined to show a clump of pinyon pines. Pinyon pines are not native to Maine and state biologists feel that the prank picture was probably taken in Colorado where pinyon pine grow. The picture shows an adult cougar emerging from the woods with two hunting dogs at its side. It is a clear and vivid image, and the animals are well contrasted against the snow.[67]

In mid-September of 2000, Roddy Glover, age 39, was scouting an area for deer when he caught sight of a large tan-colored animal walking unconcerned along a railroad trestle. Central Maine's newspaper outdoor columnist Dwayne Rioux quoted Glover as follows: "It was the week before bow season, and I was scouting for deer. I had broken my ankle shortly before and was looking for a good area to set up a ground blind when this occurred." Glover was standing in a depression below a rail line and resting when he heard a piece of trap rock slip down. "I moved out to take a look, thinking it might be a deer. At first I thought it was a large bobcat walking toward me at 150 yards away. It was taking its sweet time walking down the tracks -- not a care in the world. But it looked too weird to be a bobcat." Glover knew what it was when the animal turned and he could see a long tail and a smaller lion trailing behind it. "I was not sure the animal would attack to protect its young. I didn't know what it would do. I couldn't run because of my ankle. I just lay down behind some ferns. I distinctly remember the wind was in my favor so they couldn't smell me. I had a very good view, and they definitely had long tails. There is no question in my mind I was looking at two mountain lions. They can say I am crazy. I don't care. I just wish I'd had my camera along with me."[68]

Glover immediately contacted state game warden Kevin Anderson. Anderson called an assistant regional wildlife biologist, Keel Kemper, at the Sidney office. Surprisingly, Kemper was able to meet with Glover within an hour of the sighting. He arrived at the scene with a helper, Philip A. Dugus, Jr., who had experience conducting investigations. Dugus did not think the sighting would turn out like it did. He came to believe Glover when he saw the enormous cat-like tracks in the mud. Dugus said, "You cannot discount every sighting before giving the evidence a credibility check. I knew that these were large cat tracks." Kemper quickly made a plaster cast of the track and returned to show some of his colleagues. Wardens Christopher Simmons and Daniel Murray did not recognize the track as a cougar but simply were astounded at the size of what they would only describe as a large cat print. The print measured 4 inches long and 3.5 inches across. Kemper and the others speculated on its origin, but were not so sure that it was an escaped pet partly because of the fact there was a kitten with it.[69]

In Maine, the presence of lynx complicates the verification of cougar reports with the existence of another wild feline. In addition, the large feet of the lynx leave tracks that are easily mistaken for cougar tracks by untrained observers. Walter Jakubus is sure of his observations after many years of field experience. Jakubus, a state wildlife biologist, has had a number of sightings beginning in March of 2001 that came from Hampden, Maine. Upon investigating the scene of these sightings, Jakubus was able to locate a scrape and several tracks that strongly suggested a cougar. The region lies in the southeastern part of the state, not too far from what is referred to as Down East Maine. Additional calls from the same region in September of that year gave further credibility to the evidence. Sightings continued to come from one particular swampy area, and Jakubus believes there might have been a cougar, probably an escaped pet, hiding up in that swamp. As recently as the spring of 2004, Jakubus talks of "persistent reports of a cougar in and around the swamp. It has been seen crossing roads and neighboring farms."

Jakubus doesn't think the cat represents a resident population, but he is taking all reports seriously. Including a photograph sent his way in September of 2007 of a large dark colored cat -like creature coming into investigate a bear bait station equipped with a remote camera. The photographs are convincing, but they could not be substantiated without an actual size reference study, which upon completion ruled out a cougar sized animal and concluded that it was a house cat.[70]

NEW JERSEY

The cougar was once widespread and common throughout the state. It was considered extirpated by 1840, but occasional sightings of transients from neighboring states persisted. The latest reports came from Burlington, Camden, Cape May, and Mercer counties.[71]

Presently, New Jersey receives approximately ten to fifteen sightings each year. They have no tracks, photos, video or scats to test, but on the other hand, the state admits it does not usually investigate calls. Sometimes, if there is a cluster of sightings, they will proceed to the scene in an attempt to secure evidence. The few times that they have responded revealed sign of domesticated dogs or cats. Although New Jersey has a high deer population, it is largely an urbanized and suburbanized landscape. The exception is a quiet corner along the northern border called the Kittitinny Mountain Range, which is about twenty miles long and about half as wide. Only a few summer homes and small farms can be found there.

Surprisingly, reports have never really clustered there, but instead come from places where deer densities reach over thirty per square mile. One such surprising report came during the summer of 2006 when a police officer and his wife reportedly observed a mother and her eighty-pound cub in there Vernon yard; a few miles away on another day the same pair were reported slinking unconcerned through a Highland Lakes neighborhood, and the entire area is in agreement that the beast is living undisturbed someplace really close.

NEW YORK

Rugged mountains covered with mature trees characterize the Adirondack region of New York, where many people believe the cougar has held out. While the region is superb for black bear, there is some question as to whether it is really the best habitat for the big cat, as older forests do not typically support high deer densities. However, the large expanses of seldom-visited virgin forest and the difficult terrain both make for a secluded retreat full of ambush sites that cougars depend on. In the imaginations of wildlife enthusiasts, these rocky peaks seem to be classic cougar habitat, but the fact is that there are other regions that sustain a higher deer herd. Historically, the Adirondacks did support a healthy number of cougars, but the deer habitat dynamics were different.

Young and Goldman wrote in 1946 that the cougar was "formerly abundant throughout most of New York, and particularly in the forested regions of the Adirondacks, the animal was so reduced in numbers by the variety of attacks upon it that by the close of the last century it was nearly extinct." They report the cougar still present in 1871, and between that time and 1882, a total of forty-six had been shot. These cats came from Essex, Franklin, Hamilton, Herkimer, Lewis and St. Lawrence counties. In 1899 there were still some credible sightings, as in the case of Cornelius DuBoise, Manager of Litchfield Park, who in the winter of that year saw in the snow near Tupper Lake "where a mountain lion had made several leaps being recorded in snow - the tail mark showing also."[72]

In what is obviously an exaggeration, author Sewell Newhouse wrote in his 1869 Trappers Guide: "Full grown panthers killed in northern New York have been known to measure over eleven feet from the nose to the tip of the tail, being about twenty eight inches high, and weighing near two hundred pounds." Young and Goldman documented a specimen belonging to J.H. Fleming that was killed about 1847 on Croil Island, St. Lawrence County. The cat was of the normal size and weight. Author Ebenezer Emmons wrote that the cougar was still alive and well in the St. Lawrence County, where he claimed to have seen five killed by a man and his dogs.[73]

Despite the rich history of cougars in the state of New York, the general consensus among state wildlife biologists, game wardens, and park rangers is that any cougars that may actually have been seen since those historic days represent former pets that either escaped or were intentionally released. They say there is no definitive evidence, and there has not been any in well over one hundred years. Al Hicks, a wildlife biologist with the state for close to thirty years, believes this is proof enough that there is most certainly not a breeding population. "In all these decades we have not had any confirmed cougar evidence." Hicks further supports his position on the subject by saying that "each year over 60,000 deer hunters venture into the forest, and not one cougar has ever been shot, photographed, or video taped." Yet in 1968 there was a documented kill at Saranac Lake, complete with an accompanying photograph. It was supposedly killed by a game warden in order to collect a reward for proof of a lion in the Adirondacks. The mountain lion was taken to the taxidermy shop of Jack Taylor and later displayed at Adirondack Sportsmen's Shows as a ghostly relic of Adirondack wilderness days.[74]

New York State Game Protector Richard Emperor and mountain lion which has village conjecturing.

The Saranac Lake cougar kill of 1968. It was supposedly killed by a game warden in order to collect a reward for proof of a lion in the Adirondacks. The specimen was mounted but has either been discarded or in private ownership.

If clusters of sightings were to be established, the Ellenburg, Glens Falls, and North Hudson areas would seem fitting. Hicks says he once checked out cougar reports, but after years of finding nothing, he quit and has wasted little time since then. He admits that reports are not checked out any longer. Hicks works out of the Albany office, but says that similar feelings and conclusions can be assumed as held by other members throughout the department. In the Adirondack region where there are about twenty-five sightings per year, the cougar issue is given the same priority for the same reasons. State biologists stated that the cougar is not high priority because there are simply too many false reports. Wildlife biologists almost never investigate these sightings, but if a call sounds legitimate, then they may send an untrained park ranger out to see what can be found. So far, nothing convincing has been found.[75]

Jim Close, with the Department of Environmental Conservation and one of the original founders of the Cougar Network, has a different attitude. He believes these sightings should be given more weight, and he enjoys speculating about the possible presence of these big cats in his state. In the winter of 2004, he heard news of a deer kill that was of interest until DNA work was done on the evidence and came back as bobcat. On July 25, 2004, a credible-sounding call was taken in which the witness claimed to have seen a large cougar with kittens along the Schroon River near the state beach. A day later, someone else claimed to have seen the same lions just a few miles from there. Jim Close noted the numerous sightings of cougars with kittens that year.[76]

There are four credible reports from the Adirondack region. The first a sighting from Little Tupper Lake by a state Department of Environmental Conservation Fish and Wildlife Technician named Roy Brown. Brown says he is "absolutely sure that it was a cougar." His encounter in September 1991 joins a long list from the area of Little Tupper Lake. In November 1993, another state wildlife employee came forth with a cougar report when he stumbled upon the gory remains of a deer kill. The kill was confirmed by state wildlife biologist Ed Reed who examined the site in Keene Valley. This was the most convincing evidence to come from the region.[77]

1958

WANTED !
(Dead or Alive)
$75.00 BOUNTY

panther

AGE— Adult or Near Adult.
COLOR— Tawny (Yellow Brown).
HEIGHT— Stands Approximately 27 inches at Shoulder.
WEIGHT— 100 to 150 lbs.
LENGTH— 5½ to 7 Feet Overall.
TRACKS— 4½ - 5 Inches in Snow. No Claw Marks. Distinct Pad Marks Like House Cats. Carries Tail Low, Mature Males Would Show Drag Mark in Snow.
DISTINGUISHING MARKS— Similar to Small Circus Lioness. No Tuft at End of Tail. End of Tail Darker Than Rest of Tail.
This Animal is a Game Killer and VERY RARELY Attacks Humans. If You Should See This Animal Call Your Nearest New York State Conservation Game Protector and Notify This Club.

TUPPER LAKE ROD & GUN CLUB
Tupper Lake, N. Y. — Phone 379

Today, the Tupper Lake region of New York continues to generate sightings. This old bounty poster shows how convinced residents were of the cougar's existence.

In April of 1996 Ken Kogut, a state wildlife biologist, spotted a cougar in the southwestern part of the Adirondack Park. Kogut saw the animal cross before him on Route 3. "I hate to admit it, but I had a good look at the animal, and it was a cougar." A year later, another sighting occurred in the park, this time to the north in Riverview. This cougar was also crossing Route 3 when it was witnessed by state wildlife biologist Kurt Armstrong. There were more sightings in the days that followed.[78]

Not all sightings make the news; there are many that appear credible and are never publicized. During a quiet 6:00 a.m. walk before going off to work for the day on February 24, 2004, Ryan Cheesemen happened upon an animal wailing in catlike fashion along the frozen shoreline of Lake Roxanne. Ryan had no idea he was approaching a cougar, but at thirty yards he began to figure it out. At that distance he realized he was walking straight into the space of a large predatory cat. Within twenty yards he saw that he had approached a cougar, and slowly he began to back off. The cougar continued to wander along the ice and vocalize while Ryan made his way back to safety. Later he returned to the site, but the tracks had been blown over with snow. This was yet another sighting from the Ellenburg area.[79]

In March 2004, Ed Reed had another deer kill to analyze in Elizabethtown, Essex County, off the Labdell Road near New Russia. He could not confirm this kill, but it had been sheered or skinned in the way that cougars often "clip" a deer kill. Another report from Hamilton County left residents concerned for their safety, when Richard Corvetti saw two cougars traveling together on April 8, 2004. He addressed local authorities with the following note:

> Last fall, two mountain lions were spotted on South Shore Road in Lake Pleasant, New York. Two months ago, a deer was dismembered with apparent ease by the lions. Finally, two weeks ago, the pair was spotted at the vacant Love Camp. Very soon, numerous visitors and summer residents will be returning to Lake Pleasant. I am concerned that a child, adult jogger or biker will provide an easy target. Please take whatever safety precautions you think appropriate for this urgent public safety issue.[80]

Also in March 2004, a few intriguing photos were taken of possible cougar tracks laid in snow across a road in the vicinity of Big Tupper, making that spring in the Adirondacks an exciting one for cougar enthusiasts.

The Eastern Puma Research Network reports many unverified sightings from across upstate New York. Many of these are of dark-colored cougars. The organization claims a long history of such sightings along state Route 53, Sunshine Road, and along Route 17 near Monticello. EPRN researchers Bruce and Mary Anne Thon report considerable activity around Keuka, including a possible deer kill. John Lutz says a man named Louie Williams took a plaster cast of tracks back in the 1950s that were taken to a DEC nature center and found to be a perfect cougar match by the resident naturalist.[81] Unfortunately, claims such as this, without substantial documentation, are worth little as true evidence. Nevertheless, independent researchers have made significant contributions and have added continuity to the search. One such individual is Peter O' Shea, Jr., a former New York City police sergeant.

O' Shea has made a name for himself as a local naturalist, and he pursues cougar sightings whenever he can. Although he has never seen one himself, he believes that there is something to all the attention the animal receives in the Adirondack region. "My feeling is that in the Adirondacks, they were never quite extirpated." O'Shea suspects that many sightings never get reported for fear of ridicule or because of lack of motivation. He thinks that there has to be something to the reports. "I think you have to be blind to say there's nothing there." He refers to the fact that sightings go back for decades and that the Adirondacks consists of six million acres.

O' Shea is the author of many nature guides and is guest naturalist for the New York State Adirondack Park Agency Visitors Interpretive Center and the Residents Committee to Protect the Adirondacks. He believes that the state does not want to definitively define the cougar's presence because it would demand resources from a financially strapped Fish and Game Agency -- an accusation that Al Hicks denies. Hicks points out that there has been absolutely no evidence to suggest a resident cougar population. Hicks and O'Shea have battled it out previously in open public debate. The debate is proof of only one thing, and that is that the cougar issue is alive in the Adirondacks for some very good reason.

WESTERN FRONT
OHIO

The cougar lingered on in this state until about 1850, and may have remained in isolated numbers until the end of that century. It was often called "mountain cat" or "mountain tyger." Many have suggested that the animal held out longer in the larger swamps, but only sightings or rumors have substantiated its existence in such hideouts. Native American artifacts indicate the use of the animal's bones in ornamental dress.[1]

In 1956 a search for cougars was conducted by a Hamilton County Sheriff Dan Tehan and Officer Robert Spraul. The investigation was initiated because of the high number of livestock attacks and alleged sightings. It was quickly terminated because of fiscal constraints and complaints by taxpayers. Later, a privately funded group called Animal Trackers Puma Research Group took on the challenge in 1988. The group consists of several volunteers who are looking in eight designated transects. To date, they claim to have secured evidence of track, kill, and scat. During the 2004 Eastern Cougar Conference, the group's William Reichling attempted to bring the evidence to the scientific level for review. Questions remain as to its validity.[2]

KENTUCKY

Besides a recent kill, detailed later in this book, from Floyd County in 1997, the last cougar in Kentucky was taken in 1863 near Lexington. The animal appears to have been widespread and fairly plentiful upon settlement. Imlay, in his 1793 publication on the North American topography, reported its presence among the mammals at the end of the 18 th century.[3] Although the state information office insists there are no recent reports of cougars in their state, the *Lexington Herald Newspaper* reports a sighting verified by their own Fish and Wildlife sergeant Carl Salyers. The incident took place on June 13, 1998, and tracks were left at the scene for Salyers to ponder. Salyers was reported by the paper as having commented, "The cat may have been from Florida"[4]

In December of 2006 Judy Tipton and the late Dana Hunt, in close cooperation with the U.S. Forest Service, set out all eighteen of the Eastern Cougar Foundation's remote PhotoScout cameras, originally deployed by Todd Lester, in a place called the Land Between Lakes.

This is a 170,000 acre forest wedged between two man made reservoirs located in the western end of the state along the border of Tennessee. To this date no cougars have been captured by the cameras despite the recent reports of cougars and the promising wild nature of the land.[5]

In western Kentucky an independent researcher by the name of Travis Brown conducted a cougar search within the Westvaco Wildlife Management Area; the region was selected because of recent sightings and rumors of cougars colonizing from the west. Brown set up trap cameras, but was unsuccessful at photographing a cougar.[6]

TENNESSEE

Tennessee has a confirmed kill as recently as 1971. There was also a reported kill from the Fontana Village area back in 1920, which was discussed by Donald Linzey.[7] It is considered the last cougar to have lived in the region. Little activity comes from this state except at the western edge of the Great Smoky Mountains National Park (see section on North Carolina), but an anecdotal account was recorded by federal biologists Remington Kellogg: "a panther was seen on May 30, 1937, by local residents on North Fork River near Crossville, Cumberland County."[8] During the state's settlement, Young and Goldman report the predator's occurrence along the Tellico River bottom of Monroe County and also in the forests near Nashville. The authors did not believe it was uncommon in the western part of the state. Early accounts such as those given by Samuel Rhoades for the Academy of Natural Science of Philadelphia suggest *Felis concolor's* preference during its final years for the lowlands or as noted "impassable brakes and harricanes."[9]

Sporadic sightings are thought to have taken place since 1910, and have became more common in recent years. Tennessee is one of the states that has had game officers among the list of believers. In 1975 a fisheries biologist Eugene Cobb saw what he thought was a "cougar-like" animal crossing a road in Hardeman County.[10] Not long after his sighting, another fisheries biologist spotted a large cat. Ged Petit called the animal a cougar - not "cougar-like." He was out fishing on Kentucky Lake and saw the animal slip onto the shore from some cover and take a drink.[11] In 1980 wildlife biologist Jay Story from Oak Ridge, Tennessee, saw a mountain lion while he was studying bobcats at night. A few years later, a cougar was shot and killed in Hickman County, which had been reported as stalking a child. It was without claws and was considered an escaped or abandoned pet.[12]

EASTERN CANADA
QUEBEC

Cougars were never well established in Quebec, with the exception of some southern regions along the United States border. Historically, the northwoods did not provide a healthy living for their preferred prey, the white-tailed deer. Today, the deer is abundant across southern Quebec, and cougar sightings are almost as common as they are further south in the United States. The cougar was, however, apparently found throughout the forests south of the Saint Lawrence River.[1]

In the past twenty years sightings have really increased. There are three significant events. The first, the killing of a male cougar, occurred at Lake Abitibi in 1993. The Lake Abitibi specimen was analyzed using the most recent DNA testing technology and was found to be from South American ancestry or more specifically from Chilean descent. This was therefore a former pet or zoo captive. The second case, a cougar killed near Sherbrooke was of the most interest because it was said to be pregnant and lactating.[2] Unfortunately, the actual specimen can no longer be accounted for, and there is reason to suspect this was a hoax. The third case, occurred in 2002 when there was a road kill in the Laurentides Provincial Reserve.

There was evidence taken without a kill, but it occurred much farther north, in a region not known to have many cougars historically. On the Gaspe Peninsula, a cougar was determined to have traveled through in August of 2002. Its presence was not detected by a remote sense camera or by clearly laid tracks in the snow or mud. It was instead attracted to a scent post carefully engineered and selectively placed by independent researcher Marc Gautheir.[3] His samples were sent to Dr. Virginia Stroeher, who is familiar with wildlife testing. Preliminary hair DNA analysis suggests it was of North American origin.[4] This same method acquired four other hair samples. This gives Quebec a total of eight confirmations, with three testing out to be of North American origin, three of South American and two indeterminate.

Wildlife biologist Marc Gauthier became interested in cougars when he was contacted regarding the kill in Sherbrook mentioned above. He wanted to know the origin of that cat or any others that could be detected. That curiosity inspired him to produce an attractant, a sure way to lure in cougars to detect their presence. He didn't want to use urine from female cougars in heat, knowing this kind of lure might attract extraneous animals, wasting time and analysis funding. What he came up with was a pheromone lure extracted from anal gland secretions. These secretions are then mixed with some synthetic ingredients and placed within a specialized casing, which is then enclosed in a ventilated PVC pipe. The pipe is mounted on a pole and the hair snares are immediately placed surrounding the pole. The cougar approached the pole and either rubbed the snares or incidentally left the hair sample while investigating the scent. The strategy is now being used by Anne Sophie Bertrand in nearby New Brunswick. Gauthier hopes to market the system to other researchers.

NEW BRUNSWICK

What proof does New Brunswick yield now that decades have passed since the work of Bruce Wright? Has there been enough evidence to vindicate his claim that cougars were alive in the Fundy Wilderness? Would he still believe that there were cougars in the Province? Development marched on in New Brunswick, just as it has everywhere. The Fundy Highway, which he dreaded, was built, and forests were logged, but does the great cat live on?

Libby Cade of the Department of Natural Resources and Energy says that New Brunswick receives forty to fifty sightings every year. In the winter of 2004 she commented on these sightings: "The majority are of fisher, bobcat, lynx, coyote, and domestic pets. Unfortunately, we have not had any significant evidence for many years that would strongly suggest there are cougars here."[5]

Many believers in the eastern cougar have theorized that the animal retreated into the unbroken wilderness of Maine and New Brunswick, and that it held out there until the deer and forests reclaimed New England. A cougar kill in 1932 from Kent County, that has been overlooked in the research, helps support this speculation. And if you based this theory on sightings, you might think it was fact, but for decades after the Kent killing the only solid evidence of a cougar was the famous Waasis video, along with something discovered in Deeresdale on a cold fall day in the early 1990s.

On November 18, 1992, a sighting in Deeresdale was reported and later investigated. Cougar tracks were found at the scene, which indicated a male by their size. A scat was taken that was found along the tracks and later examined under a microscope. The scat was sent to Stan Van Zyll a curator at the Canadian Museum of Nature in Ottawa. The examination proved that the scat contained cougar hair.[6] This was irrefutable proof of a cougar in the region. Each month afterward additional reports were received. In fact, hundreds of sightings have been reported since Bruce Wright's investigation; but only the Waasis video and the Deeresdale scat suggested Wright may have been correct

Then in the summer of 2003 Anne Sophie Bertrand made a fascinating discovery. Tawny hairs were found caught in a spool of barbed wire set out specifically to obtain tangible proof of the cougar's presence in New Brunswick. Then in 2004, she found that a second pole held another sample of cougar fur. Using Gauthier's scent posts and wire hair snare, some new proof of the carnivore's presence was established. One sample tested as North American cougar, but the other, South American. Bertrand was beginning to get discouraged as she had many snare traps set that had not yielded the proof she sought. The 2003 and 2004 discoveries came from a trap set in the Fundy National Park, where Wright believed cougars were living undetected.[7]

NOVA SCOTIA

There were virtually no reported encounters before 1920. From 1923 through 1964 Bruce Wright collected 27 credible reports. This may indicate range expansion following increases in deer. Today, Pamela Mills, a provincial biologist, is keeping record of sightings. From 1997 to 2000, Mills documented calls and received 98 reports. There are only five instances of tracks. The sightings have come from all over the province, but there are more in the interior and north.[8]

ONTARIO

Lil Anderson, a wildlife biologist with the province of Ontario, collected a scat that was found to be cougar by the Alberta Natural Resources

Service Forensic Lab in Edmonton using thin layered chromatography.[9] In December of 2004 Stuart Kenn, president of the Ontario Puma Network, discovered hair in two of his scent posts. Kenn had hair snares set with female cougar urine in estrus. Both samples tested positive for cougars. At the time of this book's publication, further results on the subspecies and individual identity of the cougars had not yet been determined, and the aforementioned evidence had not been publicized.[10]

SUMMARY OF EVIDENCE IN THE NORTHEAST

The Northeast has the greatest number of sightings and has the most field evidence of any region. Types of evidence range from scat with fur to DNA and tracks. Confirmed field evidence began to accumulate in the 1990s. In 2000 the U.S. Fish and Wildlife Service acknowledged that there might be a few individual mountain lions living in the wild, but held to the belief that they are of captive origin. Still, the climate has begun to allow for more serious and engaging dialogue regarding the issues. These include, but are not limited to, discussions about habitat management, natural corridor preservations, social and economic considerations and ideas on reintroduction.

The Northeast has had the blessing of independent trackers or researchers, good historical records of cougar kills, land use, and logging. Sightings dating back to the early 1930s suggest a high interest in the animal, complete with regional pride, an esteem for the creature, and an appreciation for its legendary value. Three areas offer the most likely refuge for these shy predators, the north Maine woods, Adirondack Park, and the Allegheny State Forest with contiguous north central Pennsylvania.

While these regions do produce a consistent number of sightings, Vermont's north central area and Massachusetts's Quabbin Reservoir are the only two places that we might be inclined to call cluster areas. The Adirondacks, northern Pennsylvania, and the Monmouth region of Maine are second to these other sites for repeated sightings.

The Quabbin Reservoir has produced countless sightings dating back to the 1960s. The discovery of the scat that tested affirmative for cougar has complimented this history of sightings in the protected forest surrounding the reservoir. The Quabbin scat and associated evidence found at the scene along the shores of the reservoir has been considered by many to be the best evidence to date for the Northeast. However, there are no state biologists who think a relic cougar population has existed there. A few have believed that individual cougars were present at different points in time.

1) In 1997 tracker John McCarter discovered a large scat within the Quabbin that was analyzed and tested by the Wildlife Conservation Society in New York. In the care of George Armato, DNA testing confirmed the scat came from a cougar. Later, another test was performed by Melanie Culver. Culver confirmed the original finding and was able to determine that the cougar was of the North American subspecies.

2) A few years later, in 2002, the largely decomposed remains of a cougar were found along the western shores of the reservoir. The skull, a rib, and a leg bone were retrieved and analyzed under the supervision of the Harvard Museum. The bones are being examined at Harvard, compared with historical collections, and probed for DNA.

Individually these pieces of evidence ought to arouse interests in the possibility of cougars having been in the Quabbin Reservoir area, if not using it repeatedly as part of their home ranges. Taken together with the history of sightings, some of them made by trained wildlife biologists, these pieces of evidence make for a compelling case in favor of the cougar's presence. Unfortunately, subsequent investigations into the Reservoir's acreage have not revealed additional evidence, which strongly discourages the idea of a resident female or territorial male. Currently, local students from Amherst College and the University of Massachusetts are planning additional hunts into the Quabbin. Countless students from these and other colleges nearby continually visit the Reservoir armed with their tracking guides, but to no avail.

In Vermont another case of confirmed cougar scat finds itself in the locus of repeated sightings of a mother and her two cubs. Although the sightings of this family unit has since ceased, the Craftsbury region of north central Vermont or Orleans County continues to produce sightings on a regular basis.

1) In 1994, a scat was recovered by the Vermont State Fish and Game and sent to the U.S. Fish and Wildlife Agencies Forensic Lab in

Ashland, Oregon, and confirmed as containing cougar foot hairs. Later, confusion over the sample caused officials to retract their claims.

2) In 1994 in northwestern Maine, two game wardens found tracks at the scene of a reported sighting. The tracks were found near the Saint John's River, which is northwest of the Allagash Wilderness Waterway. The tracks were officially reported to wildlife biologist Richard Hoppe as cougar.

New Brunswick has been an active place for cougar sightings. Bruce Wright established his belief in a breeding relic population while compiling a huge collection of sightings there. A cougar kill (shooting) in 1932 from Kent County is evidence that has been largely overlooked.

1) A confirmed cougar was filmed in the town of Waasis, New Brunswick, in 1990.

2) In 1992, wildlife biologist Rod Cumberland documented tracks in New Brunswick leading up to a scat, which he had analyzed. The Canadian Museum of Ottawa found the scat contained snowshoe hare bones and the leg hairs of a cougar.

Nova Scotia, Quebec, and Ontario have all had their share of sightings and alleged tracks. Evidence from these provinces is scattered around, with hundreds of miles between each site. Much of the land in these provinces was never good cougar habitat, but with climatic warming trends and growing deer herds, the likelihood of cougars in these parts is taken seriously by a few open-minded biologists.

3) There are two cases of confirmed DNA taken in Fundy National Park from a hair snare. One collected in the summer of 2003 another in the fall of 2004.

Ontario:

1) Wildlife biologist Lil Anderson of Ontario found and tested a scat at the Alberta Natural Resources Service Forensic Lab in Edmonton. Thin layer chromatography was used to determine that it was cougar.

Gaspe:

1) On the Gaspe Peninsula, there was fur taken and analyzed from a hair snare in 2002. The cougar was attracted to scent post designed by wildlife biologist Marc Gautheir.

CHAPTER FIVE

EVIDENCE in the CENTRAL APPALACHIANS

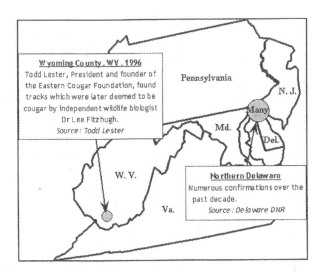

The central Appalachians yield evidence, too. The circles represent credible reports, but the confirmed reports from Delaware lack solid evidence. Each year there are hundreds of reports that cannot be confirmed.
Courtesy Cougar Network (2004-2010)

NORTH CAROLINA

This state is endowed with some of the most wooded country in the East. Much of it can be conveniently enjoyed along the Blue Ridge Parkway, which winds its way down from Virginia's Shenandoah National Park to the Great Smoky Mountains National Park. When the National Park was established during the 1930s, it was the most inaccessible piece of terrain along the Appalachians. Deer were never extirpated there, and 30 % of the forest remained uncut.[1] Occasionally, the unexpected crossing of the long-tailed cat surprises visitors.

Today, the rumors of cougar sightings persist in the same places where its presence was once common. Lawson, author of The History of North Carolina, wrote that the cougar was common throughout the state and added some comments concerning its annoyance to man. "This Beast is the greatest Enemy to the Planter, of any vermine in Carolina."[2] Not surprisingly, the animal was "nearly exterminated" by the time Audubon was to make this remark in 1851.[3]

Culbertson investigated sightings in the Great Smoky Mountains National Park and concluded that there were a few living in the park. She noticed the strong correlation between sightings and high deer densities. Downing, the researcher who conducted a federally sponsored cougar investigation, also interviewed and researched old cougar stories. He found sightings dating back to 1900 when one was allegedly trapped in Craven County. An interesting tale boasted of a cougar kill, but when investigated, proved to be an African lion carcass salvaged from a dumpster. There has been no explanation of how it got there.[4]

Despite the fact that many sightings turned out to be false, the Great Smoky National Park gave Downing much hope for the cougar's survival. He documented the observation of a cougar stalking deer by Park employees in the Cataloochee and Noland's Creek Sections of Great Smoky Mountains National Park in 1975 and 1978, respectively. There were multiple sightings of a cougar trailing cubs or kittens near Mount Pisgah from 1975 to 1977.[5] One of the witnesses was a Park naturalist. Even a game warden spotted one stalking along a fence in Catawba County; he was able to give accurate size descriptions that, when studied at the site, were credible. Dr. Donald Linzey, who has devoted a great deal of time searching for cougars in the Smokies, authored two books on wildlife within the Park and still feels compelled to remain open-minded about cougars.

The coast of North Carolina has also been a hot zone for cougar encounters. In 1980 a career engineer by the name of Charles Humphreys pursued his life-long love of nature study by examining closely the notion that a population of cougars remained in the Great Green Swamp. He collected 210 sightings and believed almost half had to be authentic. In 1994 he published a book called Panthers of the Coastal Plains in which he tried to argue convincingly that there were panthers hidden in the swamp.[6] However, photos of some of these tracks he believed were cougar have been identified as canid or other species.

David Rabon of the U.S. Fish and Wildlife Service receives calls about cougars, just as the state biologists do. Some noteworthy reports include the killing of two cougars in Tyrrell County in 1987. One of the cats had a tattoo on its inner lip. Two reports in the early 1990s came from military personnel at Fort Bragg. On August 26, 2001, a landowner in Edgecombe County sighted a cougar. The same person called again in October, and a game warden found a track at the seen.[7]

MARYLAND

Meshach Browning, an early 19th-century American trapper, found cougars throughout the region. An account of his exploits is listed in Young and Goldman's Puma -Mysterious American Cat and reads as follows:

Buffalo Gap, Deep Creek.- The country abounds in panthers.

Bloomig Rose - Directly within ten steps of me rose the head and shoulders of the largest panther I ever saw. He measured eleven feet, three inches, from the end of his nose to the tip of his tail.

Big Gap of Meadow Mountain - Instead of a wolf we found a panther upon a tree.

Meadow Mountain.- I took great care to keep a safe distance, and taking good aim I sent a ball whizzing through his brains, which put an end to a wild and furious monster.

Meadow Mountain, southern end - east slope near Savage River- I killed three out of four of the family.

Meadow Mountain, southern end - - One taken. He measured nine feet, ten inches, from end of his nose to tip of tail.[8]

The cougar was assumed extirpated by 1860, but reports lingered from the western hills. The EPRN worked closely with the state police through the 1970s and 80s, accumulating hundreds of visual reports. In the early 1990s, a home video captured what was determined to be a cougar by District Wildlife Manager Leslie Johnston.[9] The footage was taken in the western mountains near the Pennsylvania border. In the late 1990s, another video was taken in Garrett County, in the western part of the state.[10]

Maryland's wildlife biologist Glenn Therres does not think there are any undiscovered breeding cougars, but acknowledges that he "would not be surprised if a few released or liberated cougars occasionally roam the western hills."[11] Therres says there is enough woodland for a cougar to take temporary refuge in. The Savage River State Forest is 45,000 acres, and the Green River State Forest has 26,000 acres. This forestland is hunted regularly, but is attractive enough for bears. Maryland officials receive about twenty-four cougar calls each year, and about 50% originate from the western mountains. The immigrating coyote has recently accounted for many perceived sightings.

The following are some reports that sound reasonably credible:

June 10, 2004

A citizen emailed DNR the following report: "I have a sister who claims she has seen a mountain lion near her home in Westminster. She saw it on a dirt farm road and said that it was black." Westminster is in the agricultural area of Maryland.[12]

July 25, 2001

A citizen at a store in LaValle, Allegany County (western Maryland) approached a DNR biologist. The man said that he and his son had seen a large, deer-sized, tawny-colored cat with a long tail the previous week while riding 4-wheelers on Piney Mountain. He and his son stopped approximately forty yards away and looked at the cat for seconds before it bounded away. He further advised that a few days earlier, they came upon a fresh deer kill that had the throat torn away.[13]

February 26, 2001

A resident of Emmitsburg, Frederick County, reported observing two large cats having a "face-off" with her three dogs. She had heard the cats growling and hissing occasionally for the past six months.[14]

VIRGINIA

The cougar was once abundant throughout the state, having had ideal conditions from the Blue Ridge Mountains to the coast. Surprisingly, the last remaining populations were concentrated in the Great Dismal Swamp. It was believed to have been persecuted to extinction there before 1820, but sightings were noted during the early 1900s.[15]

Finally, in 1948, naturalists defended the many people who were starting to see cougars once again. It was thought that there were still cougars in the Shenandoah at that time. Reports continued to increase, and in the late 1960s became almost common. Certainly by 1970, Virginians living in the Appalachians accepted the presence of cougar and considered it common knowledge, at least in certain hunting circles. In the Jefferson National Forest there were twenty reports in 1971.[16]

There are three additional areas where cougar sightings have concentrated over the past sixty years: The Allegheny Mountains, Blue Ridge Mountains, and specifically in the Shenandoah National Park section of the Blue Ridge. Sightings are too numerous to list, and they have been received in multiple places. Some get called into the National Park Service, others to the state, and many more fall into the hands of John Lutz and the EPRN, or the ECF.

Each year, travelers report cougars along the Parkway, and dozens of visitors camping within Shenandoah National Park are dazzled with the emergence of this large predator from unexpected hiding places. Some even tell stories of cougars following them or otherwise showing total indifference to their presence. In May of 1998, two hikers and their leashed dog were traveling along the Appalachian Trail when approached by a very large cougar. They became increasingly alarmed as the cougar persisted to follow behind them. They say the cougar showed no fear and seemed absolutely intent at trailing them. The hikers made it to a road where they succeeded in flagging down a car in order to remove themselves entirely from the situation. They suspect the cougar was interested in their dog's scent.[17]

While reports do come from all across the mountains and sometimes in the flat lands, the hot spot is the Shenandoah National Park. There has been an evolution of cougar reports, marked by a gradual increase in cougar encounters and simultaneous returning deer numbers. Within the park there does not seem to be a single employee who either has not seen a cougar or has not taken a report of one. In fact, most park employees believe they exist. Ironically, the official word from the park is that there are no cougars. Like elsewhere in the East, those who are interested in the cougar find this reluctance by authorities problematic, and those in Virginia seek to have the park administration concede their presence. Donald Linzey is one such individual who has set out to do just that.

Linzey has devoted much of his free time through the years to try to document the presence of cougars in the Park. In 1985 he found tracks that he thinks are convincing. He keeps the plaster cast of these tracks in his home office, along with a map of sightings adorning his wall. Linzey, a professor of biology, has a collection of pins marking sightings in specific places on his regional Appalachian map. A few years back, he noticed the map was collecting color pins in one place called Peaks of Otter. Another cluster of pins pointed out Mountain Lakes, and in recent years he has seen the pins spreading out. The total number of reports is almost 440, and of these he considers approximately 180 to be credible. In recent years Linzey continued to receive reports and enjoyed several good hikes into the region for the purpose of photographing the elusive predator. He worked not by sitting quietly and hoping for a lion to walk by, but by setting up remote motion-activated cameras in strategic locations.[18]

Much to his chagrin, a cougar has not triggered any of the cameras. Linzey is not alone in his disappointment. Others have been hoping for better results with their camera snares. Jim Atkinson is the Director of Shenandoah National Park and has had several cameras positioned in different locations throughout the park. He was hoping to secure at least one good photo. If these cameras do capture the image of a cougar, it might be enough to persuade Atkinson and everybody else to admit their presence publicly. Atkinson has employed bait stations using road-killed deer in hopes of attracting hungry cougars. The bait stations are sophisticated, complete with scent lures and state-of-the-art night vision motion-activated video recorders aimed at the bait. This ought to reduce so much of the ambiguity that has been seen in other remote camera pictures. He has photographs of bears, coyotes and bobcats, but no cougars yet.[19]

Richard Reynolds is a wildlife biologist with the Virginia Department of Game and Inland Fisheries. When he is asked his opinion on the sightings in the Shenandoah National Park-Blue Ridge Parkway, he postures that, as with any other area, they are waiting for pictures or tracks to verify reports. Reynolds does not believe that there are free-roaming, wild-born cougars in his state. He collects and plots reports of cougars on a map obtained from emails solicited through the Department of Game and Inland Fisheries website. Interestingly, he has yet to go out in the field to investigate a sighting because as he says, "we have yet to receive sufficient evidence to warrant an investigation."[20]

He mentions the incident near the Grottos in the early 1990s where two cougars were captured and quickly verified that they had been released from captivity. A more recent sighting in Craigville made the news and attracted a great deal of attention; this particular animal was photographed, but the picture was not clear enough for either a quick confirmation or dismissal. Instead, it drew more speculation. Finally some definitive words were given by some DGIF personnel who went to the site. They were able to locate objects in the photo that gave them an idea of the size of the animal. They felt it was too small to be a cougar. There were credible witnesses but no tracks to fortify the claim.[21]

An animal compound near Natural Bridge keeps wild cats, and this is where visitors have reported large cats outside the small zoo enclosure. They even found tracks that looked like those seen inside the pen and covered them with buckets until they could be photographed. The photos were sent to the DGIF and were clearly canid, with well-defined claw marks.[22] In 2001, residents of Lexington reported what was perceived to be a cougar, and they became fearful enough to hold a town meeting.

It turns out, that John Lutz who was mentioned earlier, is not the only person suspicious of a cover-up in this region. Many people have a feeling that state and federal wildlife officials do not want to admit that the cougar exists. It is difficult to figure, but the Shenandoah National Park has not announced the presence of cougars, which all of their employees believe are there. Rumors have it that a park employee asked his superintendent why they would not disclose the existence of the cougars in the park. He was told that the park did not want to contradict the state agencies, with which they work, and therefore must deny the cougars' presence. They also told him not to disclose the cougars' presence because people might react with fear.[23]

WEST VIRGINIA

The rugged mountains of the central Appalachians are home to a variety of wildlife species including coyote, bear, and turkey. Each spring thousands of brilliantly colored neotropical migrant birds work their way over the dense canopy of deciduous trees. Below, bobcats hunting for small rodents are sometimes seen. They are frequently mistaken for their larger cousin - *Puma concolor*. But a confirmed wild cougar has not been known since 1887 when the last cat was shot in Pocahontas County.[24]

According to Young and Goldman, cougars were said to be common in the western part of the state. Many were taken by hunters, especially in the mid-1800s. One noted panther hunter was Adam Harper (1779-1870). He killed nineteen on Clover Run in Tucker County and killed almost that many more in adjacent areas. He also waged an unrelenting war on the local wolves, losing track of how many he had extinguished. According to statistical tabulations at the time, eleven panthers were killed in Randolph County in 1853, fourteen in 1856, eleven in 1858, and six in 1859. In 1910, Brooks said a "few may still exist in our more secluded forests."[25]

Two historic specimens are known to exist, both in the mammal collection of the Smithsonian Institution -- a skeleton and incomplete skull from a cougar killed in Capon Springs in 1850 (USNM A00848), and a skull and partial skeleton (USNM31438) found in a cave in Greenbrier County in August, 1959. The Greenbrier County skull was discovered in Higginbothams Cave # 4, located 1.3 miles west of Frankford. The skeleton lay on a surface of a mudbank, thirty feet above a subterranean stream. The bones were sent to the National Museum and were considered to be *Puma concolor*, and the teeth matched closely to those of a skeleton from Capon Springs, West Virginia (USNM 848).[26]

In the spring of 1936, a party from the Smithsonian Institute completed arrangements for a group from the United States National Museum to make a collection of birds and mammals in West Virginia. During this trip, Fred T. Galford, a skilled worker at Camp Black Mountain in the Monongahela National Forest, told the party that he'd found panther tracks on Black Mountain during the winters of 1935 and 1936. In the summer, he and members of a Civilian Conservation Corps (CCC) camp saw one in the same locality while they were on a trail. Forest employees said they were convinced that one or more panthers went over Black Mountain in Pocahontas County about twice every ten days. Two members of the Smithsonian party saw panther tracks on Kennison Mountain in late June of 1936.[27] Black Mountain and Kennison Mountain are in the vicinity of the Cranberry Backcountry and Cranberry Wilderness Areas. The two men also saw panther tracks on Middle Mountain in Randolph County. Arthur A. Wood, Supervisor of the Monongahela National Forest, wrote that a few panthers might exist on Middle Mountain in Randolph and Pocahontas County.[28]

By the 1950s, the number of reported sightings was probably increasing because *West Virginia Conservation Magazine* published more articles on them. Ron Nowak, who worked for the U.S. Fish and Wildlife Service, reported that the Director of the West Virginia Department of Natural Resources believed the report of a conservation officer who said he saw one in 1972 in Watoga State Park, Pocahontas County. Nowak researched sightings for all the eastern states, but much of the information from his notes has never been published previously. The most notable recent West Virginia sighting occurred on August 28, 1980, when John Gottschalk, a former director of the U.S. Fish and Wildlife Service, and his grandson saw a cougar on the edge of the Dolly Sods. The Dolly Sods has long been a hot area for sightings.[29]

More than two years earlier, however, incontestable evidence surfaced of free-ranging cougars in the state. Todd Lester expended much time and energy investigating the incident that occurred on April 11, 1976, when Kessler Pritt, a farmer near Droop Mountain Battlefield in Pocahontas County spotted a large cat about 100 yards away among his flock of sheep. Lester shared the story: "It caught one and jumped a rail fence with it and went down over the hill." The farmer ran inside and got his rifle and took a shortcut across the hill to head off the predator. From 125 yards away, he spotted the cat eating on the sheep. He shot and killed the 100-pound male cougar. In Pritt's own words, "I still wasn't too sure what it was. I was afraid to go down there for a long time."[30]

Larry Guthrie, the Department of Natural Resources (DNR) conservation officer who picked up the cougar where it was shot, told the Charleston Gazette that the cougar was in excellent condition. "It apparently had been eating well lately," he added. Since that time, it's become "common knowledge" that this animal was tame, but the original description of the event doesn't support this perception.[31]

A necropsy performed by the Southern Cooperative Wildlife Disease Center in Georgia allegedly revealed that the dead cougar contained a parasite associated with captive cougars.[32] Years later, Lester discovered that the DNR had destroyed all the paperwork on the alleged necropsy. Two days after the male was killed, a female cougar was seen on Bruffey Creek. She was bedded down near a fence under a rocky ledge. The DNR was called, officers arrived to observe the cat and keep people from disturbing it. Around 1:00 am she was shot with a tranquilizer gun, ran about eighty yards and collapsed, according to Pocahontas County Times October, 1976. She was loaded into a truck and taken to the French Creek Game Farm.[33]

What happened to her after that is a mystery. Lester was unable to find any documents on that subject, but under the Freedom of Information Act, he did see several letters stating that the female appeared to be pregnant. The U.S. Fish and Wildlife Service (USFWS) advised the DNR to release her in the Cranberry Backcountry. He also has a letter from Dan Cantner, Chief of the Division of Wildlife Resources of the DNR to the Regional Director of the USFWS stating that the DNR did not want to keep the female and asking the USFWS to pick her up. The best-case scenario is that the DNR took the USFWS' advice and quietly released her in the Cranberry Backcountry. If this happened, it would have had to involve officials of the DNR, USFWS and United States Forest Service. The unofficial word is that she died in captivity without producing kittens. Sadly, the true story may never be known.[34]

In his recent book A Valley Called Canaan 1885-2002, Dr. Ed Michael, a retired professor of wildlife biology at West Virginia University, states that he found the carcass of a beaver in the Canaan Valley that had been killed by a cougar. He told Helen McGinnis:

> I personally found a beaver that had been killed by a predator. Based on the sign around the carcass, I identified the predator as a mountain lion. In addition, I found a predator-killed deer on Dolly Sods that I was convinced had been killed by a mountain lion. Although there were not enough tracks to positively identify the predator as a mountain lion, I had no doubt in my own mind.[35]

Dr. Michael is best known for his knowledge of flying squirrels and snapping turtles and is not a carnivore expert. Todd Lester, being the founder of the Eastern Cougar Foundation, is the leading figure in the search for evidence of cougars in West Virginia. As mentioned, Lester searched relentlessly for evidence of cougars, and on March 3, 1996, was successful. He found and cast tracks in Wyoming County, which were verified as cougar by Dr. Lee Fitzhugh and Dr. David Maehr, two well-known cougar biologists.[36] Todd reflects on his work:

> On March 30, 1996, I did an all day field search in that area where I found the track and found a deer kill, which I have pictures of. Although it was nothing but hair and bone, I found and photographed three different sites where it had been dragged and covered up.[37]

Lester continued to travel about the state and in 1998 he discovered another set of tracks. These looked promising but they could not be given the same degree of certitude. In his own words Lester recounts the discovery: "In August 1998 in Mingo County, I found tracks in which there were at least three animals traveling together. Lee Fitzhugh and Dave could not say positively they were cougar, but they could not rule them out either. And the same goes for the track I found in nine inches of snow on Red Spruce Knob off Route 150 in Pocahontas County."[38]

Some wildlife officials believe cougars may roam the mountains of West Virginia and neighboring states, but many of them also believe that any cougars present are feral escaped or released former captives, or even western wanderers. The Eastern Cougar Foundation hoped its network of remote motion-sensing cameras would catch a glimpse of a free-ranging cougar, regardless of its origin. "No cougars were photographed , but a lot of good habitat remained unsurveyed," said Lester, the organization did not set cameras out in 2011.[39] Concurrently with the camera study, Lester also submitted ten possible cougar scats he and others had collected in the state to a DNA laboratory, Wildlife Genetics International, of Nelson, British Columbia. None of the scats were confirmed as those of a cougar, but one may have come from a red wolf.[40]

This camera trap photo stimulates interest -- possible cougar? But note the wooly un-cougar like appearance of the fur. Was it a result of being too close to the flash?

SOUTH CAROLINA

According to the written accounts of the early settlers, the cougar, or panther as it is preferred in these parts, was rather abundant. Experts theorize that the bulk of the animals were found in the coastal lowlands and swamps.[41] During settlement it was noted that the cat was retreating into these coastal swamps and becoming exceedingly rare. Audubon mentions in his journal in 1851 that an older native Carolinian witnessed a cougar trapped on an island during a flood: "...two or three deer on a small mound not twenty feet in diameter surrounded by a wide sea of waters, with a cougar seated in the midst of them; both parties having entered into a truce at a time when their lives seemed equally in jeopardy."[42] Their lives definitely were in danger. The relationship between panther and deer in the Carolinas would soon end, as they both faded from the landscape soon after. The panther, it seemed, would never again so casually expose itself the way that unfortunate animal on the mound did.

Yet one panther obviously did, as it was killed in the Camden region. It is significant in that the killing took place so late -- about 1916.[43] Again, these late killings are potent fuel for debates in favor of surviving pre-settlement colonies because they suggest that hidden wild corners were available. Deer had begun to rebound and might have been in those areas. Bruce Wright mentions sightings from 1948, and Ron Nowak said there were reliable sightings as late as 1950.[44] Shortly after 1970 the sightings increased and continued through that decade into the early 1980s. The decades following reveal a consistent number of them, as well.[45]

Although there are many more recent sightings, a series that took place in the new developments of suburban South Carolina are of interest. Did the event suggest another case of displaced wildlife, or were people seeing things? In October, 2003, there was an unidentified large cat-like creature lurking in the woodlands around the town of Maudlin. The region had just converted wildlife habitat into neatly laid housing. The big cat caused such alarm that residents were put on alert. The Ricelan Subdivision, Maudlin Elementary, Middle and High School were all notified of the unknown animal by police officers. The flurry of sightings was significant and memorable among the recently recorded big cat claims.[46]

It began with the sighting by a Maudlin police officer on October 7 at about 2 a.m. and was followed by another the next night on the 8th. Then on the 11th a resident saw the cat jumping a tall security fence at 5 p.m. On October 13 and 14 the cat was spotted in the early a.m. During the next two days there were additional reports, and by then the animal was being called a cougar. An article that ran in the *Greenville Newspaper* quoted witnesses in the area where the cat had been frequenting on October 23: "Duppstadt stood in the yard of his home surveying the edge of the woods Wednesday with his girlfriend, Melissa Crompton, and their neighbor, Betty Lambert. 'We're scared to go out at night', he said." The group had been looking at large paw prints and places where some large animal had slipped through the tall grass. Only the day before, Duppstadt discovered the cat crouched in tall weeds as if ready to pounce on his small dog that he was walking.[47]

South Carolina, incidentally, is the northern fringe of what was historically defined as the range of the Florida panther or *Puma concolor coryi*. In the lowland swamps and coastal plains, the so-called true eastern cougar, formerly known as *Puma concolor couguar* and the coryi subspecies would have exchanged genetic information.[48]

THE SOUTHERN STATES
GEORGIA

The cougar once ranged widely, from the land of the great Okefenokee Swamp through the pine and palmetto flat lands, up into the western mountains. In time its range was reduced to the Okefenokee and western mountains.

In Georgia the cougar is presently known as panther, as it is in Florida, but Bartram, when describing the animal, used the word "tyger" for his 1773 account described in The Travels of William Bartram. "Bears, 'tygers,' wolves, and wild cats are numerous enough. This creature is called in Pennsylvania and northern states 'panther,' but in Carolina, and southern States, is called 'Tyger'; it is very strong, much larger than any dog, of a yellow brown, or clay colour, having a very long tail; it is mischievous animal, and preys on calves, young colts, etc..."[1] (This example is an exception, as "tiger" or "tyger" in the New World almost always refers to jaguar, which conceivably could have been here in early historic times.) Young and Goldman held that the panther was still widespread even into 1880. Proof of its presence was last established in the Okefenokee, where it is last mentioned in 1927.[2] Since then, however, sightings have continued until the present day. Today, many believe the cougar still lurks among the unapproachable strands deep in the swamp.

Authorities disagree and join the long list of state wildlife people who do not believe that the cougar can still be found. This position is understandable, the big rumor in Georgia has it that in 2000 a hunter shot a panther out of a tree. The hunter was out looking for fair game when he came upon a pair of glowing eyes staring at him from a tree branch. He didn't look closely, to re-confirm the animal -- but instead fired, a dead 73-pound cougar fell to the ground. The incident is said to have occurred near Rock Spring, Georgia. The hunter allegedly notified state wardens who went to the scene and took the carcass to Atlanta for review.[3] When the incident was recently mentioned to Georgia authorities, no one had any recollection of the event.

There was a confirmed shooting in north Georgia in April of 2000; however, this animal was definitely a former captive. Interestingly, it had survived several weeks in the wild. Eight years later there was another cougar kill, this one occurred in November of 2008 at West Point Lake near Abbottsford within Troop County. Genetic testing was able to identified the cat as a Florida panther. The testing even linked the cat to its father living in southwest Florida. It was a 7 foot 140 pound male and it had made the journey from south Florida through all kinds of developed areas without incident until its untimely death by gunshot. The panther was spotted from a tree stand and fired upon by a muzzleloader, killing the endangered species instantly. The panther was in excellent health and most likely dispersing in search of a female and new territory. It is estimated that the cat had traveled some 600 miles.

The hunter was not prosecuted as of early 2011. It is reported that the incident is still under review but because of the unlikelihood of a Florida panther being that far north in Georgia, it does not appear there will be legal action against this crime. While this case offers a challenge, far to often similar crimes escape justice. Since this incident the state of Georgia has made an effort to alert hunters that Florida panthers may appear in the state and to hold fire.

ALABAMA AND MISSISSIPPI

In this harsh, humid environment the panther once lived unmolested in what Young and Goldman considered low numbers. With the advance of European settlement and the persecution that came with it, the panther retreated into the swamps. Much like in Florida, it was known to continue in these refuges for some time, and rumors of its presence persist to this day.

Audubon wrote of its occurrence in the lowland swamps of Mississippi as late as 1851, and other naturalists also noted in 1854 that the "panther is now rarely met with, except in dense and extensive swamps and canebrakes."[4] In 1877 the panther was considered plentiful enough to hunt in Tunica and Washington County of Alabama.[5] Later, Howell, a researcher for the U.S. Dept of Agriculture, wrote in 1921 that although most considered the panther extirpated in Alabama, "recent reports, although rather indefinite, indicated that a very few still remain in the big swamps of the southern counties."[6]

Place names attest that pumas once occurred in Mississippi. Coahoma County's name is derived from a Choctaw Indian word meaning "Red Panther." Copiah County means "Calling Panther." There is a small town, Panther Burn, in Sharkey County. In Hancock County we find Dead Tiger Creek, and there once was a town named Tigerville there. This suggests jaguars may have lived there. Unfortunately, not a single skin or skull of a Mississippi puma has been preserved in a museum collection, nor is known to be in private hands. No specific kills have been recorded for Mississippi, but there is a 1948 killing for Alabama. Stanley Young found mention of pumas in the state as early as 1758 and into the 1800s, but apparently they were not common.[7]

Sightings persist in these two states as they do farther east. Some have been rather believable. Helen McGinnis was intrigued by several alleged sightings in Mississippi. One in particular came from a lumberman who had spent a great deal of time in the backwoods where he claims to have seen several panthers over the years. She reports his closest encounter took place in August of 1986. The lumbermen's son saw the panther first, and then they investigated it together. They saw what they believe was the same cat the next day across the road from their house, where it had been the night before. It was in a stream valley and seemed to ignore them initially. The other report that grabbed McGinnis' interest came from a clergyman who said he saw a panther walk up to within fifty feet of him when he noticed it was carrying a kitten in its mouth. McGinnis soon found herself immersed in a thorough research of Mississippi.[8]

One of the most promising areas is the Stennis Space Center and a surrounding buffer zone near the Gulf of Mexico in Hancock County. The western edge of the area encompasses the swamps of the Pearl River, a notoriously difficult terrain and the same region of the recent

Ivory-billed Woodpecker sighting. Many cat sightings were reported, beginning in the 1960s. One of the most convincing reports came from six men who saw a cougar walk along the bank of a canal and come down to drink on November 3, 1978. Five of the men wrote independent reports on what they had seen.[9]

However, Texas cat hunter Roy McBride searched the area in December 1977 and concluded that no pumas lived there, although there was plenty of prey.[10] McGinnis searched the area for tracks again in 1987. She found no tracks and concluded that pumas probably did not inhabit the area.

Carter and Rummel (1980) reviewed the status of the puma in the state. They initiated a publicity campaign asking wildlife professionals and foresters as well as the general public for reports. They received 150 responses from as far back as 1940, not all of them credible. They were scattered across the state; the most likely ones were along the Mississippi River and in Hancock County. In their opinion, the most likely habitat for pumas in the state was an arc from the Lower Delta, south along the Mississippi River, eastward across the Homochitto National Forest, and south to the coastal swamps.[11]

SUMMARY OF THE EVIDENCE IN THE CENTRAL APPALACHIANS

There are several cases of sightings recorded on video from this area, as well as a few credible sets of tracks. The closest thing to a cluster occurs in North Carolina, Virginia, and West Virginia. The geographic area includes the site where Robert Downing conducted his investigation and the region where Todd Lester utilized remote cameras in an attempt to document cougars in the mountainous parts of West Virginia. The Great Smoky Mountain National Park and the Shenandoah National Park are all within this region and have had long histories of cougar sightings. Both Downing and Culbertson believed cougars could have made it through European settlement and clearing within the central Appalachians. Cultbertson believed a few cougars were in fact living in Great Smoky National Park.

1) In 1976 a male cougar was killed while killing sheep and was pictured in local newspapers with West Virginia Department of Natural Resources officer Larry Guthrie. Two days later, a pregnant female

was captured alive in Pocahontas County. There is a paper trail that conveyed ambivalence as to the cat's origin and what to do with it. It ends suddenly and leaves the fate of the cat unknown. Todd Lester is working to find out what happened to the animal.

2) In 1990 Donald Linzey discovered tracks that he felt were made by a cougar. Linzey took photographs of the tracks and set them in cement casts.

3) A home video was taken in 1991 in the western mountains of Maryland and verified as being footage of a cougar.

4) In the Great Smoky Mountains National Park, a video was taken in 1991 of a healthy cougar. The video was shown to many experts, including Donald Linzey.

5) In 1996 Todd Lester found tracks in West Virginia. Lester made casts of the tracks and had them re-confirmed by wildlife specialists Lee Fitzhugh of the Extension Wildlife Service at the University of California at Davis and by David Maehr.

CHAPTER SIX

VERMONT CATAMOUNTS and DNA

While all the eastern states have had exciting sightings, most of the recent indisputable scientific proof has come from New England and Canada. Today documenting cougars has taken on new meaning with advancements in DNA analysis, making the tracks and blurry photographs from the south and central Appalachian states less meaningful. With these advancements the quest of the cougar in the East changed, and this change began in a small town of Vermont.

From 1990 to 1997 there were dozens of reported cougar sightings in Vermont.[1] Many of these offered evidence, and in 1994 there was a sighting that made national news. The information gained from these sightings were the result of one curious state biologist's efforts. Biologist Cedric Alexander began organizing these sightings, using a form he designed and sent out to the state game offices in 1991. Alexander initiated this procedure because of the large volume of calls being received statewide.[2]

The first convincing sighting came from the town of Craftsbury in the central-northern part of the state. On the 20th of May in 1992, a Rutland resident by the name of Mr. Roy was traveling along Route 14 near Lake Eligo. The traveler stopped his car to observe a pair of large, spotted, tawny kittens playing in the sand beside the road. Roy said he watched for about fifteen minutes and observed these beagle-sized animals at play. Roy said, "these cubs had spots and were in the sand playing; until after about fifteen minutes a car came along and scared them off."[3]

Cedric and his father, Wayne Alexander, investigated this sighting the next morning. Although they found tracks, the sandy soil preserved little in the way of interior detail or contour, which is important for identification; thus, no positive identification could be made.[4] The significance of this sighting is that there were cubs. The importance of this would later take shape with subsequent reports.

In August of the following year, another impressive sighting of a possible cougar came from the same area. The sighting occurred in the remote town of Elmore, where there seem to be more deer and moose than people. The report came from Elmore State Park, situated at the edge of the seldom-hiked Elmore Mountain. In this part of Vermont there is a mix of deeply forested mountains and farm country. The campsite, nestled beneath Elmore Mountain, is in one of the wildest parts of the state, just east of the Worcester Mountain Range. There, the arrival of night brings out an assortment of wild creatures.

These mountains are rich with bear and snowshoe hare. A high deer population exists along the edges, where the hills intermingle with the farms. On the western side of the park, one finds a more rugged terrain. Here, the forest stretches for miles into the town of Stowe. Continuing in this direction, one leaves the ramshackle charm of the Elmore region in Washington County and encounters the sophisticated ski areas.

Here, in the shadow of Elmore Mountain, another sighting involving kittens occurred. A couple from Texas, familiar with cougars, claimed to experience an exciting night on the edge of the mountain. They described their exciting moment to Ranger Warren Griffith, while other campers told of loud, unearthly screams during the previous night. On August 6, 1993, this couple, camping in a trailer at the further edge of the park near the base of the Summit Trail, spotted a large cougar in plain view. It was near dusk at 8:30 p.m. The Vermont Catamount Sighting Form reads as follows:

> Mrs. Jones observed the adult within 50 feet of campsite walking along a 6x8 timber laid on ground to block off road. Catamount looked at her for a while and she then called her husband to come out with the camera. He

did just that and was able to focus on the catamount still staring from the log. Then the catamount turned and walked away with cubs revealed and following her. Pictures will be sent to Warren Griffith.[5]

The observer was quoted as saying, "no doubt as to what I was observing."[6] Unfortunately, they did not forward the photographs, and this report, taken secondhand, was not followed up with any further effort in an attempt to secure the photographs.

Of all the dozens of sightings on file with Cedric Alexander, the most scientifically significant is the one from Craftsbury in 1994, reported on a cold and typically cloudy, twenty-degree Vermont morning. Mark Walker walked 150 feet from his house, on his way to fill his grandmother's birdfeeder. He was not prepared for the sight before him. He stood, partially hidden by balsam firs, and saw what he believed to be three mountain lions only seventy feet away from him. They were walking on snow amid open hardwood forest. It was April 2, 1994, at 8:00 a.m., Mark looked at these lions for about half a minute before fear swept over him. Terrified, Walker says, "I just ran like hell."[7]

Cedric Alexander's father, Wayne, and brothers, Peter and Paul, went out to investigate. They found a 30-inch deep snow cover. Tracking would prove difficult because it was spring, and the top layer was frozen crust. Nevertheless, the brothers were determined and on snowshoes they set out to discover a clear trail with fairly good lion tracks. They hiked for nearly an hour over all kinds of terrain. Then ahead of them scattered a bit among the tracks were several droppings. Some empirical evidence had finally been found.

However, Cedric Alexander had to confirm that these scats were from the cats just observed. They were fresh, and Cedric Alexander placed them in airtight bags and continued to keep them close to frozen. Alexander recorded the event thoroughly on videotape, and the written report reads as follows: "Walker was interviewed on VCR tape and Peter and Paul Alexander trailed the animals on snowshoe up from the lake. They came upon fresh scat a mile up the hill. Scat appeared very fresh, dark brown with at least one longer hair. In general not much hair was in the scat although the scat was not dissected."[8] Cedric Alexander was to prove their authenticity and origin by air-drying them and sending them out to Bonnie Yates, a senior scientist, with the United States Fish and Wildlife Services Forensic Lab, in Ashland, Oregon. The purpose of this examination, explained Alexander, was to identify the contents.

Bonnie Yates examined the scats, checking the origins of any hair by looking for medulla and scale patterns, length, and color. After examining the hair in the scats, it was determined that these were indeed the scats of the mountain lions seen by Mark Walker. Alexander explained, "...in September of 1994 the results came back as cougar. Felines have a habit of ingesting hair while cleaning themselves. The lab identified cougar hair in the scat."[9] While the sighting alone offers significant scientific evidence of the presence of mountain lions in New England, two key questions remain unanswered: Does this confirmed mountain lion sighting prove there is a viable breeding population in the Northeast, and does it represent survivors of the original native subspecies?

Although Cedric Alexander is skeptical of the cougar surviving in the East, he is intrigued by the possibility that there is a chance of a family unit existing in his state and seemingly breeding in the wild. Alexander refers to his file and the two other reports of a cougar with cubs in this forested region. He mentions the significance of the Elmore sighting and the one by Roy from Lake Eligo.

These sightings, all near Craftsbury, Vermont, and all involving what may be a family unit, hint at the possibility of puma presence and perhaps reproduction in the region. But, warned Cedric Alexander, "the possible sighting of a cougar with kittens is not proof of the presence of a viable breeding population of native cats."[10] After reviewing the Alexander file, the state of Vermont went on to announce the existence of the mountain lion there.[11]

Meanwhile, the hype and publicity in Vermont led the public to believe that "the cat is back." As the mascot of the University of Vermont, the catamount is a visible symbol in the state. Here, where the charm and beauty of New England reaches its peak on every country road, the tourist industry has used the cat's purported return as a way of luring wildlife-loving flatlanders to its trails and parks. After all, the presence of something wild and free like the lion sells the image of a clean state awaiting outdoor enthusiasts. The Middlebury College Panthers, White River's Catamount Beer, Stowe Resort's "catamount returns" slogan --

all are examples of Vermont institutions utilizing the catamount as an icon of Vermont's essence.[12] But could this be evidence of the fuel that may have motivated some group of individuals to intentionally release western lions into the state?

It was, after all, during this time in 1994 that huge tracts of Vermont went up for sale. The giant paper companies had, for years, held vast acreages of these mountains for the external benefit of the public that has utilized them. In the early 1990s, they unleashed vast acreages. The Champion Paper Company alone had put up140,000 acres for sale. Surely the presence of a big endangered cat would change the political winds in favor of protecting these vulnerable tracts of Vermont, and in the following years that land did gain protection. It is now set aside for Vermont's residents to use in a multiple-use fashion; a tract large enough to keep the hope alive for a people and a cat that favor open space.

Dr. Thomas Altherr, a historian at the State College of Denver, finds this aspect of the controversy very interesting: "The existence of the catamount, supposed or real, has become integral to issues of regional self identity for Vermonters and other northern New Englanders." A region known for its fierce need for freedom and independence, Vermont has always had a close relationship with the catamount. One symbol of this was the stuffed catamount placed in front of the Catamount Tavern during the eighteenth century. In the words of Vermont writer Rowland Robinson, it was "a tawny monster that grinned a menace to all intruders." This catamount faced west so as to frighten the "Yorkers" from entering the state.[13]

In 1994, when the scat evidence was gathered and sent to the federal lab in Oregon, the technology for extracting DNA from scat had not been perfected. Not until 1997 was the process of DNA extraction available so that the preserved Craftsbury scat could again be sent out for testing in the forensic lab. This time the lab procedure was headed by Dr. Holly Earnest at the University of California in Davis. Earnest developed the extraction process of DNA from scat, which now made an analysis of the Craftsbury sighting possible. A member of the Veterinary Science Department, Earnest was the leading expert on DNA extraction from wildlife scat. She had completed the process hundreds of times. In fact, DNA extraction had been completed on mountain lions over

500 times by the time the Oregon lab was asked to test the Craftsbury sample.[14]

The specimen tested positive as canine. Originally, it was believed the wrong sample was sent from the lab that did the initial testing, and the true Craftsbury sample was accidentally discarded. Confusion over the matter through time may be another form of back peddling; but Doug Blodget, the biologist on top of the issue, clearly believes the correct sample was tested. It is a thought provoking question, as to why a scat sample containing cougar fur tested as canine? Needless to say, close followers of the cougar issue and biologists were disappointed. For years, such evidence had awaited definitive testing and now the results offer only more questions.[15] The unfortunate lab issue was yet another event making the controversy that much more difficult to resolve. With the Craftsbury sample remaining questionable, Mark Walker's sighting will never have a confirmed known identity, but at least the technology had come of age.

That technology was soon employed when, in 1997, a professional tracker was hiking through the Quabbin Reservoir in central Massachusetts and discovered a mountain lion scat. John McCarter recognized the signs of the lion while preparing for a tracking class he was about to give for nature instructor Paul Rezendes. Rezendes and his team of instructors offer tracking and photography classes and often use the wild acres of Quabbin as their living classroom.

McCarter was in a remote part of the reservoir's 80,000 acres when he noticed a mound of dirt, which he figured was another of many bobcat scrapes he had seen over the years. When he uncovered it and revealed a larger than bobcat-sized scat, he began to wonder, "Was it? There aren't suppose to be any this far east." The scat measured 7/8" in diameter and confirmed his initial suspicions, as it was bigger than any previously observed bobcat scat he had ever noted. But what really excited him was the length of a second scat located beneath a similar mound and measuring nearly a foot long. A few yards away, beneath some hemlocks, at the edge of the reservoir, he found more evidence.[16] It was the upper and lower portions of what he believed comprised a beaver jaw.

This scat found at the Quabbin Reservoir in 1997 by John
Mc Carter tested positive for North American cougar.
Photo by John Mc Carter, courtesy Mass Div Fish and Game

An experienced tracker and naturalist, McCarter now knew what
to look for, and he searched the area of the kill very carefully. After
several minutes of wandering around beneath a canopy of hemlocks
with his eyes on the ground, he found what he was after. Beneath that
quiet shade of hemlocks was an impressive cache that, when scrutinized,
gave him an eerie feeling of profound discovery. Bobcats and mountain
lions both have a habit of covering their kills and returning to them.
He knew this and had seen several bobcat caches, but this one was too
large to be a bobcat's. It measured over eight feet, and when he pushed
back the debris covering he found whole entrails of a beaver. The scrape
marks were drawn over the entrails, and they too seemed quite a stretch
for a bobcat's shorter foreleg.[17]

Realizing this could be the lucky find that so many had been
looking for in this cougar hot spot, he took some sample of the scat and
returned home. A day later he returned to obtain more. McCarter said,
"having this kind of evidence is not something you just realize right
away even when you are holding it in your hand."[18] Initially, the scat was
sent to the forensic lab in Oregon; it showed no evidence in the form of
cougar fur as did the Craftsbury sample, but McCarter and Rezendes
did not stop there. They sent it out for the DNA test, but nearly two
years were to pass before they finally had a definitive answer.

The scats were sent to the Science Resource Center at the Wildlife
Conservation Society in New York City. Using Earnest's methods, the
researchers determined it to be that of a mountain lion, *Puma concolor*.[19]
Thus, McCarter became the first man to find such strong, scientifically

irrefutable, DNA evidence in the Northeast. Furthermore, the analysis was also able to prove that the specimen had a North American ancestry. This is significant since most escapees, released or unwanted pets, are very often of South American origin or bloodline.[20]

DNA scat analysis is a lengthy process because scat contains countless DNA that derive from the micro-flora in the cougar's digestive tract and include DNA of the animals the cougar has eaten. Using probes that identify the correct DNA, Earnest and others using her method are then able to sort through the extraneous DNA information. The process, incidentally, is expected to change some of the ways wildlife biologists are conducting their studies.[21] Earnest says, "This process now makes so much research open to new possibilities and in some cases much quicker."[22] She uses the scats of mountain lions in southern California, where the species hunts big horn sheep. The method is used to study cougar family structure and feeding specialization of individual cougars.[23]

Earnest has gained tremendous respect for her revolutionary changes in the science of wildlife biology. A veterinarian, she also holds a Ph.D. in genetics. She explains, "the technique has provided me with so much more access into this population of mountain lions than would have been derived from traditional hunting techniques using hounds and darts. These large carnivores are almost impossible to observe, and the use of DNA has made the research so much easier. But more importantly, it is also a great deal less disruptive to the mountain lions."[24]

DNA research on cougars also caught the interest of another innovative geneticist named Melanie Culver, who had done some profound work at the National Cancer Institute's Center for Genetic Diversity. Culver noted the large number of subspecies in North American cougars and efficiently collected skin samples from a number of these representative specimens.[25] She examined six pumas from each of the 52 geographic regions in the Americas and compared genes to establish differences. In January of 2000, Culver's research at the Institute in Maryland completed the genetic testing of these geographic samples of mountain lion. Dr. Culver was able to decisively conclude what had been anticipated by a few biologists who knew cougars well: she discovered that the so-called unique original *Puma concolor couguar* or termed then as *Felis concolor couguar* is indistinguishable from other

North American cougars, and that they could all be considered a single subspecies of cougar.[26]

Through historical research, biologists were able to find that the original and historic classification of these subspecies was determined with a limited sample size of often incomplete specimens. Thus it was apparent that their conclusions were based on insufficient representations of the cougar within the geographic area.[27] The eastern subspecies, *Felis concolor couguar* had been defined by only seven samples and was simply based on the measurements of their skulls and superficial appearance. To make matters worse, some of these specimens were of very young lions that had not fully developed characteristic bone features.[28]

Culver obtained the skin tissue of a mounted specimen in Quebec to begin her analysis. The tissue she used came from an 1828 specimen that had been collecting dust in a Canadian museum.[29] This base sample was analyzed for unique genetic markers to genetically define the eastern subspecies against other samples.

Today, Culver has advanced techniques at her disposal, with which she is able to test preserved specimens from the East. According to Culver, who has employed the latest gene-mapping techniques to determine the evolutionary genetic relations between the historical subspecies in question: "Analysis suggests moderate levels of gene flow among all phylogeographic regions. There is no basis for maintaining 32 subspecies. Instead the use of six is recommended. All temperate North American (north of Nicaragua) subspecies should be recognized as a single subspecies, *Puma concolor cougar*. The similarity among the six groups is perhaps more important to consider than the differences." [30]

It remains to be seen how her work will be received in the future. Many zoologists feel that outward appearance and behavior ought to determine subspecies. David Maehr, who died tragically in 2008 in a plane crash while tracking bears, was one who believed the acknowledgement of the subspecies is important and that there are distinct, although often small differences, that nature has bestowed for survival within definable regions.

> I believe that the recent suggestion of a single North American subspecies is quite dangerous. The early naturalists recognized distinct differences among

different geographic populations of species. While many of the differences may have been influenced directly by environment, others were certainly the result of genetic differences that were the result of varying degrees of isolation and adaptation to unique environmental and climatological conditions. Thus, the fact that a Florida panther has (had) expanded nasal passageways and a rougher coat of slightly different color is no accident.[31]

Maehr feared that the idea of a single subspecies will result in poor conservation decisions as agencies faced with difficult problems such as in Florida will seek the easy way out and promote biodiversity homogenization. Florida introduced Texas cougars into their dwindling population as a way of saving the all but 40 panthers still remaining. The case of the Florida panther has been widely criticized by politicians, citizens, and environmentalists. Maehr believed that habitat connectivity enhancement is all that was needed to allow the panther greater range and genetic health.

So, does Culver's suggestion indicate slight differences that can be overlooked in order to simplify classification? Will it change the policies and affect the way cougars are managed in the future? Her work is a part of a trend, as more analysis with subspecies has been taking place lately. In light of the Craftsbury and Quabbin evidence, the question no longer has as much to do with the genetic history of these sightings in the East, as it does with whether there is a breeding population. The question still remains - are there free-ranging, wild bred cougars in the eastern United States?

Unfortunately, the trend in Vermont has not lent itself to more substantiated evidence. The use of DNA testing to rule out non-native origins has largely been confined to cougars in the West. Nothing convincing has occurred in Vermont since that 1994 incident in Craftsbury.[32] But Cedric Alexander and other biologists in Vermont continue to fill out sighting reports. The rash of cougar sightings with kittens in the Craftsbury area has long since ended, but it is interesting that the area in and around Craftsbury continues to produce a significantly greater number of sightings than other parts of the state. Many will continue to ponder the fate of the supposed mother and her kittens who slipped quietly into the spruce-covered hills on that winter day.

Having learned from the mishap of the Craftsbury evidence, McCarter and Rezendes archived some of their Quabbin sample for future assays and even had the scat tested twice in two different labs, a system recommended by Tischendorf. Now that tests can vindicate a witness's claim of a sighting, it is more likely that such events will be investigated. Sightings and tracks cannot stand up to the scientific rigor that is demanding of true evidence. Yet, for decades, tracks and sightings was all there was to support the presence of these phantoms called eastern cougars. Maybe now there is a real chance of solving the riddle of the "Ghost Cat."

Today, with DNA analysis available, investigators can look for repeated activity in specific locations as an indicator of resident cougars or a breeding population. Without proof of a breeding population, such occasional pieces of scat really mean nothing other than that a puma was traveling through. Animal identification taken down to the subspecific or even individual level using DNA testing of scat is an unequivocal method when the sample is double-tested, uncontaminated, and subject to a fail-proof chain of custody.[33]

PART THREE:

THE GREAT CONTROVERSY

CHAPTER SEVEN

WHERE ARE THEY COMING FROM?

There are three prevailing explanations for the Craftsbury cougars and all other sightings east of the Mississippi. One explanation proposes that escaped pets or intentional releases account for cougar sightings. The second proclaims that cougars never became extirpated. The third explanation for the mountain lions in the East is that they are transients from western populations. In the past, most authorities agreed that this latter explanation was an unlikely scenario. Today, however, it is becoming more apparent that mountain lions are indeed moving east, and while they may not account for evidence as far east as New England, it seems that the progression of this predator into areas of abundant prey is likely, if not inevitable.

Mountain lions have been increasing quickly since 2000. Recent lion populations have not extended beyond the eastern foothills of the Rockies, and this has been considered their range for the past sixty years. However, mountain lions have recently shown up in the prairie states, and they continue to generate evidence further east. There is strong evidence of occasional mountain lions in the mid-western states and in the middle southern states adjacent to Texas.

Many researchers, such as Mark Dowling of the Cougar Network and Harley Shaw, a prominent cougar biologist, believe that saturated populations in the Rockies are spilling into the Plains states and are moving toward the east.[1] As will be mentioned in the chapter on biology, male lions are forced out of their birth territories in search of their own.

They will travel extensively in search of a female and suitable habitat. With the abundance of their preferred prey, the western cougars might migrate as far east as there are deer herds to support them.

It is apparent that western cougar populations began increasing as early as the 1960s, largely due to increased legal protection and the increase in the deer herds. Recent eye-witness accounts and cougar kills offer further support that the states of South Dakota, North Dakota, Nebraska, and Oklahoma are likely experiencing the overflow of these healthy cat populations, where they are evidently taking advantage of high deer numbers. A pioneer population, now established, can be located in the Black Hills region of South Dakota.[2] Most likely, the mountain lions are traveling out from the Black Hills' population and attempting to re-colonize further east in the neighboring states. According to the Cougar Network, the South Dakota Game, Fish, and Parks Commission is working closely with South Dakota State University, where there has been an extensive research project taking place on this population since 1998. Wildlife officials have been tracking one animal through a radio collar attached late in the winter of 2004. North Dakota biologist Jacquie Ermer says the collar sent off a signal near Karlstad, Minnesota, about 40 miles into that state, indicating that the lion had dispersed approximately 450 miles at that time. Biologists wonder how far this cougar will travel, as they have documentation of another cougar from the Black Hills traveling close to 700 miles in 2004. It is estimated that the Black Hills population consisted of 50 animals or 10 males and 40 females in 2000. They now estimate the population to be closer to 200 as determined in 2010.[3]

In 2004 a male cougar was shot by police in the residential area near Yankton. A few years after that kill, about 300 miles from the Black Hills, a 70 pound female was destroyed in the town of Howard. In October of 2008 there was another male cougar kill. Reports have become so numerous throughout South Dakota that the state has removed the animal from its endangered species list, and allowed a limited cougar hunt. Although controversial and upsetting to some, the hunt provided biologists with several specimens that offered important data on the new Black Hills population. Prior to the hunt, confirmed reports consisted mostly of tracks, along with eye-witness accounts, such as an encounter at Ipswitch, off Route 212, and the Turkey Creek

Drainage tracks found in November of 2002. In 1998 there was a kill in Charles Mix County.

Across the border, in North Dakota, an 81-pound female was shot in December 1990. It was the first cougar kill there since 1902. Recently, there has been more talk of cougars ever since a male cougar was shot by a rancher in February of 2001. In August 2001 there was even more excitement when a conservation officer snapped a photo of an adult. Later, in December 2002, a county sheriff took video footage of a cougar. A young female was shot by a hunter in 2004.[4] There were three more cougar kills in 2006. A male, shot in the town of Washburn weighed 107 pounds, a female was hit by a car in November near Bismark and a three year-old male was taken in New Salem. There were two more fatalities in 2008, when a 100 pound male was killed in Cogswell and another 100 pound male was shot by police, as it approached homes near Bismark. They now have an experimental cougar hunting season in the southwest part of the state.

In Nebraska, there have been sightings since the 1950s, but not until the 1990s was there a confirmed sighting. In 1991, evidence of cougar-killed deer were found. Later, a hunter in Souix County shot an adult. Following these incidents were five more killings. In May of 1999, a conservation officer shot an injured male, and then in September of that year, a hunter shot another male. A male cougar was shot in a junk-yard after having been sighted throughout residential areas in Saint Paul. This occurred in November of 2000. A live capture took place on October 3, 2003, when a large mountain lion ran wild through a west Omaha commercial district. With the police, Humane Society, and zoo officials chasing it, the animal was eventually captured on 114th street, which is the busiest in the city. In the excitement, one police officer sent a bullet into the flank of the cat when it seemed to want to lunge at him. The 108-pound male was eventually caught after being hit with a tranquilizing dart. The wounded animal was quickly cared for and recovered fully. Years later, officials were skeptical when they received calls describing a large predatory cat near Highway 370, but the next day a woman confidently directed police to a dead cougar on nearby Interstate 80. The 100 pound male was found fatally hit and sprawled out alongside the expressway on November 6, 2005 near the Gretna-Louisville exchange.

Since then, cougar confirmations have escalated. The Game and Parks Commission collected 96 confirmations to date. Most of these reports, shootings, and other close encounters have been connected with transient males that show a preference for travel along riverbeds. Apparently, they are using the river corridors as highways, because they lead east and offer cover. Mace Hack, who heads the Nebraska Game and Parks Commission says, "The river corridors that connect Nebraska with Wyoming, Colorado, and South Dakota are excellent funnels for mountain lions migrating into and through the state."[5] He believes that there is probably a small population in the Wild Cat Hills area of Nebraska.

Oklahoma has had numerous sightings, too. Game biologists suspect that a small population lives in the Wichita Mountains Wildlife Refuge and in the Fort Sill Military Reservation. Each area comprises a cougar habitat rich in available prey and totaling 150,000 acres. Several young males have been killed in the far western part of the state. Interestingly, a confirmed kill of a cougar that had been radio collared in the Black Hills had to have traveled through Kansas before it was hit by a train in Red Rock Oklahoma during May of 2004. This incident is proof that the cougar remained unreported after having crossed countless roads and human inhabited properties.

Kansas, to the north, has probably hosted many other lions during their travels, as credible reports have been consistently forthcoming from there including a DNA confirmation. Although a hunter spotted a cougar below his deer stand and took several confirmed photos in 2009, the Cougar Network's remote sensing cameras set to capture such transient individuals has not yet photographed any. In November of 2007 there was a confirmed kill in Barber County.

Western Texas has long been known for harboring an established breeding population, but evidence suggests that the animals are expanding eastward to take advantage of the available prey. Eastern Texas has had plenty of cougar excitement in the past few years. Several cougars have been shot, beginning in 1990, when an adult was taken down in the Pinewoods Ecological Region. Two more cougars were killed in 1991; a female of 120 pounds was destroyed while attacking a dog, and a male of 125 pounds was killed in the Pinewoods Ecological Region. There were two more cougar killings in Texas between 1991 and 2000, another from the Pinewoods Region and one from a different location, known as Cross-Prairie Timber Ecological Region. In 2001 there was an additional cougar mortality in that location. These cougar deaths have been centered in the north and northeastern part of the state. This puts lions along the Arkansas border, where there has been much activity.[6]

Arkansas has long been a hot zone for cougar sightings, and although recent cougar evidence may be attributed to the obvious immigration from the west Texas populations, it may be that some of these cats have remained hidden in this state. If that is the case, those beleaguered relic gene pools might find relief, as fresh bloodlines begin to mix in. A few pieces of evidence worth mentioning have come from Pulaski County, where in 1998 scat was analyzed by thin-layer chromatography tests as "probable" for cougar. Then in February of 1999 more scat tested as "probable," but this time with tracks also discovered nearby. In March of 1999, a deer kill was dragged over a fence and through mud that revealed confirmed cougar tracks. In 2000 Game and Fish staff caught a cougar in the light shine of a boat in a creek near Lake Maumelle. In August of 2003, a hunter discovered an image of a cougar on his film taken from a remote sensor camera set up in the wild to monitor deer. A number of search missions and peer-reviewed papers have been generated because of the strong suspicion of cougars in Arkansas. According to Tischendorf, "The mountain lion is expanding east and using the cover of river bottoms like the coyote did -- it is taking advantage of the abundance of deer. If we see them in eastern Texas, then what will stop them from turning up in Arkansas, and from Kansas into Missouri, from the Dakotas to Minnesota, and from there, why not into Wisconsin, and into Ontario or the northern reaches of New England?"[7]

Despite Tischendorf's words, everyone was caught by surprise when on a warm June day in 2011 a 140 pound male cougar was hit and killed by an SUV in Connecticut. Speculations ran wild but when the complete necropsy was finished the DNA work showed the cougar had originated from the Black Hills population of South Dakota. It made an epic journey across all kinds of developed and undeveloped terrain to meet its end over 1,700 miles away. It may be many years before cougars make the headlines again -- but this wayward cougar will not be the last to turn up in the East. Cougars may not immigrate into the

East as quickly as coyotes did, but both of these large carnivores are capable of long distance travel. In the 1950s when the coyote began to move eastward, their presence went largely unnoticed. A decade later, however, they were beginning to produce some alarming encounters. While many sightings of cougars have turned out to be coyotes, there was a time when such an occurrence was as controversial as if these sightings had been of actual cougars. Back then the coyote created quite an uproar and left those seeing them feeling as foolish as those who report cougars today. As far as anyone knew, the nearest coyote was someplace west of the Mississippi. When rural residents and hunters saw these larger than life canines, their reports were dismissed and ridiculed by those who should have known better. Wildlife authorities had little faith in reports of large wolf-like canines, brushing them off as cases of mistaken identity. These reports were considered to be of large feral dogs, and like cougar sightings, they went uninvestigated.

Eventually, there were too many reports to ignore, and state game officials began investigating the sightings. They would soon vindicate these observers and make a fascinating scientific discovery that took years to puzzle out. They found evidence of large wild free-roaming canines colonizing the river valleys in northern New England. Biologists could not quite identify these canines as coyotes, dogs or wolves. The term "coydog" seemed fitting, as these new coyote specimens were larger than their western counterparts. They were, in fact, often a mix, but today coyote dog hybrids are uncommon. As time went on, the number of coyotes began to grow, and physical specimens became available. Eventually the coyote was determined to have bred with Ontario gray wolves, which accounted for their larger size and helped explain their emigration route out of the West. Their journey east created a new subspecies now known as the eastern coyote or *Canis latrans x lycaon*. Perhaps the cougar may share a similar fate and re-introduce themselves.

While migration for such individuals will be extremely precarious, there is documentation of mountain lions navigating through various kinds of dangerous settings in search of new territories. This behavior has occurred in Florida, where radio-collared panthers have been tracked through south Florida's city of Naples on route to Ten Thousand Islands, and north through one busy region of Fort Myers, including areas along the Fort Myers International Airport.[8]

The closest known cougar populations to the East are those in Florida, Texas, the Dakotas and northwest Nebraska. A few biologists suspect a small population in Minnesota. This is a highly controversial and pre-mature assumption at the moment. According to Golley and Lowery, authors on cougars in the South, vagrants from the south Florida population have occurred as far away as Georgia.[9] Dispersal of suspected but unproven populations in the Great Lakes region to parts of the East is possible, but predictable routes seem more dangerous and unlikely.

Migration into the Northeast is more likely from the north, down from the Canadian border, into the Adirondacks, along the wilder regions of the Connecticut Lakes area in New Hampshire and into Maine from across the Quebec border. Such animals would be migrating into New England via the route of the coyote from Ontario north of the Great Lakes. Although there is evidence of lions along the Great Lakes, these animals may not be likely sources of any migration. The lakes themselves, and the narrow corridors afforded to them through populated regions, discount such a theory; therefore, Minnesota becomes a more likely launching point of eastward-moving cougars.

Additionally, Minnesota has a substantial amount of suitable habitat and travel corridors. Its heavy forest cover is further increased in quality by the numerous wetlands, ponds, and lakes that make human travel and activity difficult and therefore less likely. Minnesota is also adjacent to the Dakotas, where the Black Hills population is expanding. The fact that wolves have managed to remain in many locations throughout the region of the Upper Peninsula of Michigan and in Minnesota is a strong indication that the deer population is large enough to sustain cougars and that an ecosystem is there for these migrants. "I believe there must be a small population existing within the wild northern portions of the state. We have numerous reports, many so credible and often, that sightings of offspring seem to indicate a possible breeding status," says Rich Staffon, a wildlife biologist for the state of Minnesota.[10]

Adding credibility and consistency to the larger picture are sightings such as Pat Brun's, who on May 15, 2000, observed a large tawny cat on Highway 89. Numerous reports have been generated from the Ely,

Minnesota, region. One credible report came from Dan Litchfield, a wildlife technician who said, "I found a good set of tracks going across a gravel pit just outside of Ely. The tracks were found after several reports came from the region."[11] But if that is not believable enough, then consider that in Bloomington, Minnesota, police shot and killed a 100-pound cougar after it had frightened hikers on a trail. The animal was shot because it failed to flee, showed aggression, hissed when approached, and assaulted the air with swipes from its enormous claws. A quick examination of the animal by Department of Natural Resources biologists showed no obvious signs that the cat had ever been in captivity. "The cat sported a full set of claws and had very large canine teeth," said Ed Borggess, a manager with the Department of Natural Resources Wildlife Division.[12] Borggess estimates he receives approximately 45 credible reports each year statewide.

There are also recent photographs of a cougar that appeared on two successive nights at what had seemed an obvious fresh cougar kill. Amateur photographer Kerry Kammann had set out an infrared motion detector camera and was able to secure several photos of an adult lion feasting on the deer kill at 10:00 p.m. Rumors of large cats had been circulating in that immediate area for some time. The most significant piece of evidence for cougars in Minnesota was the kill of a female in Aitkin County near Big Sandy Lake in August of 2001. The female left behind kittens that were later captured and placed in a zoo. A few years later, in 2009, a cougar was struck and killed by a car in northern Minnesota.

But if cougars were pushing east via this route, then would there not be some evidence of them in Ontario? There are historical accounts of cougar in the literature that are rather suggestive of the puma's presence in the Province. From the *Canadian Field Naturalist*, an account of a cougar is documented as leaving a track in 1973, and the journal also documents a rash of sightings in the 1950s.[13] None of these historical sightings help to document a migration to the east, but biologists working at the Ministry of Natural Resources in Thunder Bay believe that there could be a small population living along the north shore of Lake Superior, not far from the Minnesota border. Reports consistently come out of this region. For a long time the only tangible evidence was a scat collected by provincial wildlife biologist Lil Anderson and confirmed by the Alberta Natural Resources Service Forensics Lab. But then in the fall of 2004, tests on hairs captured in a scent post with a hair snare were identified as cougar. Stuart Kenn, president of the Ontario Puma Foundation, set up scent posts consisting of estrus urine from a female cougar in heat and surrounded the posts with barbed wire. Two of his posts snared hair, proving the presence of a cougar in those regions.

Another possibility is that Midwestern transients are working their way into Pennsylvania and up along the Appalachians. However, there have been no confirmations of wild free ranging cougars in this region. Current evidence of mountain lions in the Midwest, as just illustrated, suggests that western lions are entering into Kansas and turning up in Missouri and Iowa. But this route requires crossing the Mississippi River, which is not likely. For decades, Florida's panther population has been somewhat contained by the Caloosahatchee River, which is considerably smaller than the Mississippi. While crossings have taken place, the frequency at which they do is low.

However, in July of 2000, a 110-pound male cougar was found killed by a train in Randolph County, Illinois, which is just east of the Mississippi River.[14] Biopsy of the animal showed that it had all its claws and had been feeding on white-tailed deer. DNA tests later proved that it was of North American origin, strongly suggesting it had not been a captive and that it was truly wild. Alan Woolf performed the necropsy at the Cooperative Wildlife Research Laboratory at Southern Illinois University. He found the cougar was a normal male, in good health, with no tattoos, and a stomach containing 100% white-tailed deer.

Similarly, another male cougar believed to be of wild origin was happened upon by a hunter in the town of New Boston. The December 2004 discovery took place in northern Illinois where the animal had been freshly killed by an arrow and preserved by the cold before being reported. The presence of what seems to be wild, free-ranging mountain lions in Illinois does suggest that no matter how difficult and unlikely a migration from the West may be for this species, it is perhaps taking place.[15]

This male probably crossed the river from Missouri, where the Missouri Department of Conservation has documented seven credible reports. In 1994, two raccoon hunters in the southeastern corner of the state poached an adult female mountain lion. The hunters were fined $2,000 each. Then, in 1996, a state Missouri Department of Conservation (MDC) officer by the name of Jerry Elliot videotaped an adult lion feeding on a deer in the central Ozarks. That same month, another lion was videotaped in the western part of the Ozarks by a state biologist. A few years later, in 1999, hunters treed an adult.[16] State MDC biologists were able to locate their tracks and two lion-killed deer nearby. In Lewis County in December of 2000, an adult mountain lion was videotaped again.[17] Two years later, in October of 2002, a young road-killed male weighed in at 125 pounds in Clay County.[18] The animal appeared to be of wild origin and in its second year. In 2003, a car struck and killed an adult male cougar in Callaway County. This specimen also showed no signs of having been in captivity.[19] By 2010 Missouri had at least 5 confirmed cougars.

The Callaway County, Missouri cougar before being examined.
An increasing number of young transient males are moving
toward the eastern states through the Midwest.

In Iowa, cougar tracks were found in December of 1995 and confirmed by state biologists upon an investigation at the scene in Lyon County.[20] From Ringgold County in February of 2001, a cougar sighting was established by a Department of Natural Resources personnel, who was also able to find tracks and scat.[21] A few months later, in April, more tracks were confirmed by Department of Natural Resources in Webster County. In August of 2001, a 130-pound male was struck and killed by a car in the town of Harlan. The accident occurred in the rolling, forested hills of the west-central part of the state. Physical evidence indicated the cat was of wild origin.[22] This was the first confirmed killing of a cougar in Iowa since 1867. [23]

Between the time of that road kill in August of 2001 and the spring of 2002, twenty-one more sightings occurred, including one recorded by a state conservation officer in Carroll County in December.[24] During the summer of 2002, the sightings continued. These sightings, along with a fresh set of tracks, put to rest the idea of the Harlan cougar being the only one responsible for the consistent flurry of sightings that year. Since 2002 many new tracks have been confirmed by the Department of Natural Resources, and in 2003 there was another cougar kill. This animal was shot in November near the town of Ireton. The female cougar had mostly raccoon and some deer in its stomach. On January 6, 2004, in Promise City within Wayne county, raccoon hunters were given a tip about a cougar nearby and decided to run their hound on it. After a half-mile, they treed it and then shot it. Ron Adrews and James Mahaffy performed the biopsy on what appears to be a two-year old male. In December of 2009 a 125 pound male was shot during deer season in Iowa County.[25]

Some cougar biologists point out that expansion of the cougar eastward is next to impossible without the reintroduction of females at the destination point. Cougars are different from coyotes or other canines in that they are philopatric, which means that only the males disperse as transients on long distance journeys. The females remain in familiar terrain in hopes that their territories will overlap with a male. If western cougars are to immigrate and repopulate available habitat in the East, we expect the process may be very slow, as such individuals cannot reproduce immediately without resident populations already in place. Such mountain lions would continue to wander and might find other individuals by traveling in their scent or otherwise end up waiting years for such an opportunity.

Another possible scenario is that a migrant might locate another lion of a different origin, such as an escaped pet trying to live independently. Immigrant western cougars aside, the other explanation for sightings and physical evidence is that such cougars are either released or escaped from private owners. Sure enough, within the past fifty years, many cougar kills turned out to be former pets. In fact, most cougars that have been killed in the East have arrived in this way.[26] But when did the last remnant cougars give way to sightings of escaped pets? How do we know that they did? Are all the eastern sightings actually escapees?

The first of many questions that need to be cleared up is whether a mountain lion, escaped or released, has the ability to survive on its own. What methods of survival would be adopted by a carnivore of this size and strength, having been accustomed to human contact? House cats have had absolutely no problem surviving on their own. Set free or abandoned by their owners, mountain lions, it seems, could surely survive, too. Not necessarily, house cats are well equipped, while released cougar pets are almost always ill equipped for survival.

One explanation of cougars in the East is the escape or release of captive cougars. A surprisingly large number of people keep cougars as pets. Recently, laws have made this more difficult.

Generally, a captive cougar's claws are removed and their teeth are often dulled, placing them at a disadvantage in the wild. Many biologists feel these lions could make it, but others disagree. Todd Lester has said that his investigation into captive cougars revealed that 90% are de-clawed. Lester states, "I really don't think a de-clawed cougar could survive in the wild."[27] On the other hand, Tischendorf believes mountain lions could survive in the wild without claws. People in the pet trade have said that nearly all of the captive lions are declawed, and some have had teeth altered. Most feel that their cats would not do well if set free, suggesting that such animals would have a tendency to frequent human habitation and perhaps prey on domesticated animals, causing these felines to be shot or run over. Some people believe that the cats would turn up just days after release. But a case from overseas, where a clouded leopard escaped from a zoo in Great Britain, proves the adaptability of felines, as the healthy cat was not found until it was shot nine months later while stealing chickens from a farm.[28]

Nearly all wildlife experts agree that escaped pets would show little fear of humans, but this characteristic contradicts most of the sightings. However, those who know the animal say showing fear is a poor indication of whether a lion is of a captive origin or not because healthy wild mountain lions sometimes show little fear or are indifferent to humans when encountered.

Sherry Blanchard, who runs a captive cougar rehabilitation center, has said, "Captive cougars are always desensitized and often totally fearless. Most have had claws clipped and are seriously weakened; they lose the ability to hunt effectively."[29] In general, captives are probably going to be socialized with humans, exhibit abnormal behavior, lack survival skills, and seem ill-suited to make it in the wild, especially during harsh weather. However, captive-bred cougars in Florida, where the climate is warmer, were able to learn quickly how to kill prey.

Another consideration is that most sightings do not occur in residential areas but instead are documented in rural or semi-wild areas away from the suburbs.[30] This matter may cause some difficulty for those inclined to believe that all sightings are released or escaped pets, since sightings occur in the lightly populated regions. Wildlife biologists suggest that mountain lions would not make a beeline for remote areas but would act as other escapees do and would frequent the general area of release. Biologists believe that such mountain lions would stay close to humans, associating us with food and survival. It would also follow that captive raised cats would not have the experience and skills to fend for themselves so abruptly in the wild. Lacking endurance, with withered muscles from years in cages and on chains, these animals would look for easy ways to find food.

Maybe the reason we do not have as many reports from semi-wilderness locations is because of the absence of humans to make observations. As pointed out by Ted Reed, the founder of Friends of the Eastern Panther, it takes both cougar and human to make a sighting, and there just are not that many people in the wilderness late at night when cougars are active. If the cougar phenomenon can be explained completely by disillusioned pet owners who have given up on their lions and set them free, one would logically expect to see more mountain lions adjacent to populated areas. This has not been the reported trend.[31] Why, for instance, were there no sightings in Rhode Island prior to 2001? Why do they come from northwestern Connecticut, hilly and rural, and not southeastern Connecticut, where it is developed?

Perhaps, one could argue that owners bring their cats to these wilder areas when disposing of them. Owners first acquire these pets as cute and cuddly kittens, but they soon realize the fierce temperament of the feline, or become exasperated with its demanding care. Because ownership is illegal in some locations, few persons dispose of the cats in a humane way.

Since we know some pumas are being released into the wild, another way to figure out the puzzle is to match such releases /escapees with sightings. A basic comparison of reported sightings does not seem to match up with the number of known captive cougars, and certainly does not correspond to the number of those known to have been released. Even if everyone in possession of a lion simultaneously let their cat loose, would not the number of sightings still be greater? But Chris Bolgiano, author of <u>Mountain Lion : An Unnatural History of Pumas and People</u>, believed that there could well be thousands of legally and illegally captive mountain lions.[32] The ownership of exotic pets did become very popular and this explanation cannot be underestimated. In Great Britain, mountain lion sightings increased immediately after legislation was passed prohibiting their ownership.[33]

Although, there are now laws prohibiting the ownership of dangerous species, the relative ease with which these cats were obtained was striking. Ads appeared in trade magazines and on the Internet as recently as 2007. Some prices for kittens were $980, and $700 for young adults.[34] Among the animals offered included jaguars, leopards, black leopards, and even male African lions. The occasional capture of an exotic animal is proof that the illegal pet trade is alive and well. There are numerous instances of strange and amazing critters turning up. Reports include everything from the run-away wallaby that took on curious motorists on Boston's Route 128, to an African lion in Boxboro, Massachusetts.[35]

There have even been cases where cougars have been used in elaborate hoaxes. One such event took place in the fall of 1957. It began as an innocent stunt to help vindicate a local newspaperman who had been publicly proclaiming the presence of cougars near Richwood, West Virginia. A friend volunteered to import a live cougar from Mexico and let it meander the town, while the press would have ample opportunity to play up the event with stories and photos. The plans fell apart and the scheme was leaked. As a result, the town and the readers of the local paper were quite irritated. The cougar never gained its freedom and was put on display in its small cage.[36]

In another instance, cougars were illegally introduced into Newfoundland. In 1960, during the infancy of wildlife legislation, three cougars were illegally flown in from Idaho by a wealthy set of hunters who decided it would be a "great idea" to introduce cougars on the island to reduce the booming moose and caribou population.[37] The cougars, one male and two female, were set free and never accounted for again. Today, some forty years later, there are reports of cougars near the site of the release.

For some time the vast majority of evidence from specimens indicated that escaped pets must be the explanation. The Quabbin scat specimen was the only DNA evidence in the East to support the idea that maybe sightings represent wild, native born cougars. Recently, all of that changed with the four confirmed North American DNA work gathered from the hair snares in eastern Canada. Nonetheless, many of the DNA results came back as South American for many of the samples. Interestingly, a specimen from Floyd County, Kentucky, had both North American and South American DNA. In June of 1997, an eight-pound kitten was struck and killed by a 19-year old motorist on Route 850. The driver observed two other cats leaving the scene, which may have been the kitten's littermate and mother. DNA testing indicated a paternal ancestry from North America and a maternal ancestry from South America.[38] This specimen is not irrefutable evidence of a wild born cougar, as there are other possible explanations. However, those explanations seem unlikely in consideration of the motorist's observation of two other animals with the kitten.

The following is excerpted from a letter from Steve Thomas, Wildlife Biologist, Kentucky Department of Fish and Wildlife Resources, Frankfort office, and received in April 2003 by Helen McGinnis, an independent wildlife biologist and a founding member of CRF, who has studied the case of the alleged eastern cougar in great depth:

> Sometime after dark in June 1997, a 19-year-old man was heading south on KY highway 850 in western Floyd County when he hit and killed a puma kitten. He stopped, picked up the kitten and took it to Jason Plaxico regional wildlife biologist for the KY Dept. of Fish & Wildlife Resources. Jason put the kitten into his freezer. I was told about the specimen in late August 1998 and decided to have DNA analyses conducted. I sent out two tissue samples on Feb. 15, 1999. One went to Melanie Culver at the National Institutes of Health. The other was sent to Holly Ernest at the University of California. Culver found that the kitten's mother had a genetic type that is identical to a type found in South America. Ernest found that the other parent was most likely of North American ancestry.
>
> The kitten is a female, weighs 8.8 pounds, is 805 mm long, has a tail of 300 mm. All toe nails are sharp, intact, and there are no visible human markings. When I questioned the man on Feb. 27, 2001, he told me he saw a large shape and then a smaller shape cross the road in front of the kitten he hit. It seems most likely that the young kitten was following its mother and sibling(s).[39]

Another small kitten was killed in New York State. This particular animal was found in a condition highly supportive of the inability of cougars to fend for themselves after captivity, and the analysis of the body proved it a former pet. This cat was shot south of the Adirondack Park, near Desolation Lake in 1993, and it was in visibly poor health.[40]

A Tennessee cougar that was killed and mounted in 1971 had no toenails and had other obvious signs of having lived in captivity.[41] Later, in 1974, a cougar was killed in West Virginia, and it showed signs of having been in captivity. Typical signs are de-clawed paws, non-natural stomach contents, unsharpened teeth, sores from resting on cement, and specific stomach parasites commonly associated with captivity. Stomach contents of the West Virginian specimen showed the classic parasites of captive cougars.[42]

In 1967 there was that young female taken from the town of Einboro, Pennsylvania. It had deformities that were indicative of former captivity.[43] As mentioned, in 1992 a cougar was killed in Quebec and found through DNA testing to have Chilean genes.[44] The cat was shot on May 27th near Abitibi Lake, not far from the Ontario border, but a good 350 miles northwest of Montreal, Quebec. Some thought it suspicious that a cougar would be found so far north in what was never a really good stronghold for the species, yet the press ran away with the story and proclaimed the return of the mountain lion to Quebec. The 90-pound male stretched 7 1/2 feet long and seemed to be in good health.[45]

CHAPTER EIGHT

BLACK PANTHER:
THE INTRIGUE OF MELANISM

Since 1880 there have been consistent accounts of black or melanistic cougars. The percentage has remained steady over the decades, somewhere between 15 to 25 % since 1960, with some regions getting more than others.[1] While skeptics use melanistic cougars to refute the credibility of those inclined to accept the cougar's existence, the implications of this fact, and the consistent nature of it over time and geography, is of a unique curiosity. There are no known cases of melanism that can be proven in the East, but it appears that there is no scientific reason why it could not occur, if even rarely. Only one seemingly reliable case of melanism in *Puma concolor* has surfaced, and it is from the tropical climates of Central America. A second case from Colorado remains unverified. There is no other evidence to date other than sightings.

Early North American natives in the East were known to refer to two different mountain lions. They respected and revered what they referred to as "The Spirit Cat," which was described as tawny. However, they also described a black phase, which they feared and considered to be evil, deeming it the "Devil Cat," an evil version of the norm. They believed this cat stalked their camps at night and was capable of carrying off small children.[2] In the north, along what is now known as the Canadian border, the Mic Mac Indians also talked of the great cat and the fear of the "Lunk Soos" , in English, the "Indian Devil" -- its darker counterpart.[3]

While the phenomena of black phase sightings seems more recent, there are published accounts of its existence during settlement, as mentioned in a chapter on "The Black Cougar" from an 1812 English translation of a 1761 French natural history book by Count de Buffon. Historian Thomas Altherr found reference to the black phase cougar living in Vermont at the end of the 19th century. "Patricia Rush recalled in 1899, near Enosburg Falls, Vermont, a thin black animal with a long lashing tail and eyes like fire scared their wagon home."[4] Bruce Wright and Hal Hitchcock both documented sightings of the melanistic phase, dating back to the late 1940s.[5] Wright was especially intrigued by the matter and set up a few experiments using a puma skin, which he traveled to British Columbia to obtain. He was unable to make the wet skins appear black, nor could he do so by altering the lighting. Unable to explain black mountain lions from wet fur or problems of backlighting, he concluded that there had to be black individuals present in the dwindling population.

As mentioned, others commenting on this controversy have used the sightings of melanistic individuals to support their argument against the existence of the eastern mountain lion, stating that there is no such thing as black mountain lions or as they have been more commonly called, black panthers. This is proof, they say, that people are claiming to see something that in fact does not even exist. But assuming that thousands of people for the past one hundred years have not been hallucinating, what are they mistaking it for? Surely a few sightings might have been of black Labrador retrievers, but this explanation cannot account for all of the huge number of encounters dating back to the 1880s. One source of confusion may lie in the name being associated with such sightings. Early settlers often called the animal the painter cat, which as a name came from panther. Therefore, the question lends itself to the folklore that any black, long-tailed creature must be a panther. When people hear the word panther, many automatically envision a black panther, even when that is not what is meant. The term comes from the Old World, where captive leopards were exhibited in traveling zoos or circuses. Leopards are known to exhibit a melanistic phase and have been sometimes called black panthers, as has the New World jaguar. Jaguars of Central America and leopards are the only members of the large cats that exhibit the trait of melanism on a predictable basis. Recently, the tiger is rumored to have expressed this trait.[6]

Could the high number of melanistic cougars be explained by melanistic jaguars? If so, then why don't people report the regular spotted phased jaguars? Melanism is known to occur in the jaguar and other spotted cats, but not the cougar. *Reid Park Zoological*

Is it possible the sightings of "black panthers" all across the East are of escaped exotic leopards? The question is an important one worth considering. Loren Colemen is a renowned cryptozoologist that has studied this possibility through extensive research of records and sightings in hopes of discovering the origin of such an explanation. It seems that whenever a large black cat is sighted, the explanation that surfaces later is that of a circus train wreck. Coleman says, "The most often repeated explanation for reports of black panthers in America is that they escaped a circus train. This story has become a frequent rationalization for the numerous black puma accounts."[7]

This explanation has indeed been widespread across the East, where to substantiate the numerous sightings, it would have had to occur in multiple places up and down the eastern seaboard. The story of the train wreck full of black panthers has become incorporated into a modern American folklore motif. Upon investigating such crashes in Illinois, where the explanation was persistently given for 200 black lion sightings, no such accidents were discovered. There is no historical evidence of any such accident. Yet, during a November 1992 panther sighting in Northern Illinois, a reporter stated he received a call from a gentleman who claimed to have the answer for so many black panther sightings. Coleman revealed the farmer's statement that "a circus train wreck that happened in the 1950s released the panthers."[8] A different reporter for the Associated Press also quoted a similar proclamation from a zookeeper at Peoria's Glen Oak Zoo who announced that "the mystery cat was an escaped circus animal."[9]

Interestingly, the circus train explanation is a convenient one that has been used abroad, where there are also unexplained large cat sightings. This same kind of controversy is also taking place in Great Britain and in Australia. There, Coleman has discovered the same explanation used in the Australian bush, where rumors persist of a train wreck in the early 1960s. Coleman checked government records from 1958 to1974 and found no documentation of any such accident. Further investigations revealed such explanations worldwide whenever out of place large cats are sighted, but only Great Britain and Australia plead the case for mountain lions accompanied with melanistic reports. This fact is useful, however, in explaining the possible cause for black individuals. One explanation entertained by Wright and others has been that melanism is more frequent in the Northeast part of North America.[10] For instance, there are melanistic squirrels in Westfield, Massachusetts, and in Berkshire County.[11]

The theory is that this occurs in the Northeast more often because of the persistent cloud cover and heavy foliage or density of the forested landscape. The speculation that follows has to do with the fact that wild animals do not receive as much sunlight and are therefore not subject to having their coats bleached out by solar radiation. Eveland wrote, "Black pumas may not exist in the West for this reason -- too much solar radiation. If the true eastern puma does exist, I would not be surprised if black specimens did occasionally occur within the population. Although it is possible that diet and genetics may play a role, the amount of solar radiation that reaches the animal may play a larger part in determining adult color phases."[12]

However, if this theory were true, we would then see even more black panthers in the Pacific Northwest where in fact there are none reported. There are, however, black pumas reported within an isolated known and proven population of pumas, just outside of San Francisco, California, where about 15% of the sightings reported are of melanistic individuals. In fact, a booklet put out by the Las Trampas Regional Park labeled one individual cat as the "Black Mountain Lion of Devil's Hole."[13] Other than these few examples, black phased pumas have never been sighted, or are so rarely sighted, that we are unaware of their occurrence in the West.

When looking for the occurrence of the black phase, there is only one other location that has occasionally reported black phase individuals, and this is within the known documented range of the South American panther.[14] Rumors abound of Florida producing such individuals, but there is no documented proof.[15] When putting this information together, it seems to point to another explanation previously asserted, and that is the genetic factor. What do the alleged populations of Australia and Great Britain, San Francisco, and Florida all have in common? It is not wet, cloudy climates, but low numbers and isolation from greater numbers. If climate and habitat were to explain the melanism, it could explain the occurrence in England, but not in arid, sunny Australia. Isolation and low population allow the possibility of inbreeding as the cause, which means that such dark phase sightings could have some substance.

Newer studies have recently explained melanism as caused by genetic factors prompted by isolation, rather than by natural selection. Environmental factors may favor different colors. Scientists are now realizing that a trend toward dark forms is not always a survival advantage, as in the case of ground squirrels losing their regular normal camouflaged colors and becoming conspicuous to birds of prey high above them.[16]

The case of the beaded lizard is an example of this. These lizards are normally quite colorful, and predators have recognized their flashy colors as a warning that they are poisonous. However, a subspecies does exist that is melanistic, and there is nothing different about its environment. Thus, the question is raised as to why it would become melanistic, when flashy colors ought to be favored by natural selection as a defense against predators. Upon re-examination of this case, scientists discovered that the species was isolated from the rest of the colorful non-melanistic population by wide expanses of desert.[17]

Tischendorf speculated on melanism, noting that the phenomenon occurs in perhaps most felid species and that at least in some species it often seems to occur at the extremes of a species' range. For example, in a short note published in the Florida Field Naturalist, Tischendorf and Donald McAlpine described a melanistic bobcat captured in November 1983 by a trapper in New Brunswick, Canada, near the northern limit for the species. The unusual specimen, now mounted, is held at the New Brunswick Museum. Interestingly, at that time only ten other black bobcats had ever been documented, all from Florida, the most southeastern limit of the cat's range. This suggests that the phenomenon of melanism may be associated with the isolation or in-breeding that presumably is more likely to occur at the fringe of an animal's range.[18]

The case of the melanistic tiger, once considered a fantasy, now confirmed by two specimens from India in 1993, was known to have been within a population of tigers under extreme stress of inbreeding[19]. There was always a rumor of so called "indigo tigers" having lived in sections of the tiger's former range. There are even cases of melanistic coyotes, which occur in pioneer populations along the front of their expanding eastern range. While working on red wolf recovery, biologists captured twenty melanistic coyotes in North Carolina. Shared information from other states confirms melanistic coyotes in other places where they have not yet become well established. The aforementioned ground squirrel has been used as an example by author Keith A. Foster, who has also theorized that melanism is the result of inbreeding. Foster goes further and explains that in these cases it is a population under endangerment of extirpation, and that it is often associated with other changes in appearance, none of which are necessarily advantageous. He cites the thirteen-lined ground squirrel, which lives east of the Canadian Rockies, at the extreme edge of its range on the plains. An additional example is found in the black jackrabbit, found on the Espiritu Santo Island in the Gulf of California. The habitat is identical to that of the same species of normal color found on the mainland.[20]

Foster also believes that the melanistic trait, being a recessive one, is not random but is actually favored when genes of two parents are too similar. This would explain its appearance when a species is under the stress of inbreeding. Sightings of melanistic mountain lions were recorded early on, but populations were already in extreme decline in the 1800s. Foster believes it was an expressed trait before this era, as witnessed by the Native Americans, because as mentioned, the large carnivore was never over-abundant. Foster explains it like this:

"There is also a chance that melanism can occur in species that are naturally of low population numbers, such as predators at the top of the food chain. Many of the large terrestrial predators, such as large cats that do not form prides or groups, normally have large established territories and could be prone to inbreeding within the population. Persons have been ridiculed for years by the authorities for reporting sightings of 'black puma' in the eastern states. Knowing the inbreeding that must have occurred in the population lows of the eastern puma at the beginning of this century, I would expect the progeny to be melanistic in many cases."[21]

So why then, after so many mountain lions have been shot throughout its history of persecution, have we not had even one melanistic specimen? Only recently has there been a video from California of a large, pure black cat. It was reviewed by wildlife biologists there, who were forthcoming in saying that the video did indeed look authentic and seemed to capture a large mountain lion-sized cat of pure black coloration. However, neighbors informed the officials that the Hearst estate was only a few miles from the site, and that Hearst had been known to keep large exotic pets. Neighbors could recall some of the other exotic pets often escaping or being allowed to roam off the property. Therefore, it is possible this creature in the film may have originated from the estate, and the case was not investigated further.

There is a photograph of a "black cougar" that was killed in Costa Rica by Miguel Ruiz Herrero in 1959. The cougar has been estimated at about 120 pounds. One photograph of a dark-colored cougar is hardly convincing or persuasive and really cannot be used as good evidence. An amateur naturalist, who claimed he had seen the hide of a black puma (Barnes 1960), documented weak evidence of a melanistic cougar in Colorado.[22] In over one hundred years of human puma interaction, these two cases are all there is to substantiate the claims of melanistic mountain lions in North America. And while the science tells us that *Puma concolor* must have a recessive allele for melanism, there is no evidence that it has ever appeared, other than that one old photograph from Costa Rica.[23]

The only known example of a melanistic cougar is this specimen from Costa Rica killed by Miguel Ruiz Herrero in 1959. *Courtesy Jim Bob Tinsley Museum. Jim Bob Tinsley, author of The Puma: Legendary Cat of the Americas*

The documentation of the melanistic cougar raises an interesting question about whether these black cougars were imported from South America where according to the photograph, melanism may occur. This idea in turn raises again the explanation of escaped or released pet cougars, and it would indicate that they have established themselves and are breeding. Even the accounts of the melanistic squirrels have been thought by some to be the result of human importation. The significance of the photograph is, however, to document melanism occurring in the species, and escaped pets are not likely to explain melanistic cougars in colonial times.

Unfortunately for the cause of the elusive eastern mountain lion, the report of this dark phase does not seem to help the situation. In fact, when a good sighting by a credible witness describes a "black panther," it is almost instantaneously ignored. This only furthers the controversy, as such sightings are not investigated and therefore can never be proven or disproven, which in turn perpetuates the mystery. Much evidence has probably been forfeited in this manner, whereas it might possibly have been given some attention, had the witness described a tawny cat.

Another problem arises with Florida, where those who believe in black cougars cannot account for the absence of melanistic individuals in what is without doubt a population that is inbreeding. If melanism is a result of inbreeding, wouldn't there be melanistic panthers captured on videotape or radio-collared by now? Why has there not been a single case, or even a photograph, of a melanistic Florida panther? There is absolutely no question as to the fact that this population is suffering from isolation. Florida panthers are recognized by their genetic problems, which include but are not limited to: crooked tails, cowlicks, and cryptorchidism or undescended testicles.[24] With so many other traits resulting from their inbreeding, it would seem that melanism might have shown up here, and yet, it has not. Some may argue that climate plays a role in conjunction with genetic factors. Perhaps the melanistic trait, if it ever existed for cougars, never entered this population, even though it occasionally surfaces in the state's bobcat population.

A further strike in favor of the skeptics is the fact that there has never been a captive-born melanistic cougar. In-breeding ought to be a common occurrence for captive pets or zoo animals, and yet the black phase has never been observed in such situations. However, Patrick Rusz, Director of Wildlife Habitat Programs with the Michigan Wildlife Conservancy, believes in the possible existence of melanistic North American mountain lions, and cites his personal correspondence with Gary Rooney, a puma breeder of many years from Michigan.[25] Rooney claims that one of his females gave birth to a cub which was black, except in a few places on its body where puma are normally black. This would be consistent with many melanistic cases. There were other cubs in the litter that were not totally black but very dark brown. Rooney claims that the mother, who had raised other litters, would not care for these cubs, and they all died.

The fact that none of the cubs were completely black, suggests that persons could be seeing very dark-colored individuals which at a distance in certain lighting may appear to be black. This would not contradict Wright's test results with normal colored pelts.[26] If people witness a large, dark-colored cat run past them, and they only see it for a minute, they are likely to simply say it was black. Unfortunately, there are no instances of extremely dark-colored specimens being documented, either.

While the mystery may never be solved, the alleged sightings of black cougars is a real intrigue. We know that the early settlers talked of killing a certain number of panthers and a certain number of mountain lions, as though they were differentiating between the two-color phases.[27] The information on melanism and its possible explanation for these reports has to be considered because of its genetic likelihood. The consistent percentages of melanistic cougar sightings from all eastern North American regions may be a clue. Regardless of what one believes as proof for its existence, the sighting of melanistic cougars does not seem, when understanding these ideas fully, to be so absurd as to discourage the open mind.

Certainly, sightings are not entirely provoked by dark-colored dogs and cats, nor do escaped leopards from train wrecks go very far in explaining the reports; especially since the presence of melanistic leopards would lend itself to the sightings of the dominant phase or of orange and spotted leopards. Jaguars are native to the Texas area and once roamed further north, but it seems unlikely they would be able to make it into the Canadian Provinces, where black panther sightings are especially numerous. The jaguarundi is a native black cat to Central and South America, but here again it would have a long way to travel through unfamiliar habitat. The question of how much of this has to do with folklore and legend continues to nag at the phenomena as a whole. Certainly, the many different names that are used to describe this one species, along with all the confusion resulting from it, may have much to do with what people are seeing, and what they are expecting to see.

So for now, the mystery will continue. As for explanations, in-breeding of the imperiled population seems reasonable to those inclined to believe in eastern mountain lions.

CHAPTER NINE

CATS, DOGS, BOBCATS, AND COYOTES

While thousands of cougar sightings have been recorded, only a small percentage of those investigated have produced credible evidence proving a valid sighting. The vast majority of investigated reports turn out to be cases of misidentification. Many more fail to even raise suspicions, as they clearly describe something that is not a cougar. In fact, the bulk of the reports are of dogs, cats, coyotes, and bobcats. As mentioned previously, Robert Downing believed that 90-95% of sightings were false or cases of mistaken identity.[1] Why do so many people think that they have seen a cougar?

Some believe that it is because people want to see them. The cougar is regarded as the most wild of all creatures and given its generally unobtrusive nature, many think it is the ultimate wildlife sighting.[2] Others, however, believe cougars are being reported because people really are seeing them - - because they are really there. Although uncommon, a few sightings yield some form of evidence, such as possible tracks. They comprise less than 5% of all reports. A larger percentage of reports, though lacking physical proof, seem believable and come from credible persons. Finally, there are those rare instances of confirmed track, scat, DNA or video evidence, which represent less than 1% of all reported cases. Certainly, a few cougars have roamed through the eastern woodlands. But how do we account for the huge number of false reports?

Can all of these mistaken sightings come from impassioned yearnings?[3] If so, then why are people not seeing other creatures? Why don't the state and federal agencies get reports of wolverine sightings or wolf sightings? Does something in the cougar stir the soul that strongly? Has the media influenced the public? Or are wolverines and wolves less cryptic and therefore less romantic? Why has the cougar managed to remain in our cultural terrain?

Whether or not the cougar remains alive in the forests of the East, it has remained alive in the popular culture. Hundreds of news articles and reputable magazines have featured sightings of the alleged eastern cougar or cougar in the East. *The Republican*, a Springfield, Massachusetts newspaper, presented over eight articles on alleged cougar sightings in one year. None of these observations were actually confirmed.

There is a profound interest in cougars throughout the eastern United States. Such a consistent and wide-ranging campaign in favor of cat stories must certainly play a significant role in the psycho-social persistence of an animal which, for lack of better evidence, has not existed for decades. Is the answer to all this cat talk found in the articles? Are all the alleged cougar sightings due to the media?

It is true that media-driven impressions can cause people to report cougars when in fact they have seen much less "wild" creatures. It happens when journalists who are unfamiliar with cougars and sometimes other wildlife as well, draft stories for readers who are unfamiliar with their natural environs. Together, the two forces perpetuate the myth by tapping into expectations. The mystery cat phenomena is then created, people believe quite matter of factly that they exist, and the expectation is then created that any large, tawny-colored animal must be the one about which they have often read.

In many instances, outbreaks of cougar sightings have occurred shortly after a news article or a reported sighting. Several wildlife biologists reported this phenomenon while conducting investigations. Rainer Brocke is a retired wildlife biologist who now lives in the Adirondack Mountains of New York State; he authored numerous peer-reviewed articles on mountain lions, oversaw an ill-fated lynx recovery and studied a possible puma release. Brocke has noted that following a media account of a purported cougar sighting, a rash of sightings often breaks out in the Adirondacks.[4]

As mentioned previously, Virginia Fifield noted the same response and learned to avoid coverage or publicity. Eventually she ceased distributing posters asking for information on the animal's whereabouts.[5] Bob Downing and Jay Tischendorf have observed that some people prefer to believe that a briefly seen animal or fragmentary carcass is the least probable animal, such as a cougar, instead of a much more common species.[6] James Cardoza noted that, "eyewitness memory research has shown that misidentification can occur due to a combination of perceived familiarity or contextual recall and the use of conscious inferential processes, which provide rationale for selecting the most plausible choice."[7]

In other words, people have a tendency to complete a picture of something that they think they should have seen. Humans tend to fill in the missing sections of a picture based on previous information or what they may expect. Thus dogs become large cats, and small cats look bigger. Since most sightings last only seconds, the fleeting glimpse is easily transformed. Unfamiliarity with local fauna makes the metamorphosis that much quicker. It is startling, for example, how few people are aware that coyotes inhabit the East. Many still think coyotes are strictly a western species.

Cardoza believes that the coyote accounts for approximately 30% of the sightings reported in his state.[8] Coyotes are roughly the same size as a small cougar and often have similar coloration. Game biologists in Pennsylvania also put the coyote on the list of cougar misidentifications. Paul Rego, furbearer biologist for Connecticut, has taken hundreds of calls from people totally convinced that they have seen a cougar. He believes coyotes cause as many as 50% of the false sightings.[9]

Gary Donovan, a wildlife biologist from Maine, responded to countless cougar reports that inevitably panned out as mistaken identities. Usually the observer is confident, but when confronted with the illusion becomes defensive or embarrassed. Donavan identifies the coyote as the animal most commonly confused for the wild cougar, although the mysterious little known fisher and the secretive bobcat are also commonly labeled as cougars.[10] In Vermont, the State Game and Fish Department has likewise noted that the majority of sightings are mistaken and they cite the coyote, dog, and domestic cat as the cause of the confusion.[11]

Scott Van Arsdale, a wildlife biologist for the east-central part of New York State along the Massachusetts border, has been very conscientious about responding to calls and appearing at the scene. In nearly every case the evidence has been blatantly incorrect. He can produce a long list of mistaken identity cases, and has yet to find any solid physical evidence. He provides the following:

> I get numerous calls of cougars that turn out to be house cats. I remember one in particular from a women who saw a cougar frequenting her barn, but when I went to the barn there were only house cat tracks. She still did not believe me, and I brought her into the barn to see the tracks. A large tawny house cat ran out between us. I suggested that was her cougar - a mistaken identification. She became angry and said I was looking for an excuse. I think this is where people get the idea for government cover-ups.[12]

In another instance, Van Arsdale received a call from a woman who said that a large animal had been seen numerous times and was suspected of living in the barn. The caller had used a Peterson's Field Guide to identify the animal, and it had to have been a cougar. She had even taken pictures to assist her in identification. Upon arriving at the scene, Van Arsdale viewed the photographs and could see it was a picture of a house cat. He used a barn window in the picture as a size reference. The cat in the picture was half the size of the window, which measured less than two feet wide. Upon walking around the barn, inside and out, the only visible tracks were those of a house cat. On a different occasion, Van Arsdale responded to a man with a video of what he claimed was a cougar. The wildlife biologist says, "It was obviously a house cat because you could even see the collar. The tape had audio and you could hear the fellow talk himself into thinking and believing it was one of those eastern cougars. A good chuckle was earned when the man said, 'it's twice the size of Tinkerbelle,' who we later learned was his own cat."[13]

Van Arsdale fields a rash of calls in August and September when people are most likely to be in the woods. At that time of year, temperatures are getting more pleasant for outdoor activity, and there are fewer bugs. He thinks that deer produce a number of reports mistaken for cougar. "During the late summer and early fall, the deer have the reddish coat, and the grass is high, sometimes obscuring the deer's belly and long legs. From a distance, they can be mistaken for cougars, especially in the low light of afternoon or morning." Although he should be thoroughly discouraged by so many cases of mistaken identity, Van Arsdale keeps an open mind as he has found some cases that were hard to discredit. "I will never say never," he explains.[14]

A few years ago, a black cat was at the forefront of a big media hype on cougars. *The Bur*lington *Vermont Free Press* displayed some photos of the cat in question, which was later determined to be someone's house cat out for a stroll. Communities all over the East face similar situations. Several videos have been in the limelight over the years; most are of domesticated cats. At the 2004 Eastern Cougar Conference some of these videos were viewed, and according to a consensus of lay people and professionals viewing the tapes, most looked like house cats.

As far as advancing the evidence for the return of the cougar, such embarrassing videos of house cats have contributed only misdirection, controversy, and premature, ill-founded assumptions. Because of this, biologists shy away from commenting on photos and videos. With so many cases of mistaken identity, some wildlife professionals now view the public as impressionable, unreliable, and excitable. On the other side, the public looks at authorities as disinterested, arrogant, misinformed, and dishonest.[15] The truth is that wildlife professionals would like to share in the public's enthusiasm, but their own expectations have been crushed by years of false reports. Tony Gola with the Massachusetts Division of Fish and Game says that wildlife agents have learned this lesson the hard way, by chasing too many false reports and enduring many disappointments.[16] Gerry Parker, a retired wildlife biologist who spent a long and adventurous career accepting and investigating cougar reports in New Brunswick, expressed the same feelings. He dutifully investigated countless reports that turned out to be dog, coyote or domestic cat.[17]

Black Bear   Labrador Retriever

Wolf   Fisher

Coyote   Raccoon

Fox   Bobcat

The silhouette of animals often mistaken as cougars. The cougar is shown on the left of each row. *Courtesy Michigan Conservancy*

When dogs are mistaken for big cats, the situation is less difficult to explain to the viewer, and more people can accept the mistake and see it clearly for what it is. However, when other creatures are mistaken for cougars, field agents find it very difficult to tell the viewer who is uninformed about these less familiar species. To date there are few videos or photographs of canines being peddled for large felines.

Nevertheless, agencies are swamped with calls about pumas when the description indicates dog. Golden retrievers are easily mistaken for cougars when viewed from a distance or in the shadow of brushy cover. This breed comprises a large number of false reports, as do German shepherds. Certain breeds such as greyhounds, English mastiffs, whippets, and ridgehounds present cougar-like silhouettes. Since these breeds are atypical of popular canine types, they can be easily mistaken for a cougar when in certain visual contexts.

When sightings are investigated and dog tracks are found instead of cougar tracks, officials have trouble accepting the word of the eyewitness, and assume the sighting was of a dog. However, the presence of dog tracks at a cougar sighting should not discourage further inquiry. Since dog tracks can be found essentially everywhere, their appearance at a site is not sufficient evidence to conclude they were the animal in question.

Feral dogs and wild canines infected with mange also present an unfamiliar appearance and are often perceived as cougars. Just as individual humans take on unique appearances, wildlife also have unique appearances. Birders know this well; species have wide-ranging variations and are never exactly as depicted in field guides. Likewise, coyotes can vary widely in appearance and may have longer fur or thinner tails than commonly reported. These anomalies can fool viewers into believing they have seen something unusual.

A good case in point is the rare individual bobcat with a tail that is longer than usual.[18] While this is rare these individuals have deceived the most astute wildlife professionals. Bobcats with or without long tails are commonly mistaken for cougars, but the culprit is usually an abnormally large bobcat. Some of the largest bobcats weigh in at forty pounds or more. In the instant a sighting occurs, such a cat can easily be mistaken for its larger cousin.

The December 1998 sighting in Lincoln, New Hampshire, was explained as an unusually large bobcat with an exceptionally long tail. On a cold, snow-covered Christmas Eve in a small town nestled within the White Mountains near Mount Washington, Maureen Clark was preparing for the holiday celebrations with her nephew, when her boyfriend noticed a large animal walking through the backyard. At first, they thought it was just another deer or coyote, as both animals frequented their land. But the boyfriend noticed that there was something different about this animal and proceeded closer toward a window for a better look. Meanwhile, Maureen had been watching the creature from a different room and thought nothing of the large wild cat. Her boyfriend told her this was no ordinary sighting and that she ought to run for her video camera. Having been accustomed to seeing bears and moose in the yard on a regular basis, she thought nothing of the large creature and delayed her response. Her boyfriend became emphatic, however, and began yelling, "This is a mountain lion!" With much time wasted, she seized her video camera. The film captured less than a minute of a large cat-like creature.[19]

It walked slowly through a substantial amount of snow cover, passing behind withered golden-yellow beech leaves that still clung to the trees. The animal turned slowly away from the camera and headed deeper into the forest bordering Maureen's yard. At one point in the film, the faint December sun dapples the animal's fur and reveals what looks like spots; one behind each ear, a few along the legs, and some on the sides. There appears to be possible tufting of the ears, but in the glimpse the film offers, it's not possible to be certain. Bobcat-like, indeed, but what about the tail? When the animal turns, a tail is clearly revealed; it slopes down and curls slightly up at the end. It is not as long as the animal is high in snow cover but reaches halfway. There appears to be some ringing on the tail, which is characteristic of neither adult bobcat nor cougar. The tip is not dipped in burnt sienna, as is typical of cougars, but it does slope down in typical cougar fashion.

After the animal could no longer be seen, Maureen filmed what they believed to be its tracks in the Christmas snow. The tracks were unclear and filmed without a size reference. Although Fish and Game Biologists were notified, Maureen was not instructed to place a reference object to scale the alleged cougar and re-film the site. Without something to indicate the relative height and weight of the animal, the image captured in the film is of limited significance. Other evidence was also poor. There was no other sign except an odd-looking scat that was taken inside and frozen. It was given to a woman who thought she might have it tested, but this was never discussed again. Since it was recovered from a place where there is no certainty that the animal traveled, few are concerned with its contents.[20]

Maureen's film made it to the newsroom of New England Cable News. The story propelled a tremendous media event that went on for months with feature stories and daily news pieces. She had no idea of the attention the sighting would bring and became overwhelmed with phone calls and interviews.[21] It all came down to questions for the State Fish and Game, which responded weeks later with a careful analysis of the film. Christine Bontaites from the New Hampshire Fish and Game Agency, who had a mild interest in previous cougar reports, viewed the film and concluded it was a bobcat. The tail looked a little small for a cougar.[22] Others familiar with wildlife disagreed; because of the tail they felt it ironic for Bontaities to deem it a bobcat.

Did the event showcase one of those unusual examples of an animal that does not fit a typical mold? The public, unaware of the fact that bobcats can have an anomalously long tail, criticized the state for denying yet another cougar report. In the years that followed, other biologists disagreed with Bontaites. Some thought it was indeterminate, and others thought it was either a house cat or cougar but not a bobcat.

To make matters worse, the New England Cable News aired the tape in a delayed format, so the details would be more visible. When this film was slowed down, the animal appeared even more like a cougar, because the tail could clearly be seen. There was ample opportunity for it to be reviewed, as the news clip ran on a twenty-four minute continuous reel. Each time it played thousands more viewed it, firing-up the debate.

No one will ever know how many bobcat tracks have stirred the imagination. Bobcat tracks encourage newspaper columnists to remind readers of the cougar controversy. Tracks and sightings are at the core of the controversy; on the other hand, video coverage is rare. Bontaites, who has spent many hours in the New Hampshire mountains, talked about the Lincoln film candidly and admitted how confusing it could be to the less informed. Bontaites felt the typical bobcat pelage and the markings behind the ears as strong proof that the animal was not a cougar. Bontaites explained how easy it is to make misidentifications of wild creatures. She said, "Biologists do it, and average citizens do it. I once mistook a pair of fawns for a pair of coyotes. It can happen, especially during those tranquil moments in the forest where lighting is difficult and viewing time is instantaneous."[23]

Understandably, Bontaites and many other professionals express caution over using sightings due to their lack of scientific criteria. Subject to memory failure and viewer veracity, sightings never hold up to scientific standards. They often take place in poor lighting and are susceptible to emotional response. If the cougar is to be proven to exist in the East, it will only be done through methods that eliminate this ambiguity.

Edward Hoagland said it best in his <u>Walking the Dead Diamond River</u>,

> There is a precious privacy about seeing wildlife, too. Like meeting a fantastically dressed mute on the road, the fact that no words are exchanged and that he's not going to give an account makes the experience light-hearted: it's wholly ours. Besides, if anything out of the ordinary happened, we know we can't be expected to be believed, and since it's rather fun to be disbelieved -- fishermen know this--the privacy is even more complete. Deer, otter, foxes are messengers from another condition of life, another mentality, and bring us to places where we don't go.[24]

Hoagland's romantic analogy of a cougar sighting in New England re-affirms what we know is true about seeing rare wildlife on their own terms in wild settings. The encounters stir the excitement of being out of our everyday surroundings. There is that hint of fear that we may encounter the unexpected -- bear, wolf or cougar, and the subconscious knowledge that we are not the invincible predator but potential prey for larger creatures. In this setting the human mind may run wild with imagination. People may be inclined to see things when they are in the woods.

Helen McGinnis once maintained a cougar discussion group and circulated a photograph of a four-legged unidentified animal. Half the group firmly believed it was feline with a long tail. The other half adamantly professed it a canine, perhaps a coyote. McGinnis' conclusion: "People see what they want to see."[25] Fred Van Dyke, a cougar biologist who authored work that dealt with aspects of the eastern cougar, did not use sightings for his cougar surveys.[26] Although sightings are being used in many research efforts, he did not think they were of credible use. Today, ornithologists are using birders' sightings to collect data that will show trends and population changes. Public sightings are used in Oklahoma for cougar surveys; however, they are compiled with a full understanding of viewer bias.[27]

Long-tailed bobcats are not the only unusual occurrences that cause confusion. For instance, there are fox that can climb trees. The gray fox can climb trees with great agility and have often incited rumors of cougars. Just as people are prone to interpret events based on previous expectations, they can also be thrown off by the unexpected. The sighting of a canine climbing a tree can quickly be converted into what the human mind is accustomed to -- a feline climbing a tree.

In this case, someone certainly might glimpse the gray fox in a tree and immediately assume it was a mountain lion. The gray fox is native to the Northeast and prefers a more heavily wooded habitat than its cousin, the red fox. These feline-like canids are usually silvery gray with sprays of auburn and chocolate brown. A handsome creature, the gray fox is a swift and agile hunter of small rodents. Gray fox even catch their kills the way cougars and bobcats do. They have evolved some of the highly successful hunting styles of felids -- namely the ambush. Grays also use the house cat method of "stalk and pounce." Very few people are aware of this canine's existence, and even fewer are aware of its ability to climb trees. Similarly, they are unfamiliar with the fisher, an emerging member of the Northeast's forests.

The fisher has been expanding its range in areas
where cougar sightings are increasing.
Photo by Fusco CT DEP

Fisher were once widespread, their numbers fell as a result of habitat loss and trapping. While a few did survive in northern New England, the fisher was widely extirpated in the Northeast by 1880. Recently, they have made a comeback. An odd-looking creature, the fisher seems a cross between a dog and a cat. Instead, they are actually *mustelidae*, members of the weasel family.

The fisher's return to the Northeast has correlated with the increase in cougar sightings that increased in the seventies, grew through the eighties and into the nineties.[28] Is this a coincidence, or has the fisher been responsible for recent attention given to the eastern cougar? Both fisher and lion have long tails roughly equal to the length of the body, and both travel alone in similar habitat. Both are nocturnal and can climb trees. Neither is inclined to leave evidence of its travels, and both travel widely. They each require large territories and have never been numerous in one location.

Further confusion arises with the many names given to the fisher, which include polecat, fitch ferret, pekan cat, black cat, and fisher cat.[29] But the fisher is neither a cat nor a ferret, nor does it catch fish except on rare occasion or when starving. At one time, science even mistakenly classified this animal. The debate as to how it acquired its name continues to this day. Some have said that it perhaps raided traps baited with fish; others claim the name was bestowed upon it because it stole fish from anglers.

Regardless of what you may call it, the fisher is a fast, secretive, and quiet hunter of the Northeast, so it doesn't take much imagination, especially when one is within a forested or secluded site, to think that in a fleeting glimpse, the fisher is a cat, perhaps even a black colored puma. Although they lack the rounded face, they are cat-like in appearance. They move through the landscape in a cat-like way, staying close to cover, traveling on logs, and often choosing ridges or streams as travel corridors.

However, to experienced outdoors people who have even the slightest bit of knowledge about cougars, it seems like a significant stretch mistaking a ten-pound fisher for a 110-pound cougar. But it happens, rather frequently at that. According to the Maine Fish and Wildlife Department, the fisher accounts for approximately 30% of the big cat reports.[30] Wildlife sightings, often fleeting, do not provide viewers with access to size references and improved lighting. Without size references in the deep shade of the forest, even experienced biologists have noted candidly that they have often done double-takes at the fisher.

For its small size, the fisher has managed to carry a large reputation, much of it shrouded in a mystique as enchanting as the forests in which it dwells. It has been attributed to domestic dog kills and sheep slaughters, and has been rumored through the ages to have carried off small children. While it is an efficient and able nocturnal predator, such fears are unfounded. Make no mistake, the fisher can and often does take a small house cat, but its reputation for ferocity is derived from its close cousin, the larger and more formidable wolverine.

Fisher do prey on porcupine. While not as large as a human child or full-grown ram, the porcupine requires a certain finesse if the predator is to secure it safely, without assault from its quilted spines. A fearless terror of the tree tops, the little fisher does not flip its prickly prey over until it has chased it up a tree and forced it to fall or drop after which it is finally taken belly-up. The fisher's liking for porcupines made it an attractive animal to import and foster back into its original haunts. In an effort to cull the number of porcupines, which are notorious for destroying commercial timber stands via its dietary preference for the tree cambium, or inner bark, fishers were introduced much more quickly than they otherwise might have been. Although its luxuriant pelt has been valued at many times that of the beaver, but for its taste for the porcupine, it would probably not have received such care and attention.

Beginning in 1959 and ending in 1967, 124 fishers were trapped in Maine and released in porcupine "problem areas" of Vermont.[31] The fishers quickly re-established themselves, possibly aided by a few hidden survivors of the original population. Fishers prefer an advancing, aged forest rather than a successional growth, and they also prefer habitat with many snags or blow downs and a healthy understory. This is precisely the kind of forest character that we see so much of today, and it is one reason that the animal is doing well. The fisher is even appearing in suburban areas, where it takes advantage of the overabundant gray squirrel. These factors will insure its expanding population, at least into the immediate future.

Larger than the mink but closely related, the fisher weighs in at an average of eight pounds. Males may weigh as much as thirteen pounds. They are almost always a dark chocolate brown but occasionally show slight variations. Such an appearance might help to explain why many of the cougar sightings are of black individuals.[32] Tischendorf once investigated a report of a 75 pound black panther; tracks photographed at the scene, in snow, were found to be those of a fisher.

Massachusetts's biologist Jim Cardoza also explains, "Many people are experiencing the fisher and mistaking it for the cougar. It is because of the cat-like appearance of the fisher and the fact that they know little about either animal and have in fact heard or read more about the cougar than about this reasonably common furbearer."[33] Yet fisher sightings cannot explain the long history of alleged cougar sightings in the southern Appalachians, where the fisher does not yet exist. So while fisher may often be reported as cougars, they cannot account for the majority of reports through the Appalachians.

Dogs, cats, bobcats, fox, and fisher-- they all have something in common with the cougar, if not in physiology, then in some way with their behavior or physical appearance. It is not too difficult to see how a fisher can be mistaken for a cougar, but some investigations cited otters, squirrels and weasels. Obviously, these cases are the exception, and they in no way account for the 100 year-long phenomena of sightings. They are, however, worth mentioning, if not for amusement, than to illustrate the public's degree of unfamiliarity with wildlife resources.

The sightings come from all geographic regions. Massachusetts's wildlife biologist Thomas French refers to a call reporting a cougar roaming a suburban residence. The person described the animal as having a long tail and powerful looking shoulders. They were absolutely, positively certain the animal was a cougar, and they were adamant that a biologist should "get to the scene and make the neighborhood safe." After much questioning, the person was still firm they had a cougar that needed to be attended. The state biologist was reluctant to pursue, since the animal described was behaving unlike a cougar. After much pleading, the biologist responded to the request and to his amazement found a full-grown otter.[34]

In other instances callers describe cougars too well. "It is as if they have just opened their field guide and started to read from it. We can always tell with these calls," says Al Hicks, a non-game wildlife biologist.[35] In these cases it's usually something that in no way resembles a cougar. Such reports are strong indications that the viewers have been predisposed to interpret other living things as eastern cougars. Whether through exposure to the media or by more direct stimulation, such individuals are acting out expectations or impassioned yearnings.

Reports from suburbia could be expressions of modern angst; a cougar sighting might sooth that angst. Some people may have a sense of responsibility about the environmental destruction and experience guilt. Living in the suburbs, many human beings yearn for more wild environs and subconsciously lament their tortured landscapes. Such conscientious persons look about their world and see the advancing development and the lowering of quality of life that often accompanies it. They see roads and acres of toppled trees, and therefore wish to see cougars as a way to alleviate the guilt.

Humans are prone to romanticizing nature; there is something in all of us that wants to believe the eastern cougar was a pure and distinct subspecies, an indigenous creation to the familiar Northeast landscape. We want to believe that this creature, the most wild of all, has not left us but has in fact been able to survive. Such a survival would mean that wilderness has somehow endured, and because of that, the wildest of all has remained, mysteriously, unobtrusively hidden. Sportsmen and sportswomen especially take pride in thinking the woods they hunt are capable of sustaining and hiding a wild creature such as the cougar. Hunters are inclined to perpetuate the legends of the Alexander Crowell brand, Vermont's cougar killer. In doing so, they in fact turn the cougar into more than a mythical beast; it becomes part of the cultural terrain. It is a phenomenon.

In any rural part of the Appalachians, especially in the central and New England states, hunters can be found conversing about the cougar or can be easily prompted into a discussion of the cougar. It is part of the local lore, a part of the regional pride, a hot issue for some, and for others an excuse to fabricate an exciting tall tale. Eavesdroppers catch a word or two now and again in local diners on cold December days during the deer season or during personal confessions between hunters regarding spiritual desires. They talk about wildlife sightings and the possibility of the cougar. Even someone who doesn't have his or her own sighting to discuss knows someone who does. So the cougar is out there, whether in physical form or not. It's just under the surface and it's real.

Unfortunately, the huge number of mistaken sightings make it that much more difficult for biologists to remain open-minded and pursue sightings that might be valid and capable of offering significant information. Sightings usually lack additional information, and the vast majority offer absolutely no hard evidence. There is often very little that biologists can do with the accumulating sightings other than file them or note them with a pin on a map.

The question as to why so many people think they have seen a cougar will remain, but the media has definitely played a role in all of this by keeping cougars on our minds. Who knows how many of these sightings are valid or mistakenly contrived? Some of them, if only a very few, are most certainly real, and that is all that is needed to make the rest components of the investigation. Nevertheless, some peculiar spiritual need turns ordinary dogs and cats into cougars. These "transformations" account for the vast majority of alleged cougar sightings; and if sudden enchanting encounters with unfamiliar creatures such as the coyote, bobcat, lynx, and fisher are not thrilling enough, then these also become the elusive cougar. A variety of explanations then, are behind cougar sightings that turn out to have been other species.

CHAPTER TEN

AN UNDETECTED PRESENCE

History is filled with accounts of animals having been mistakenly, prematurely declared extinct. The rediscovery of the cougar in the East would not be the first case of a species that quietly, surreptitiously blended into its habitat only to be discovered later. In almost all of these instances the species declined, became infrequently observed, was declared extinct then reappeared once or twice before completely disappearing for years or even decades.

The most astounding case is the discovery of the coelacanth, which was never before seen by human eyes. Its story is too fascinating to pass over. Author of The Great New England Sea Serpent, June Pusbach O'Neil says, "One of the most astounding finds of the twentieth century, the discovery of the coelacanth in 1938, startled the scientific world. Not only was there no hint that this 400 million year old fish might still exist, but fossil evidence suggested it had perished at the end of the Cretaceous period."[1]

Other cases are not so dramatic, but prove that animals can remain hidden in their habitats and go undetected for a long time. On September 4, 1996, villagers in a rural part of Vietnam were searching for dinner and caught two examples of a type of native pheasant long thought to be extinct. These birds were minutes from becoming soup when a local forester recognized the pair as male and female Edward's pheasants. These birds were exceptionally rare when first reported in 1923 by French ornithologist Jean Delcour.[2]

On three separate occasions between 1994 and 1998, ornithologists had attempted to find these birds on organized search missions. They failed to produce any and found no evidence of their existence. As in the case with the cougar, there were persistent rumors within local villages that the birds continued to live. These search missions were well organized and professionally conducted, and yet they failed.

Vietnam has been an active site for such discoveries. In 1992 the World Wildlife Fund ran surveys to discover other creatures presumed lost to the driving force of extinction. The survey discovered the Sao La oxen or spindle horn oxen. This same investigation caught word of a report published in *The Saigon Times Daily News* which mentioned that an official had heard of villagers sighting rhinos in a salty marsh. The footprints of a Java rhino were confirmed near a marsh in the Cat Loc Forest in Lam Dong Province in 2002. These rhinos had been assumed extinct by some and were thought to be nearly so by others. Further investigations revealed that a dozen or more might exist in that area, but then in 2010 officials actually found the carcass of one rhino. It was later confirmed to be a Java rhino and it had been shot by poachers.[3]

A more recent discovery presented itself in August of 1999 in southeast Asia. A deer like mammal, found in dense cover and completely unknown to modern science was discovered and called a muntjac. Several other mammal species have recently been discovered in southeast Asia, including the rediscovery of a type of pig thought extinct over a hundred years ago. A banner decade for rediscovery, the 1990s also revealed other species previously unknown to western science. In Hanoi, a biologist is desperately trying to save a giant turtle that he believes lives in the dirty muddy waters of the Han Kim Lake. Peter Pritchard, a renowned turtle expert, believes a few have been living there undetected for centuries. Pritchard bases his belief on photographs that show the turtle's head and shell. He theorizes that it is the biggest soft-shelled turtle in the world. If estimates about its age are accurate, it is also the oldest.[4]

In India there are many cases of wildlife being rediscovered. The case of a forest owl mimics our eastern cougar hunt because local people swore it existed but scientists could not confirm it. Suddenly in 1997, American researchers in India happened upon the bird which had been written off as extinct some 118 years earlier. The bird was photographed and unmistakably identified as the Indian forest owlett. Another set of surprises from India were the rediscovery of the Jerdon's courser, a bird found in Andra Pradesh, and the sighting of the grey and black streaked quail, in 2006 within the state of Assam. In the same year a new species of bird was confirmed in Arunachal Prudesh, a remote region of India. This bird, was named bugun liocichla, and is a close relative to the babblers, a small species found in China.[5]

There are others -- the Arabian tahr, an agile, horned mountain goat type of creature, was considered extinct outside of Oman since 1982. It reappeared in 1995 during a survey on behalf of the Arabian Leopard Trust when a female and her kid were photographed at a waterhole. Tahrs have long reddish-brown hair with a black stripe down the spine. Their natural enemy was the Arabian leopard, but the domesticated goat has dealt them a blow instead with the complete destruction of their delicate habitat by over-grazing.[6] In Africa, the last white-necked rock fowl was suppose to have disappeared in 1965 but was well documented in 2003.[7]

Such amazing discoveries in less developed countries are one thing, but when lost species are rediscovered in developed nations, it bears a second look. In the United States few people realize that the common Canada goose has many subspecies. A large subspecies, *Branta canadensis maximus,* the brazen goose of parks, community fishing ponds, and golf courses was once considered extinct. *Branta canadensis maximus* was hunted for its meat and grand feathers.[8] The passing of the historic Migratory Bird Act in 1916 protected the dwindling subspecies, but it was not enough to keep this bird from the brink.[9] It was generally accepted that the bird had followed the dodo. But then in the early 1960s, a small flock was happened upon. Federal and state wildlife agencies joined together in an effort to save the big goose. The agencies' work was a tremendous success, and land use changes, detrimental to other species, now favored the bird. The suburban/urban landscape is much to its liking.

On the North American prairie, many millions of prairie dogs once thrived. Like the cougar and the deer, the prairie dog was inextricably linked with a predator, a *mustelid* called the black-footed ferret. When the prairie dog was relentlessly persecuted and the habitat upon which it lived was converted to crops and grazing land, their decline spelled death for the black-footed ferret. Believed extinct for decades, biologists were astounded when contacted in 1981 by a taxidermist who was asked to mount a two foot, black-masked, weasel-like creature that a ranch dog brought home in Meeteetse, Wyoming.[10] Authorities recognized the long-lost ferret and found the ferrets among 37 colonies of white-tailed prairie dogs scattered across a 30,000-acre area. The ferret population expanded for some time unassisted. Then an epidemic swept through the prairie dogs, and a decline soon followed. Biologists began capturing the ferrets, and today they have been re-established in the wild through captive breeding programs throughout the West.[11]

Finally, the most remarkable discovery took place only a few years ago when the beautiful ivory-billed woodpecker was documented as existing in a remote Arkansas bottomland. Despite countless sightings of this huge woodpecker, the bird could not be proven to exist anywhere in the United States. In the early 1800s naturalist John James Audubon and his apprentice Joseph Mason reported the occurrence of the ivory-billed woodpecker along the Ohio, Arkansas, and Mississippi Rivers. He also discovered healthy numbers along a stream in Texas called the Buffalo Bayou.

In the years to follow, bird lovers were concerned that the unique bird was extinct. By the early 1900s, the vast majority of ornithologists accepted this as fact. However, Cornell ornithologists Arthur Allen and his wife Elsa soon found the bird again in Florida near the Taylor River.[12] Allen considered the sighting one of the greatest moments in his life because he saw what everybody said could not be seen. No sooner did he announce his discovery when greedy taxidermists found the pair and shot them dead, plunging the woodpecker under a shroud again.[13]

In 1932 another ivory-billed was shot. This specimen was taken in a large Louisiana forest called the Singer Tract by an attorney eager to prove his sighting.[14] A few years later a team was sent into the tract, and a nesting pair was actually found and documented with film footage and sound recordings. The pair was quickly absorbed into the forest. Although notes and observations were made, the species ceased to offer any more sightings until 1944.[15]

After the last credible sighting in 1944 in the Singer Tract, hope faded fast for this unusual woodpecker, and only isolated rumors persisted of their existence. Although Cuba claims to have retained the birds, there has been no irrefutable evidence from that country in many decades to substantiate such rumors. Then suddenly in 1999, David Kulivan, a forestry student at Louisiana State, claimed to have seen an ivory-billed in the Pearl River region of Louisiana.[16] The sighting reinvigorated interest in the bird's possible survival, much like the media attention to frequent cougar sightings. While sightings have surfaced consistently throughout the south, this report strikes the authorities as more credible than those in the past. At places like south Florida's Corkscrew Swamp Sanctuary, blurry pictures and long-winded tales have always been taken in good faith. Kulivan's sighting, however, was believable.[17]

His sighting inspired the investigation into the Pearl River Basin in 2002. It was ultimately unsuccessful at uncovering the missing bird. Fortunately, two years later Gene Sparling of Hot Springs, Arkansas, identified an ivory-billed with chilling accuracy, and a new search went back on. In a matter of days, Sparling was interviewed by Tim Gallagher, editor of the Cornell Lab of Ornithology's *"Living Bird"* publication, and by Robert Harrison, an associate professor at Oakwood College, Huntsville, Alabama. On February 27, during a recognizance the men observed a large black and white woodpecker and simultaneously cried out "ivory-billed!" After comparing notes they were convinced their initial response was correct. Before long, the woodpecker was sighted three more times by different biologists during a carefully planned and well executed scientific search mission into the Cache River National Wildlife Refuge.[18]

During 7,000 hours of search time, the bird was reportedly seen a total of 15 times. On April 28, the woodpecker was finally documented with four seconds of film footage. The film was carefully analyzed, and a full year after its discovery, the news was released, and it seemed to rest all doubts. Typically, with such announcements there are those who will challenge, and since more evidence has not been forth coming, the challenge is likely to remain. Nevertheless, Cornell stands behind their claim with confidence. The rediscovery of this incredible bird after its disappearance for some 60 years is nothing short of amazing. The history of the cougar has followed a similar pattern of lingering reports, and assumed extirpation followed by unexpected proof such as the 1938 cougar shooting in Maine. A long silence with nothing but flimsy sporadic evidence followed until more compelling evidence recently emerged.[19]

Eventually sightings with and without corroborative tracks or other evidence mounted to impressive numbers throughout the East. Between 1970 and 1983, the Eastern Cougar Survey Team of Massachusetts recorded over 150 reports--a significant number, considering the small size of the state. In North Carolina 300 reports were made between 1975 and 1979, and 600 reports were received from Canadian Maritime Provinces through 1993.[20] Since July of 1983 the Eastern Puma Research Network has collected 2,200 reports. Since 1965, when they first began recording sightings, EPRN has taken in a total of 7,500 reports.[21] With so many reports coming in from different regions, it would seem that a healthy population must be in attendance. In fact, EPRN estimated that 1,500 to 2,000 cougars survive in the East.[22] Such an estimate seems too generous, lacks logic and betrays reason, but if it were at all accurate, it would strongly imply that the cougar ought to have been discovered. Yet somehow, from some peculiarity, the animal has managed to remain undetected. Is it likely that a breeding population of a large carnivore could remain undiscovered while inside a region with a high human population? If so, how could this happen?

The mountain lion has been called the most elusive of all North American land mammals. Often referred to as "Ghost Cat" or "Mystery Cat," the sight of this large carnivore is thought to be, as previously mentioned, the wildest and rarest encounter there is. While the literature is not replete with cases of cougars living undetected, some examples do exist.

Perhaps one of the best-known and widely cited examples of the cougar's stealth originates from a 530-acre park situated on a peninsula in Seattle. The event occurred in August of 1981 when five people saw a good-sized cougar. Officials then closed the park to everyone except the 300 people who lived in it. From the Eastern Puma Research Network Newsletter, an account of the search reads as follows:

> One Game agent and one park employee looked for it 2 hours on Saturday night. On Sunday, two state game officers, three park employees, and a hunting family with three hounds spent all day looking for it to no avail. On Monday, the cougar was seen sunning itself in

the road by police, firefighters, and maintenance crews, so six more dogs that 'can smell a cougar a mile away' were brought in, joined by two State Game Department employees with a tranquilizer gun. At the end of the day, one official said, 'I'm not calling anybody a liar; the dogs are,' then gave a lecture on 'cougar hysteria' and how it makes you see things that aren't there. The hunt was called off because 'if there had been a cougar in there, my dogs would have gone wild.' Finally, on Tuesday, someone saw it again and found a good track and a scat, the first definite evidence the Game Department people had seen in 3 days of hunting. The six dogs were released in the vicinity again and after 9 hours, they finally flushed the cougar at 1:30 a.m. Wednesday morning, a 95-pound male cougar was darted and captured. This last hunt involved several Game Department people, half a dozen park employees, several Navy security personnel, and numerous news people.[23]

In California, where Holly Ernest conducts her DNA research, studies have shown that the cougar can use areas frequented by humans yet remain unseen. Specific examples include trails heavily used by hikers and bikers, that lions use at night to hunt and travel, then rest only yards away during the day. Unaware and unconcerned, cyclists and hikers pass within a few feet of these giant carnivores.[24]

At the University of California at Davis, James Bauer is working on a project to monitor and analyze cougar activity in human dominated landscapes. Bauer says cougars are presently living alongside people and often remain completely undetected. They live in densely populated areas without anyone having the slightest clue of their presence.[25] Another California researcher, the late Eric York, studied the movements of cougars in highly fragmented and urbanizing landscapes. In doing so, he noted that despite the close proximity of the radio-collared cougars to residential settings, they are practically invisible. He once stated, "The collared animals are almost never seen by anyone, including the researchers tracking them, even though they cross numerous roads and trails and sometimes venture close to residential areas."[26]

Harley Shaw, a cougar biologist, has said, "Sometimes, where a healthy cougar population exists, its secretive nature often leads less informed individuals to believe the species is endangered."[27] He believes that in some situations they can go undetected even when living within close proximity to man. He is not implying that cougars might remain undetectable to the trained professional but rather invisible to the untrained.

Florida provides another example. Considered extirpated for several decades, a search conducted by scientist Ronald Nowak in 1973 confirmed the panther's existence there.[28] Had the World Wildlife Fund not funded this investigation, we might not have discovered the cat's presence.[29]

Does this suggest that cougars may have remained undetected north of Florida? Central South Florida was basically a wilderness before the now-famous Alligator Alley (Interstate 75) was constructed. The absence of proof for panthers there can be compared best to the situation in the north for specific locations where similar sized near-wilderness conditions presently exist. As in the north, hunters reported panthers throughout 1940s up to the 1960s. During this time period, few people gave sightings much thought as there were no kills. The panther was assumed to be absent.[30] Maehr, who was in charge of the Florida panther recovery in its early years, observed the following:

> The big culprit was Alligator Alley or I-75 that was built in the late 1960s. Before then, most of south Florida was pretty remote wilderness, and even after Alligator Alley was built, traffic levels were not that high compared to the 1980s and beyond. Outdoorsmen saw panthers from time to time in the swamps and forests, and there may have been a roadkill someplace, but nobody focused until it was officially looked for in the 1970s with an organized hunt. Traffic began to increase on Alligator Alley in the 1980s and the roadkills soon followed.[31]

A crucial component to the " prove cougars exist" argument has been that roadkills should occur in places claimed to harbor cougars because they occur in places cougars are known to inhabit. Florida panthers are the only proven population of *Puma concolor* east of the Mississippi.[32] There are believed to be about 100 Florida panthers living in the wild. Despite the small population of these cats, collisions with cars occur often enough to be considered a real threat to this endangered population. Similarly, the mid-western states that harbor sparse populations or wandering individuals also produce roadkills with some frequency. So why are there no roadkills in the East?

Discussions have failed to point out that the Florida panther remained undetected for years because none had been reported killed by automobile strikes. Roadkills do not necessarily occur or get reported everywhere cougars live. This is a good defense in favor of hidden relic populations, but it is not the only defense. South Dakota's Black Hills cougar population went without a reported road kill for twenty years. The number of cougars there has grown steadily. Presently, they are being killed on an annual basis. However, before the population reached the carrying capacity, no roadkills were reported.[33]

The Black Hills National Forest has the highest human population of all the national forests in the United States.[34] While cougars there show a tolerance for human disturbance and an absence of road fatality, this does not support the creature's lack of detection. The Department of Game, Fish and Parks in South Dakota has known about and verified the presence of these carnivores since the 1960s. Later, deer kills in the 1980s became frequent.[35] Eventually, a trapper accidentally captured one. In 1980, the State biologists began recording sightings. If cougars can survive there and breed successfully without a road fatality for thirty years, the same thing could be possible in any of the less populated National Forests in the East.

Likewise, conditions similar to those in southwest Florida between 1935 to 1973 are found in at least a few places throughout the Appalachians. Several locations offer similar protection in the central Appalachians, the Northeast and in eastern Canada. Many people are unaware of these facts, and the debate continues because each side focuses on the rate of roadkills now occurring in south Florida.

Many years ago Robert Downing said, "If cougars everywhere are as susceptible to being killed by automobiles as they are in Florida, where since 1978 there have been an average of 1.2 road-kill per year out of a population of 30-50 animals, then we should occasionally experience a road kill elsewhere in the East."[36] Tischendorf, however, disagreed with this comparison:

The roadkills in Florida occur because of a unique situation. They have a population of animals stuck in a limited amount of habitat with a major freeway running directly through the middle of it. They must cross this highway in order to exist as a population. This is a different setting altogether and cannot be accurately compared to the kind of country found further north.[37]

Nevertheless, Tischendorf believes that if cougars were present in the East, there would be roadkills, but he does not believe the situation in Florida is comparable. He contrasts the lack of road kills in the East to the growing number of transients killed on roads in the Midwestern states:

> If the pumas killed in the Midwest and elsewhere represent transients, and transients represent the lowest possible cougar density - - then what does that say about the East where there are no kills? In the Great Plains and Midwest, pumas today are routinely being confirmed. These are bodies - - pumas being shot by farmers and hunters and hit by trains and automobiles - - not just reliable sightings. If there were as many pumas in the remainder of the East as sightings today and over the years suggest, then there should also be a relatively comparable number of specimens documented. There are not.[38]

Brocke supports this thinking, yet he makes a direct comparison to Florida and continues to defend his reasoning to this day. Arguments in defense of the lack of roadkills are far less cogent than Brocke's.[39] For decades those who discount the existence of cougars in the East have used the lack of roadkills as ammunition. Indeed, the lack of such kills has been especially difficult to explain.

Less convincing arguments have included considerations of road surfaces, road systems, and misinformation. Could Florida's flat, fast, straight expressways be different enough to explain why there have been no kills on the slower, twisting, undulating country roads of the Northeast? Slower roads create slower driving conditions, and this means less severe impact injuries. It also means that the odds of an animal being hit are smaller, because they have more time to react and to hear approaching vehicles. Cougar densities are also significantly less than the non-predatory creatures frequently killed on roads. While dead deer may be found regularly along high-risk roads, coyotes and fox are seldom hit. Bobcats are even more unlikely to be hit by an automobile. Nevertheless, as one might guess, these are all very weak arguments to explain the absence of road killed cougars in the East north of Florida.

Other issues defining the differences between the Florida panther and the alleged cougar populations to the north involve public awareness and attentiveness. Public knowledge about the Florida panther is high, but few people know to look for the cougar in the Northeast.[40] David Maehr said the following in regards to the sudden appearance of roadkills in Florida: "The apparent suddenness of roadkills coincided with the first radio telemetry study that began at the time. Now resident animals could be tracked to their untimely ends, whereas before, carcasses went unreported, or were scavenged by critters and people."[41] Some believers claim that people in the Northeast have a much lower awareness of the animal's appearance or endangered status. Therefore, highway cleaning crews might not realize the significance of a cougar kill. Public works employees are not generally experienced with wildlife identification. Conceivably, but not likely, a cougar kill could be removed from a road and discarded without knowledge of its extirpated status, comment or concern. In Florida, on the other hand, the panther now makes the newspaper almost weekly. There are panthers on license plates, T-shirts, and posters at tourist sites. Furthermore, as just mentioned, the panthers are radio-tagged and their whereabouts known.

This is not the case in the Northeast. Wildlife biologist Thomas French said he received word of a cougar road kill from western Massachusetts, but the incident remained a rumor as nobody came forward. Rumors do not stand as evidence. Yet many more rumors abound and claim that several roadkills have never been properly documented. These claims, however, come forth with zero documentation.[42]

In 1992 a roadkill was reported in Vermont but the animal was presumably removed before authorities could secure it. The following report was sent to Dr. Hitchcock a few weeks after the incident:

> On approximately September 15, 1992, I was driving south on Route 7 at about 6:20 in the morning. I had driven across the long straightway in Salisbury over the river and just past the large pull-off area for parking on the right. I was traveling at about 65-70 miles per hour. Just as I had passed the parking area to the right, a large cat jumped out in front of me, traveling west to the east. I missed it. However, a second cat following right behind it hit the middle of my car. I pulled my car over, as did a man driving a dump truck behind me, to take a look-see. It was a cat, solid brown in color with a thick tail about 15 to 18 inches long. It weighed about 40 to 50 pounds. I know this because I picked the cat up by his tail to move him out of the middle of the road. I used a rag out of my trunk because I was concerned about the rabies outbreak in Vermont. Finally, when I draped the cat over the metal guardrail its paws touched the ground on either side.[43]

Kevin Korkins, of Rutland, Vermont, returned later to retrieve the specimen but it had been removed. Hal Hitchcock returned to the site months later with someone to help him locate the carcass but nothing was found. Ted Reed also believed there were a few roadkills over the years, and he presented this Vermont case as an example of what he believed was happening whenever such accidents occurred.

Clearly, the absence of roadkills is a difficult one to counterpoint, but believers can cling to the fact that there is to date no conclusive study to correlate cougar roadkills to cougar densities other than anecdotal data. The lack of data to indicate the likelihood of a cougar being struck by an auto based on traffic volume, cougar density, land use, trails and dirt tracks, topography, and other variables consoles those who want to believe the cats exist. In addition, the previously mentioned roadkill of a juvenile cougar in Kentucky counts as a plus for defending the cougar's presence. It is something that has occurred recently that critics said would have to in order to suggest the cat's existence. One might also think the roadkill in Connecticut bolsters the defense for cougars, too. Actually, it is a case that can be argued either way. Some may say it proves a cougar can travel close to 2,000 miles across countless roads without being hit. Yet, others may point out that the roadkill was inevitable and revealing of the cat's presence. In either case, the necropsy ruled out the possibility of the cougar being of a more local wild origin. Nevertheless, true believers in government cover-ups may suggest the obvious wild appearance of the cat left authorities no choice but to lie and claim it came from the West, since no one would believe it if they tried to pass it off as an escaped pet.

There is, however, plenty of evidence from California that cougars are capable of crossing heavily traveled roads with little or no incident. Fred Scott, a Nova Scotian biologist, concluded that,

> The documented occurrence of roadkilled cougars has been positioned as necessary to prove their existence in the East. However, in light of the 1992 confirmation from Quebec (shot animal) and New Brunswick (confirmed track with associated scat) where no roadkills or even vehicle strikes are reported to have occurred, the absence of roadkill proves nothing (except that none have been recorded).[44]

The lack of many roadkills is a strong point for those who do not believe cougars still exist—and you may take the recent roadkill in Milford, Connecticut any way you choose. Roadkills are an excellent way to detect cougars but there are other indicators worthy of this debate. Skeptics cite the searches of Downing, Fifield and others as proof that cougars do not exist. Most cougar biologists will admit that as cryptic as the cat is, evidence of its presence can be found with a proper search. They leave sign of their travels and activities just like any other creature. According to the skeptics, if Downing or Fifield had searched for the admittedly rare Florida panther, they would have found them. In response, believers say that the investigations of Downing, Fifield, and others involved only a handful of places within a very large land area.

When looking for cougars in an area as vast as the East, the chances of pinpointing the most likely location are small. Many of the previous efforts to locate these big cats may have been conducted in less-than-ideal settings with sightings or rumors of sightings to support the choice. An excellent example is the search conducted with Ted Reed in New Brunswick, which was based on old sightings. The argument can be made that previously held searches conducted by professionals acting alone, as well as by individual enthusiasts working in nonscientific ways, were too limited to have completed the job. Until each potentially promising area is searched independently, it is the same as looking for a needle in a haystack. It can be compared to taking a cup of water from one of the Great Lakes and making the claim the lake contains no fish because the cup sample did not contain any.

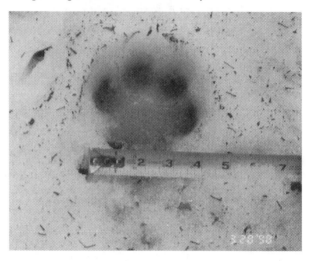

Tracks are not always reliable pieces of evidence. This track found in Maine shows features of both felids and canids. The track is representative of the marginal evidence state biologists are presented with each year. *Photo courtesy Maine Fish and Game*

Furthermore, the search methods employed in the past relied heavily on tracks. James Cardoza, a wildlife biologist with the Massachusetts Department of Fish and Game, who is among the few state biologists with an intense interest and knowledge on the topic, has said in his article published in the *Wildlife Society Bulletin* that cougar tracks are often presented as "evidence". Moreover, he claims that such statements are misleading and that cougar tracks "are best used as a component of a package including gait, stride, and behavior, not as a sole identifier." He does not feel that tracks give much weight to the alleged cougar presence because, like Brocke, he feels that other sign can and should be readily available where the cougar has left tracks. He writes, "Additionally, food caches, scrapes and mounds are typical cougar field sign. These features are obvious where cougars are present."[45]

Downing also felt that the use of tracks by themselves was not a reliable indicator. He recommended that their use be considered alongside other methods. Microscopic and genetic analysis of hair and scat samples are among the other indices. Food caches can be identified as distinctly cougar when found soon after burial, but are difficult to identify after other creatures have begun to scavenge.[46]

Rainer Brocke, on the other hand, does believe in the use of tracks to define the presence of a cougar. He has said it should take only "a matter of hours" to locate an individual in cougar habitat. Brocke states that females with kittens are especially easy to locate, even though the kittens may go undetected. "If a cougar with cubs is roaming an area, she is not going to travel too far, rather she will keep to about thirty square miles. If she is sighted one day she is going to be nearby for a few more. Anybody with any kind of knowledge of these animals should be able to locate a kill site within a short period of time. Tracks ought to be found in the area and scat will, too."[47]

Bruce Wright once asserted that cougars were probably avoiding roads altogether and that this made their presence undetectable in places they frequented. Brocke and his student Fred Van Dyke believed this was false. "The most important segment of an eastern mountain lion population, its resident females, should be relatively easy to detect through track surveys. We found no support for the idea that resident lions exist in the East but remain undetected by deliberately avoiding roads."[48]

Several sets of tracks have been found in the East, and a few have been verified. But it is more difficult to detect evidence of breeding populations needed to prove the existence of cougars east of the Rockies. The probability of detecting kittens with females is only 19% in ideal conditions. Yet kittens travel with their mothers over 63% of the time. According to Dan Barnhurst and Frederick Lindzey, both widely published wildlife biologists, the probability of detecting kittens more than doubles after the kittens are about six months of age but is still less than 50 percent.[49] In short, the females are easier to detect than the kittens that follow them.

Skeptics will view this information differently. They suggest thinking in terms of prey kill rates, which increase dramatically when a female is providing for young kittens. According to Bruce Ackerman, a renowned cougar researcher, a female with kittens has to kill a deer every three days while kittens are less than fifteen months old.[50] Considering this kill rate, evidence of a resident cougar in a home range ought to be detectable. Even though kitten tracks are difficult to find, nursing mothers ought to be easily located by her kill sites.[51] The question is, would casual observers recognize such kills? How would humans happen to find them? Cougar kills are cached, which means hidden. They are usually tucked under branches among dense vegetation and covered with detritus.[52]

From the Van Dyke study in Utah, published under the title *"Use of Road Track Counts as Indices of Mountain Lion Presence,"* the author states that:

> Our study of wild transmitted cougars in southern Utah has shown that where cougars are present in a resident population, their tracks will be found. For example, under good tracking conditions on dirt roads, there is a 95% probability of detecting the presence of a resident female if 19.7 mi (31.6km) of trail in the cougar's range is searched. This can be done by auto in one day. Conversely, if no cougar is found at this level of effort, there is a 95% probability that no resident female is present in the area. On the basis of this study and other data, it is very unlikely that the endangered eastern cougar subspecies still exists as a viable or declining population in the Northeast.[53]

These findings cannot, however, be applied to transient males or cubs. Track surveys were less successful at detecting transient lions. Transients, by definition, tend to wander erratically and do not remain long in a local area. If transients account for the phenomenon of eastern mountain lion sightings, it is possible that such lions might go undetected by track surveys. In Arizona about thirty-one miles of roads were needed to detect resident females; more mileage was necessary to find sign of other cougars. In another study, it was suggested that 225 miles of road per 195 square miles of territory was needed to find cougar sign.[54] All of these studies have taken place in the West. Are those findings applicable to conditions in the East?

There are those who assert that tracking conditions in the Northeast and Canada are vastly different and are commonly referred to as poor. Robert Downing, Helen McGinnis, and Virginia Fifield all reported poor tracking conditions. Many biologists do not feel such findings can be applied to the East. However, the Van Dyke study states that the search must take place on a good substrate. In his study, Van Dyke attempted to find a sound method to verify the presence of cougars in the East. Unfortunately, it has yet to be tested, and one reason is because the necessary stretch of road with good track substrate is difficult to find except maybe in winter. In reference to cougar habits and tracks in the eastern United States, Brocke wrote the following:

> There are similarities and differences between our study population and the target population of eastern mountain lions to which we wished to apply our inferences. There is no reason to suspect that mountain lions in the East would not leave tracks, deposit scat, treat killed prey, or make scrapes or mounds differently than the western mountain lions. Differences in site conditions are more serious. We studied in a dry climate with long intervals between precipitation events. Search sites often had little ground cover. Sighting locations in eastern areas may often experience precipitation between reporting of a sighting and the investigation of the site. Eastern locations are also more likely to have heavy undergrowth and abundant ground cover.[55]

In the Midwest, tracking conditions encountered by independent non-profit organizations were so poor that most of the work took place in winter, with the exception of sites along the Great Lakes. Similarly, Downing restricted the bulk of his research to winter. Downing did have other agency biologists out tracking and none were successful finding cougar sign. As mentioned, he himself found no pronounceable evidence of a resident population. But in light of the Brocke studies, Downing stated that, "If laid end to end, the mileage searched on roads would not equal the length to even find resident females."[56] This statement implies that Downing searched less than twenty miles on suitable substrate. Nevertheless, several peer-reviewed journal articles refer blindly to Downing's search and use it as proof that cougars could not be found.[57] Thus, each time the Downing study is mentioned, the implication is that cougars have been proven not to exist in the East because an extensive search was conducted.

Nevertheless, whether Brocke or any other highly experienced cougar authority can find sign is not the question here. Rather, the concern is whether the average eastern state biologist with a mind-set for deer and turkey would recognize cougar evidence. It is true that several states have specifically sent biologists out west to train with top cougar trackers. However, in the past many were unfamiliar with the large cat because most agencies took the stand that they did not exist; therefore, the number of biologists with cougar tracking experience was small. Could this unfamiliarity be the reason why cougars have escaped detection?

Surveys have been conducted with lay people to see how familiar they are with cougar tracks. A high percentage of western cougar hunters correctly identified a cougar track; only a small percentage of western deer hunters could do the same. Neither western deer hunters nor campers did well at identifying or drawing mountain lion tracks. Only 45 of 236 western deer hunters (19%) and 42 of 211 campers (20%) selected the correct track. A significant number who drew a mountain lion track did not show the correct number of toes and/or drew claw marks above the toes -- 43 of 63 western deer hunters (68%), 35 of 47 eastern deer hunters (74%), and 66 of 112 campers (59%). Most people who declined to draw a track said that they could not identify a mountain lion track. Selecting the correct mountain lion track from illustrations and the drawing score were both independent of respondent category for campers and deer hunters.[58]

These are nicely preserved cougar tracks used for tracking education. Tracks are rarely set in such ideal condition. Most deer hunters and campers cannot identify cougar tracks even when clearly cast. *Photo by Jay Tischendorf*

There is an alleged instance or well circulated rumor regarding a federal wildlife biologist who was shown a defined set of tracks previously set by a cougar on a leash and asked to identify them. The official was hesitant and unsure but eventually said they were dog tracks.[59] Be that as it may, but Bruce Wright had his panther tracks misidentified by the American Museum of Natural History. Track identification can be difficult.

This is because the academic degree in wildlife biology does little to educate the aspiring student about specific species, especially if they are not considered a part of the local fauna. Instead, students learn the mechanics of managing wildlife populations and implementing the appropriate studies and policies. Thus, if biologists have had no prior experience with cougars, they may know no more than the typical lay person with an interest in wildlife. Van Dyke commented in his "Searching Technique for Mountain Lion Sign" in the Wildlife Society Bulletin that "...eastern biologists inexperienced with lion sign may be less likely to spot lion sign."[60] Therefore, if a small population of cougars was scattered widely or nestled tightly in some forgotten haven, detection may be unlikely.

Little discussion has explored the adaptations cougars might make in order to remain undetected, although this response has been observed in other species such as wolves in Europe. The European countryside does not seem like a probable place for wolves, but small packs are living alongside man in densely populated regions. They are able to do so by concentrating their activities during times when the local human populations are inactive.[61] Van Dyke discovered some similar behavioral modifications in cougars:

It is possible that the mountain lion's ability to adjust its activity pattern may be an important behavioral compensation mechanism for dealing with human disturbance. The basic activity pattern of lions in undisturbed environments is already disposed toward minimizing encounters with humans. Lions tended to be inactive during mid-day; more active during some mid-evening hours and at sunset, and most active at or just prior to sunrise. Lions in the immediate vicinity of human disturbance shifted activity peaks to after sunset, concentrated other activity during evening hours, and were inactive rather than active at sunrise.[62]

Even though the cougar is elusive and secretive enough to challenge the most experienced hunters and biologists alike, it can be found, as Fifield stated, in places where it is established and breeding. The re-discovery of the cougar in Florida proves the point. It also suggests that the cougar may exist unverified by science for a long time, even when there are sightings and tracks. In addition, poor training and unfamiliarity in the East could allow the big cat to remain hidden even when actively sought. Few people can recognize cougar sign and identify their tracks. Tracks have historically been used to answer the cougar question, but have never proven anything. It is even possible that search efforts may have been conducted in the wrong sites or were too limited in size. Fortunately, speculation on how cougars might remain without detection is assisted by knowledge gained from research and experiences in Florida and the West. The examples from Florida and the Black Hills are the only strong defense against the well-made point that cougars could not survive east of the Mississippi without occasionally yielding a roadkill; they lived in each of those sites for many years without such a fatality. While the lack of roadkills is difficult to explain, unfamiliarity with cougar tracks and other sign seems a stronger argument for their continued lack of detection.

CHAPTER ELEVEN

MICHIGAN:
PARALLELS OR CONTROVERSY?

In Michigan, as in the eastern United States, cougars are thought to be extirpated. The last physical evidence of a cougar in Michigan was in 1906, but since then rumors have persisted of their presence in a few locations. In 1998 a non-profit organization called the Michigan Wildlife Conservancy, formerly Michigan Habitat Foundation, began discussing the large number of cougar sightings in the state and the need to verify what some have suspected is a small remnant population of cougars existing undetected. The group went looking and claims to have found irrefutable evidence of cougars in seven counties in both the Upper and Lower Peninsulas. Unfortunately, the evidence that includes DNA has been subject to suspicion, and many wildlife biologists have been reluctant to back the MWC claims.

As for the locals, they accept that cougars have been there existing undocumented all along in hidden corners throughout the state. In the Upper Peninsula alone there were over 600 reports between 1960 and 2005.[1] Most were unverifiable, but some came with tracks and later there were a few photographs. A heated debate ensued and continues today.

Since cougar reports to the Michigan Department of Natural Resources were often brushed off, the Michigan Wildlife Conservancy seemed the most fitting organization to give the sightings some attention. In 1998, the PHD wildlife biologist Patrick Rusz of the Michigan

Wildlife Conservancy was asked if he would get involved. At first he was hesitant, thinking, "We'd just spin our wheels, never get to the bottom of it and never accomplish anything. I was initially reluctant to do it."[2] Soon, however, Rusz had put together an organized method for investigating cougars in Michigan. He immediately began to find evidence in Seul Choix Point, which is on Lake Michigan in the Upper Peninsula.[3]

His cougar quest took him to the people of the Upper Peninsula and northwest Lower Peninsula. "I was told these people were seeing things....that they must have mistaken dogs or cats for full-grown lions," Rusz said. "Then I interviewed the people in these areas, and I was overwhelmed with the response. There were photos, tracks, perceived caches, and I learned to listen to the collective claims of local residents."[4]

Footage of the controversial Michigan cougar video depicting two cougars in tandem. The one at the rear appears to be "spraying", but skeptics have noted the inability of cougars to raise their tails that high. The video was given low credibility based on additional less specific observations. The Conservancy insists it is real.
Stokes video (Michigan Conservancy)

He chose the remote shoreline of Lake Michigan, about forty miles from the site of the 1906 cougar kill, because there was a long history of sightings there. Seul Choix Point is a 33-mile stretch of wild, inaccessible sand dunes and mixed forest adjacent to thick cedar groves. This is a rugged coastline with dense dark swamps along a prominent point, jutting out like the bow of a Great lakes ore ship, into the frigid wind-swept waters of Lake Michigan. Rusz exclaims, "Within the morning we had found sign! It was all over the place. We had everything from fresh scat to fresh deer kills. Before the search was done we had thirty fresh scats."[5]

Rusz used captive cougars as study aids. He literally brought the substrate, or beach sand, upon which he was looking for tracks, into the cages of captive cougars and let them walk over it, accumulating tracks to examine. Simultaneously, he had dogs do the same and compared the two. This also allowed him to study the tracks of cougars in different weather conditions. Eventually his eye became keen to the tracks of cougars in a variety of conditions and gaits.[6]

He used the same method for other sites as well. Before the year was through, Rusz had located fifteen probable sites that contained incriminating scat. "We picked places noted by hunters for many years. These were sites with long histories of sightings and tracks. By putting it all together, I was able to see clusters and then set out to investigate the best part of each area."[7]

Unlike other eastern and midwestern investigations, where tracks had not been convincing, this one focused on obtaining DNA-containing material. But the scat had to be analyzed for more than content; it had to be taken to the molecular level. Rusz explains, "We knew we would have skeptics. So I sent out the samples for definitive testing to the Wyoming State Fish and Game Laboratory in Laramie. I also wanted to find out more about the population and individual cougars. The DNA testing was positive for cougar."[8]

It was at this point that Rusz went ahead and announced that the Conservancy had definitely proven the presence of cougars. "We have a wild, remnant breeding population."[9] But the lab that did the testing expressed it differently. "There are eight of thirteen samples of scat being examined at this lab that we firmly believe came from the feline family, most probably a mountain lion."[10]

However, by November of 2001, the story began appearing in publications such as *The New York Times, The Detroit Free Press, Grand Rapids Press,* and *The Traverse City Record Eagle.* Each article presented the cougar as residing in Michigan. Thus began a controversy regarding the cougar's status in Michigan, the outcome of which has a direct influence on parallels made to the cougar question further east.[11] According to Michigan journalist, Tom Carney, who publicly criticized the MWC at the Eastern Cougar Conference of April 28, 2004, Rusz has repeatedly used words like "irrefutable" and "conclusive."[12] Carney's critique about the MWC findings and statements to the Associated Press came a day after Rusz presented his evidence at the Conference in Morgantown, West Virginia. According to one biologist at the conference, "It was an uncomfortable setting - with Rusz seated before Carney and the journalist picking apart his scientific research. It seemed to expose, however, some major holes in the Conservancy's approach and of course the scientific credibility of their central figure Patrick Rusz."[13]

Rhetoric was unquestionably a component of the confusion, as the Wyoming lab had only said "most probable."[14] The Conservancy, on the other hand, has used phrases such as "indisputable physical evidence" and "verified as cougar."[15] Yet as the Conservancy points out, "most probable" means that there is a remote statistical possibility or a small infinitesimal percentage that the test could be inaccurate (1x10-6 or a one in a million chance). They claim that the right interpretation of the tests was made.[16] There were other misunderstandings, which resulted from some technical difficulties that the Wyoming lab was having. Rusz claims these technical difficulties helped to create additional controversy. The Wyoming lab had been in the process of determining how many individual cougars might inhabit specific sites, when they suddenly resigned from the task.

Nevertheless, the Conservancy continued to press on with their mission and they eventually established a new working relationship with a different lab. So, now all subsequent scats were eventually sent along to the Central Michigan University lab where Brad Swanson was responsible for performing the tests that would take the evidence to more specific levels. Swanson's testing would supposedly determine if scats came from a cougar or other feline, and whether or not the cougar or cougars were of North American origin. When completed, true statements could be accurately made and announced -- or so they believed.[17]

Rusz collected 297 scats over a three year period and presented all of them for testing. The scats were collected in remote areas from the Upper and Lower Peninsula.[18] The scats came from a total of twelve different sites and after analysis only twelve scats were suitable for testing. Most specimens were in poor condition, having been left in the elements, where sun, rain, freezing and thawing acted over time to degrade the DNA contained within. However, some of the specimens were nicely preserved and some were almost fresh. In 2006 Rusz and Swanson published their long awaited, peer reviewed article in the *American Midland Naturalist* where the results and conclusions were presented with the testing methodology.[19]

Their paper stated that the twelve scats yielded ten identified as cougar, one as bobcat and one as canine. Only one of the ten cougar scats could be determined as coming from a North American cougar -- the others could not be tested to that level. From this data, they stated that there were eight individual cougars living in the state. This conclusion was derived by the distances between the sites where samples were obtained and then ruling out the likelihood of an individual cougar depositing any of these scats in more than one area.[20]

Their paper came under immediate attack. Cougar biologists from around the nation criticized the methodology, and enthusiasts found fault in their conclusions regarding the eight resident cougars. Eventually, in 2007 a rebuttal appeared in the same journal. Basically, its authors fault the testing procedures and the lack of controls to rule out the possibility that any of these scats may have come from a domestic house cat or a lynx. In addition, they feel that if ten out of the twelve testable specimens were cougar scats or 83%, then had all 297 scats been testable, the mathematical logic would have 223 or 83% of those scats coming from cougars.[21]

Their testing for cougar, with the lack of controls for domestic cat and lynx, does seem reckless. Claiming that distance can define these cougar scats as individuals is another assumption, especially when the samples were taken over a three year period of time. Cougars are known, as noted in previous chapters, to travel widely and do so in short periods of time. However, the large number of scats, 223, may not be such a stretch, when considering the three year long collection time.

The Conservancy article leaves one wondering. Is the Conservancy looking to entice more funding by claiming the existence of cougars via a huge publicity campaign? Could it be it is just the very nature of the issue and the difficulty of detecting the species and the methods used? Is there some really sloppy science coming from the Conservancy or are journalists trying to further their careers by finagling information to create illusions in the hope of debunking or creating bellwether science articles? In light of the scant and flimsy physical proof of these animals in the state, it just seems the conclusions made in Rusz's journal piece and the number of cougars they think are present, are too extravagant.

As in New England, Michigan's deer-hunting season yields an invasion of thousands of sportsmen and women into areas that are otherwise vacant of human presence. One would expect a few encounters to have happened if the cougars were there as claimed and in such numbers. This point is frequently made in the Northeast to refute the existence of cougars, but skeptics will be at a loss should cougars be proven beyond a doubt in Michigan. Each season, hunters report moose, wolves, and bobcats -- and cougars are sometimes on the list. Wolves, moose and even sportsmen are inevitably struck down by cars or errant projectiles, but so far no cougars have been shot. Some sportsmen and sportswomen reserve judgement, but many are outspoken.

Houndsmen are on top of that list. "We hunt the whole area up by Seul Point, where they did their study, and there are no cougars there," claims John Cryderman of Sault Sainte Marie, a long time houndsman.[22] Cryderman believes that if cougars were there, one would have been treed. He says, "There are too many good houndsmen running dogs all over the Upper Peninsula for a cougar to hide from."[23] It has been said that there are several houndsmen spending up to 200 days of the year in the woods and swamps of the UP and, like Crydermen, they just cannot believe that a cougar population could have escaped their detection. "Cougars are not homebodies; they travel," says Cryderman. "I can tell you when a cougar hits a road he is going to travel. Wolves do the same thing. Someone running his or her dogs would have crossed a track. They're just not there." Cryderman has been outspoken about this experience with cougars and cougar tracking. An active houndsmen, he has spent a lot of his time in the UP and says, "There are 580 wolves in the Upper Peninsula, and they get hit by cars, and deer hunters kill wolves every year. Where are the lions? Where are the dead ones?"[24]

Mel Guntzviller is another houndsman who also feels the cougar is not elusive enough to outsmart him or his dogs. "I've been around a lot of lions in California," Guntzviller said. "I have been in on depredation hunts and had them everyday on my trap lines killing coyotes, bobcats, and fox. You just can't mistake a lion track, especially in the snow."[25] Winter snows are his pivot point when arguing against cougars. He believes the deeryards would have to yield a cougar or two or some sign of them if there were any. Guntzviller explains: "During the winter in the Upper Peninsula., the deer "yard up"; they are in the cedar swamps. That's where houndsmen spend all their time in the winter, running the cedar swamps, chasing the bobcats and coyotes. If they were in there, somebody would run one."[26]

Rusz believes that cougars have been able to survive because of impenetrable swamps that were avoided and never logged. He believes the cougars at Suel Choix Point are remnants from pre-settlement populations. They held out from persecution in these large impenetrable regions and were able to find enough deer to feed their young by using the landscape in the surrounding woodlands to their advantage. He claims that at the Lake Michigan site, the cougars have been ambushing the deer along the coast by hiding in-between dunes and behind rocks and cornering the prey along the water before retreating into the thick of the swamps to consume the prey.[27] He has much historical research to prove that cougars could have survived the lean years when the land was cleared. Deer survived especially well in the Country Club Region of northwestern Michigan where huge acreages were closed off and turned into camps. Some of these landowners restricted hunting and began to feed deer.[28] With the help of a local historian named Nelson Yoder, Rusz has been able to uncover reports of cougar sightings as early as 1930, and he claims to have seen a photograph of a killing in 1919. "Here is evidence of a cougar a full thirteen years after they are suppose to be extinct," Rusz said.[29] It should be mentioned that apparently no one has actually seen this photograph other than the MWC team.

While many sportsmen in the UP doubt that there are cougars, others have been emphatic about their existence. On the warm summer night of August 8, 2002, some believe a cougar slipped into a corral and pounced on horses in South Boardman. "In such a case where there is so much emotion, you know somebody has got something worth looking into," exclaims Rusz.[30] A distraught Bill and Linda George called in the attack on their horses by what they were sure was a cougar.[31]

According to the Detroit News: "Both animals have bite and claw marks along the back, neck, rump, and sides."[32] An animal also attacked a dog and a mule owned by the George's neighbors, the Strouss family. In the words of Larry Strouse, "There were two cats, one large, about six feet long, and another half the size."[33] Rusz observed the wounds on the George's animals and stated, "a cougar kills by jumping on its victim's back, digging claws in, and biting through the neck vertebrae or breaking the neck."[34] He could not say if the animals had survived a cougar attack, but did not feel that the scars were made from barbed wire, another logical explanation. Skeptics noticed the George's account of track marks, "the tracks path zigzags down our drive."[35] Cougars are known to travel in deliberate straight lines, not zigzags. Rusz claims he collected different corroborative evidence several weeks later -- not the zigzag tracks that he never saw.[36]

As in the East, the incident proved little, yet fueled the debate, and probably gave Rusz further reason to proceed with his work. His work also revealed what the Conservancy believes is a small population within the heavily used Sleeping Bear Dunes National Park along the eastern shores of Lake Michigan.[37] The lakeshore has had consistent sightings for many years. Although Mike De Capita with the United States Fish and Wildlife Service said the agency does not recognize cougars in Michigan, it acknowledged at one time that the Sleeping Bear Dunes had one cougar.[38]

United States Fish and Wildlife officials argue that the animal was probably released in the area but has nevertheless caused great concern for visitor safety. Kim Mukavetz, a park ranger at Sleeping Bear for fourteen years, describes the large cougar she believes lives in the region: "I was driving north on highway M-22 to Empire in 1997 when the grayish-brown cougar jumped across the road and ran toward the Lake."[39] On another occasion, Bill Herd, who also works for the park, was driving the same road in 2002 when he saw the animal cross before his vehicle. "It crossed twenty five yards in front of me and vanished into a swamp."[40]

The Michigan Department of Natural Resources acknowledges that there could be an individual cougar in the National Park, but does not feel that it represents a population. Interestingly, the National Park Service conducted a thorough search in the park for cougars a few years later in 2006 and did not find any sign of them. The investigation included camera traps and miles of track surveys. Sightings were investigated and only sign of dog and bobcat could be confirmed.

That finding did little to support the MWC and the credibility of Rusz. Albeit, the Conservancy has not appeared to have put too much time into researching cougar spoor and public claims in the park. Like so many discussions about cougars in the East, people often become embroiled in heated arguments of frustration. The Michigan study is no exception. On one side, you have the Conservancy proclaiming viable populations of cougars in different locations. On the other, the Michigan DNR doubts the Conservancy's assumption that there are breeding populations. Consequently, you have a state agency refusing to do anything about the MWC findings, and the reason is that there are errors with DNA testing, disbelief over photographs, and tracks obtained. Meanwhile, the Conservancy is shouting for acknowledgment, calling the state irresponsible if they take no interest or action in defining these alleged populations further.[41]

Outraged, the Conservancy cites the issuance of a kill permit to shoot a cougar that was said to be killing livestock. "We find cougars and ask for the State's help in protecting them, and the first thing they do after denying their presence is to issue a kill permit. How can they issue a kill permit for something they are telling us does not exist?" Rusz refers to the Wildlife Damage Investigation and Control Permit signed by Penny Melchoir, issued by DNR staff Tim Web, following the George and Strouse incident in Kalkaska County, citing that DNR believed the animal was a cougar.[42]

Rusz quotes the Michigan DNR, "We do not believe this is proof enough to verify a viable population with which we could be expected to do something about."[43] Perhaps the DNR is simply being cautious in an area where there is controversy. After all, Michigan has yet to produce a single specimen. On the other hand, it seems ironic that the first specimen might come through a control action. So, whether one is inclined to accept the claims that cougars are in Michigan or not, the case there, at the very least, goes a long way toward showing how even in places with a possibility, state officials are likely to have them remain undetected simply by lack of resources.

It is not clear whose side one should believe, but the DNR has admitted that even if there was irrefutable proof of cougars breeding in their state, there is little they could do about it, because they have absolutely no funding. Rare as a cougar may be in their part of the nation, the list of endangered species is well over one hundred, and there is no possible way that the state can attend to each of these individual cases.[44] The Conservancy, meanwhile, has been busy defending what seems like premature claims on Rusz's part. The Conservancy's credibility has been crippled by excessive back-peddling, rhetorical contradictions from the lab scientist's findings of scat evidence, and questions of Rusz's interpretations.[45] Some may wonder why the Conservancy ever came forward with its cougar evidence, since it would only seem to incite controversy. But the Conservancy had hoped to educate the public and let them know that these are not escaped pets; that they are endangered, or at the very least, a part of the ecosystem, regardless of origin.

The concern of the Conservancy is that the DNR has led people to believe that all cougars in the State are escaped pets and are therefore permissible to shoot. Legally, the ramifications of viable cougar populations hinge on where the population actually is. Cougars in Michigan's Upper Peninsula were historically considered to be of the western subspecies *Puma concolor hippolestes*, while those in the lower Peninsula were thought of as members of the eastern subspecies *Puma concolor couguar*.[46] According to the outdated wording of the Federal Endangered Species Act, it is only the latter grouping that is afforded formal protection.[47]

While Rusz's work has been steeped in controversy, there seemed to be a breakthrough at one point. Rusz claims that with the retirement of certain hardcore skeptics within the DNR in 2005-2006 came a breath of fresh air for his followers. The DNR sent several wildlife biologists out west to train with Harley Shaw on detecting cougar spoor. Later, the DNR re-examined the evidence of photo, track, anecdotal and DNA and had a more accommodating attitude regarding the claims of the Conservancy. In fact, they publicly admitted that hair samples taken from a car that struck a cougar tested positive. The sample was obtained in November of 2004 by a state trooper responding to an animal strike call.[48]

In 2008 there were finally some tracks found in the Upper Peninsula that the DNR accepted as being cougar. These tracks, found in Delta County, were impressed in snow and verified as cougar. Then another set of tracks was discovered in June of that year and determined to be made by an average size cougar. Later, in 2009 more tracks were found in Marquette County. These were followed by more sets in October from Sault Sainte Marie, and in November from School Craft and Chippewa Counties. The official position on these from the DNR is that they do not represent a resident breeding population, but probably indicate the occurrence of transients. They suspect that they have arrived from the Black Hills, but this is only a speculation.

Photograph of a cougar allegedly taken in August 1997 in western Alcona County. *Courtesy Michigan Conservancy*

Sadly, the Conservancy continued to bash the DNR and make more bold statements about these cougars being resident animals. Why they continue to do this, even today, is uncertain, but they have not convinced anyone of official or reputable stature. None of the evidence they claim from the Lower Peninsula has been accepted. This includes two photos, scats and tracks. Both photos seem fake, the cat resting, photographed in Alcona County is suspected to be a mounted taxidermy specimen, and the other from Oscoda shows belly flab, a sign that the cougar is probably a pet. The scats, as just mentioned are discredited and the tracks, indeterminate at best. Unfortunately, it appears that the Michigan Wildlife Conservancy will not gain much credibility in the years to come.

Rusz hopes this will not be the case. He warns, "the cougar is not on a comeback but has probably never been so endangered."[49] Rusz is not the first person to assert that cougars are breeding in his state. In fact, his methods of research relied heavily on clusters of sightings over time. The cougar was, after all, placed on the state endangered species list in 1987.[50] This was done because the DNR felt there was adequate evidence and common knowledge of cougars in the state. In 1994 a DNR-sponsored publication recognized the presence of cougars in the Upper Peninsula, but over time skeptics within the agency convinced others that this was perhaps a mistake.[51] Rusz claims he is the first person, however, to finally put it all together, resurrect and confirm the state's earlier reports and to gather the evidence, and formally present it. In doing so, he truly came to believe the presence of cougars could be proven and specific answers answered about the eight individual cougars that the Conservancy believes are living in Michigan, as well as hypothesize over the eighty or more they suspect to make up the breeding population.[52]

While there are many factual disputes and disagreements between the Conservancy, the Michigan DNR, and individuals aligned with journalist Carney, it is very clear that little progress has been made in unequivocally answering the real question and protecting the resource. The cat of today and tomorrow could slip through the rhetoric, remaining officially undetected and unrecognized. The Michigan controversy is an example of how the cougar has managed to remain truly elusive in almost every imaginable use of the word. For certain, should a Great Lakes population of cougars be proven, it would answer any doubts that a resident cougar population could remain undetected.

Many lessons can be learned from the Michigan situation, and this ought to be what is finally taken from all of this. Primarily, any search effort for cougars in the East must be done jointly with the accepted wildlife authorities and government game departments to maintain credibility and avoid conflict. The other consideration involves the presentation of evidence in scientifically acceptable terms; for example, publication in a reputable, peer-reviewed journal, and findings introduced this way from the very beginning. Tracks and photos should only act to supplement other findings and be offered for interpretation. Publicity should be limited until such evidence has been offered for scientific review. In this case, the DNA evidence presented by the Conservancy does not contradict the test results disclosed by the Central Michigan

University lab -- rather none of the tests are accepted by the scientific community. The best evidence today seems to favor the presence of only transient cougars in upper Michigan; better proof of a breeding population is desired. The statements and findings of the Conservancy will likely remain suspect. There is, however, no way to ascertain the origin of any Michigan cougars to date. Should the Conservancy be correct, then the East could theoretically also harbor cougars.

CHAPTER TWELVE

THIS IS COUGAR COUNTRY

Perhaps the biggest misconception regarding cougars is that cougars require wilderness to live. Consequently, many people, including wildlife personnel, immediately react negatively to claims of their existence in the East. The truth is that these cats require large territories, but they are not necessarily wilderness dependent. Cougars are highly adaptable, and their survival depends on three things: an adequate prey supply, sufficient cover, and protection from persecution.

Cougars are ambush-style hunters who utilize cover and topography accordingly; this is why certain kinds of terrain and plant life are more important than outright wilderness. They need the cover for travel and shelter for their young, too. When these conditions are met, along with a good prey base, the cougar will adapt to human activity. While the idea of mountain lions existing in densely populated states like Massachusetts and Pennsylvania may seem absurd, the fact is that these basic requirements do exist there.

But just how developed might a cougar's home range actually be before the animal is stressed into departing? Can they persist in the segmented and drastically disturbed woodlands across much of the Northeast? It would seem that the East would not have the suitable habitats for this, the wildest of all animals, but the cougar is an adaptable creature, capable of living in regions where humans are active and have altered the land with roads, farms, and suburbs. In fact, there is much evidence to support their tolerance of fragmented habitat and their ability to make use of such marginal forestland.

Documentation of the animal's ability to persist in developed areas can be taken from cases in the West and Florida. For as long as anyone can remember, the cougar had been found only in the wilderness, but more recently, there has been a sudden change in the animal's behavior. Cougars are making an appearance in the suburbs. Theories vary on the reasons for this, but human-cougar encounters are increasing at an alarming rate. Basically, biologists have summarized the situation as an increase in cougars and an increase in humans traveling or residing in areas that were once frequented only by the cougar.

Maurice Hornocker, founder of the Hornocker Institute, studied cougars for decades in the Idaho wilderness. He is recognized as a leading authority on the animal. Hornocker himself substantiates the case. "We have a very, very adaptable animal. This is an animal that lives at sea level, it can live in the desert, and it can live in the rain forest. It will change to its environment and that means it's a survivor. The environment has changed out west, and if the cougar is to survive it will have to change as well," says Hornocker.[1]

David Baron reported in *The Boston Globe* on the increased presence of *Puma concolor* in suburbia throughout the West. He stated, "In suburbs of Seattle, Sacramento, and Salt Lake City, deer have made subdivisions their homes, and the mountain lion has followed."[2] Baron went on to document these kinds of situations across the West until he discovered Boulder, Colorado. Based on what happened in that city, Baron wrote his acclaimed book Beast in the Garden, a gripping account of specific events that led to the killing of a young man by a cougar in Idaho Springs, Colorado.

Baron brings to light a study conducted by Michael Sanders and Jim Halfpenny. These two biologists strived to explain the existence of cougars near humans and tried to find out how often cougars were frequenting these areas. The occurrence of cougars in suburbia increased drastically during the mid-1980s and continues today. Halfpenny explains that "the number of cougar sightings outside of large cities was increasing."[3] Sanders and Halfpenny determined that cougars were in fact able to live alongside humans. Nowhere can this point be better made than in California. Morgan Wethje, a wildlife biologist with the

California Department of Fish and Game, stated that cougars are living successfully alongside humans in subdivisions.[4] They are able to adapt, and their behavior may change as these adaptations do.

There are others in California who, like Wethje, can document cougars living in semi-urban settings where there are deer and a few forgotten acres. Craig Dorrough, who works in the state's Sacramento Fish and Game Office, says that cougars are living along the Interstate highway buffers. "They have a sustained presence along the Interstates, where incidentally there are hardly any roadkills. These areas are full of deer, and while only a few thousand feet wide, they stretch for miles."[5] Linda Sweanor is an extensively published puma biologist studying the animal in the West. She noted their use of deer-rich areas among high human densities, such as Cuyamaca Rancho State Park, where there are a half million visitors each year. Outside of the park, cougars would approach the properties within a town of some 10,000 residents.[6] California's reputable biologist Steve Torres also noted cougars living where there are high human densities.[7]

Studies have shown that these reclusive predators can tolerate and cross the roads intersecting their habitats, although in some regions it has been seen that females avoid them.[8] Reports are common now of cougars crossing lawns and frequenting suburban woodlots.[9] These observations further support the view that human disturbance can be tolerated to some extent. In California the animal is turning up regularly in developments, and depredation on pets is now being considered a tool to measure how frequently and how intimately the cougar will use these settings.[10] Baron wrote in Beast in the Garden that cougars were frequenting backyards without fear and approaching humans in daylight hours. Halfpenny noted extreme cases where cougars had dens underneath backyard porches.[11]

As pointed out by Maehr, the cougar is not confined to vast areas. "One of the biggest misconceptions about *Puma concolor* is its need for true wilderness. My studies in Florida expose this and show that the panther is not the wilderness species we think it is."[12] In his monograph "*The Comparative Ecology of Black Bears, Bobcats and Panthers*", Maehr discusses the panther's adaptability to marginal habitat and the greater significance of prey abundance over remoteness. Most people tend to associate the cat with the wide-open spaces of the West -- but those who have worked closely with cougars, such as Maehr, will tell you otherwise. Maehr revealed data on the Florida panther that supports the cougar's tolerance of humans in his rebuttal to Langlios and Cardoza, "*The Eastern Mountain Lion: A Management Failure*". Maehr states the following:

"It can also tolerate human activities and subsist in suburban settings if sufficient habitat is available nearby. Thus it is not strictly a wilderness obligate, even though, like many large mammals it embodies wilderness values. As experimental work in Florida has demonstrated, there is little doubt that the species can survive and reproduce successfully in forest landscapes that support a variety of human activities."[13]

Today there are more white-tailed deer than ever before. While the landscape in the East has changed dramatically from the days when cougars commonly roamed the region, they would enjoy a greater supply of prey today. They would find survival in areas of adequate refuge easier because of the high deer densities. We have been conditioned to think of the cougar as the symbol of the wilderness; the popular literature is brimming with reference to the cougar's need for huge wilderness tracts, void of human disturbance, but in fact there is no scientific basis for this view. While forest fragmentation is commonly blamed for the paucity of cougars -- there are no studies that prove this as an absolute. Van Dyke demonstrated in his study "*Reactions of Mountain Lions*" that some lions will incorporate human disturbance into their home ranges.[14]

The Northeast Corridor, from Boston south to Washington D.C., comprises the most densely populated area in the country, but surprisingly some of the best evidence for cougars can actually be found there. Massachusetts is one place in particular that has been mentioned. About two hours drive from the Greater Boston area, the foothills of the Berkshires rise up in western Massachusetts. These hills are forested and contain a few extensive tracts that are seemingly suitable for the cougar when taking into account the adjacent Green Mountain National Forest to the north in Vermont. In Massachusetts most of the human population is confined to the region east of the Connecticut River. Likewise, other parts of the East are set up this way, where the majority of the people are concentrated, and thus much of the outlying areas remain quiet.

While the cougar may not need wilderness, it most certainly cannot thrive in suburban-urban environs as the eastern coyote does. Van Dyke showed that places, "...where there is continuous concentralized human presence, or residence, are essentially lost to the lion population, even if there is little impact on the habitat itself."[15] Even in places where there is some distance and time between human disturbance, mountain lion activity was determined to be altered according to Van Dyke's studies. Van Dyke used two study areas in the West which each had human disturbances, primarily logging, and mountain lions were found to avoid these sites. "A comparison of mountain lion reaction to logging activity on two study areas revealed several trends. Most residents appeared to restrict their activities to areas outside of timber sale areas, whether logging activity was taking place or not."[16] Van Dyke observed only one individual lion utilize a logging site as a central part of its range; all other lions which had been collared avoided timber sale areas -- some completely, most others only partially.

The study showed that disturbed areas were more often utilized by young mountain lions, transients in search of their own home ranges and other lions. Their presence in disturbed regions strongly indicated the marginality of these sites, as they were the only free and open hunting grounds available to these inexperienced wanderers. There were notable differences between types of disturbed habitats used by residents and transients. Transients were more likely to be involved in close human contact than were residents.[17]

The utilization of human impacted landscapes is contingent on the fact that there is an adjacent forest available. Cougars could survive successfully in the East, as there is a great deal of peripheral corridor habitat or loosely associated deeper wooded private and public lands. Contrary to popular belief, eastern states do offer extensive woodlands. For example, Vermont offers large expanses of forest within its Northeast Kingdom. New York has habitat so attractive it has been considered by many to be suitable for wolf restoration. To the south, Pennsylvania, also a heavily populated state containing twelve million people, has 43 of its 67 counties with more than 50% forest cover. This means there are 17,000,000 acres under forest cover.[18] United States Department of Agriculture statistics reveal that there are 384,000,000 forested acres east of the Mississippi. If the total land areas of these forested acres were consolidated, they would approximate an area the size of Pennsylvania and New York State combined.[19]

Consider further that some of the nation's largest parks can be found in the East -- Great Smoky National Park, Washington and Jefferson National Forests, Monongahela National Forest, Adirondack Park, and the Green and White Mountains National Forests. In Virginia, forested land by broad definition approximates 11,000,000 or 1,690,000 acres of protected rural forest, North Carolina has 736,000 protected acres, and Tennessee 630,000. In the southern Appalachians, there are 47 Congressionally-designated wilderness areas, many of which are very remote and still contain old growth forest. A habitat study using GIS analysis of road, human and deer densities showed that good cougar habitat existed in several locations.[20] In addition, there is the vast private acreage of individual citizens and paper company holdings.

In the central Appalachians, United States Forest Service lands account for large amounts of contiguous forest in West Virginia, Virginia and North Carolina. This land is more expansive than the public land that is presently sustaining the Florida panther; such federal land is supported in many areas by adjacent or adjoining state wildlife management areas, national park land, state parks, and smaller conservation parcels.

Western and northern Maine is especially noteworthy. In northern Maine alone, there are well over 3.2 million acres that are largely undeveloped, aside from a few small villages and isolated hunting cabins.[21] This is more than the size of Yosemite and Yellowstone National Parks combined. The grassroots organization RESTORE has proposed that this region, Maine's north woods, be set aside as a national park and preserve. Their efforts include the restoration of the wolf, which has been considered a potential candidate for trap and transfer into the region. If the region is ecologically sound enough for potential wolf restoration projects, then it ought to be attractive as cougar habitat. In addition to the millions of acres under debate are adjacent lands of equal size. Some of these lands are even more remote.

Another area of promise for the eastern cougar might be the Allegheny National Forest, where Renee Davis of the International Society for Endangered Cats conducted a feasibility study on re-introducing cougars.[22] From her research she found a white-tailed deer population that was exploding and in great need of a predator such as the cougar. The study looked at many factors before arriving at a single conclusion -- sustained survival. The study assessed the potential of Allegheny National Forest to support a viable reintroduction population. Biological considerations included home range sizes, food sources of many types, and adequate cover. Davis wrote, "According to the findings of this study, I conclude that cougar reintroduction in Allegheny National Forest is ecologically feasible."[23]

As convincing as all of this may seem, there are those such as Brocke who have compared these wild areas with others known to support cougar populations, and have determined that road densities and human populations are measurably higher in the so-called wilderness sites of the East.[24] The implication of this is that these sites are not regions that could sustain viable cougar populations. Brocke believes there would be human-cougar conflicts, roadkills, and shootings. He thinks they would take place often enough to cause eventual extirpation. How then does the Brocke study explain the cougars living in California suburbs? Presumably such cats would be considered victims of habitat fragmentation, and represent a population of animals with an uncertain future, complicated by human-caused mortality. Such individuals are in jeopardy of illegal kills, car strikes, conflicts with humans, pets or livestock.[25]

Understanding this, Brocke has calculated the human density of the Adirondack Park, which is considered one of the least populated regions in the Northeast. He states the following: "Human density in the central Adirondacks, perhaps the most sparsely populated area in the Northeast, is 3.35 human/mi2 (1.29 humans/km2). By contrast, in two areas where cougars were known to occur, namely in southern Florida and southern Utah, human densities are 0.50/mi2 (0.19/km2) and 1.60/mi2 (0.62/km2), respectively."[26]

Brocke also calculated road densities for a hypothetical area within the Adirondack Mountains. The road density he arrived at was 0.42/km2 and compared this to the densities of Florida panther habitat of 0.06/ km2.[27] His conclusions made from such comparisons become questionable when the road densities of the Black Hills cougar population of South Dakota are looked at. This last comparison reveals that road densities and their implied human densities may not be the only factor at work. The road densities within the Black Hills site are 0.8 /km2 or two times greater than the Adirondacks and yet cougars are thriving there. There has to be a number of other factors then that determine what disturbances are acceptable to this carnivore, and hunting activity is most definitely one of them. Cardoza's response to these figures: "These presumed road effects may reflect a behavioral response to hunting, rather than an innate intolerance of development and human related activity."[28]

Likewise, Van Dyke's observations of collared lions might have more to do with the opening of habitat or the lack of cover in a logging site than the presence or disruption of humans. His study did, however, reveal the preference of lions for forested areas with less than average road densities. The building of roads, even small logging tracks, brings in human activity. Jim Halfpenny concluded while studying the cougar in the West that persecution had the biggest effect on cougars and where they may establish themselves, rather than human influences or land use. He said, "These are carnivores designed to eat deer, and when left alone and protected from persecution, they do fine with adequate deer numbers, cover, and a reasonable space from humans."[29]

Similarly, Gerry Parker, a wildlife biologist who has studied and written about the panther of the East, agrees that if left alone the cougar would probably not need wilderness to hide in. Parker says the following:

> Throughout much of the northeast we have large areas of suitable forested habitat and abundant supplies of white-tailed deer, the panther's preferred food. And I do not necessarily subscribe to the concern expressed by some that there are too many roads and too little wilderness left for panthers in the east. The panther, like many predators, is capable of adapting to specific environmental conditions. Yes, I initially blamed its demise on its inability to be ecologically flexible and adapt and cope with changing conditions of the eighteenth and nineteenth centuries. But times and humans attitudes have changed. We recognize and respect the growing public intolerance of widespread deforestation ... No, the main threat to mountain lion,

wherever it is found, is the trap, the gun, and the dog. An exception may be in Florida where large tracts of remaining wilderness and panther habitat are being lost to urban and agricultural sprawl. In California, a moratorium on hunting has seen a significant increase in mountain lions there, and an increase in the number of lion-human encounters. If not shot, trapped, and pursued on sight, I really question the often-repeated assumption that mountain lions require wilderness sanctuaries. Once, when all hands were raised against them, they needed somewhere to hide. But today, when they receive the benefit of conservative hunting regulations, and total moratoriums, that need is not nearly so great.[30]

And there are others, many with notable credentials, who also strongly believe that there is sufficient room for mountain lions in the eastern woodlands. Two among the group are Helen McGinnis and Susan Morse. Susan Morse is not a true believer in eastern cougars; she has searched high and low for tracks with her group of trained volunteers, but she firmly believes there is room for these creatures. "I am not saying they are out there; my guess -- many sightings are of far and wide wanderers and escapees or intentional releases, however, I do not believe for a minute what some people may try to assert -- there is enough woodland, and in some places, near wilderness conditions to support cougar populations."[31]

Helen McGinnis knows the issue very well, and she postulates the following: " The Black Hills cougar population represents a viable breeding population in the most densely human populated National Forest in the entire country. I think this is a good indication they could endure in many locations east of the Mississippi."[32] Tischendorf agrees with McGinnis and has been a long time believer in reintroducing cougars to the East, which is why he made this point clear at the recent Eastern Cougar Conference.

"From an ecological standpoint, I feel there is no question that pumas could survive in many areas of eastern North America. The recovery in this region of many predator species and other wildlife that we see today support this claim. Also keep in mind that panthers continue to survive in Florida, which in many respects represents one of the more challenged ecosystems in eastern North America. If panthers or cougars can survive there, they can do so in more favorable habitat and ecoregions to the north."[33]

While Brocke's analysis cannot explain the Black Hills pumas, the difference between the presence of cougars at a site such as that and the discovery of a similar, hypothetical group in an equally human-altered habitat in the East, is that pioneer populations have continuous new recruits. Van Dyke believed that mountain lions needed a central wild area to maintain an overall regional population health.[34] The Black Hills population, as previously mentioned, is likely the direct result of immigrants from saturated populations immediately to the west. On the other hand, a group in the East would be predominately isolated, except for a few instances where an escaped or transient cat happened, against all odds, to find the group and mate successfully. So there is a difference between what constitutes enough habitat protection in a pioneer population and that of a relic population.[35]

One significant difference may be that relic populations are less mobile than pioneer groups. Assuming, for the moment, the Michigan studies are true, one would have to wonder why the cats there do not get into human conflicts, while the Black Hills cougars do. Again, if the situation in Michigan can be accepted as true, then the sites that harbor those cougars could be used as a guideline, albeit crude, of what size "wilderness" is needed to support the undiscovered cougars in the East. The question can be answered with maps.

Much of southern Michigan can be compared to places such as the Berkshires; although the terrain is more rugged in Massachusetts, the human populations and road densities are similar. Maine can be compared to the Upper Peninsula, except that it offers more isolation and is in fact a near wilderness, depending on definitions. The Seul Choix site as mentioned does have some year round homes and roads near it.[36] However, even though a 33-mile stretch harbors these cougars, an expanse that can be found in many places in the East, the site is different in that it has nearly impenetrable swamps. Large, nearly unapproachable swamps are fewer in the East. But regions of old growth, places untouched through history, and inaccessible terrain, can nevertheless be found up and down the Appalachians.

One cannot speculate about the suitability of eastern woodlands without considering the factors that determine a cougar's territory. Since we are accustomed to the studies and books about cougars in places where they are known to exist, instead of those -- such as this book -- that discuss where they might exist, our knowledge of the cougar is in the context of habitats drastically different than those in the East. Much of the recent cougar studies have been conducted in dry regions of California, Idaho, Utah, and Colorado. The East is essentially humid and wet, with significant rainfall averages each year. The forests are dense with plenty of deciduous cover, evergreens, and rugged, rocky, hilly terrain. Finally, deer densities are extremely high, as is the total prey base. The biomass of the eastern forest is tremendous. These are all factors that favor the cougar, as they offer ambush sites among lush green cover within places full of deer and supplemental prey. Thus, the cougar has little reason to travel far in search of prey and consequently requires less territory in comparison. If the range of a female out in the West is fifteen square miles, it might be half that in the East. Abundance of prey is a standard in figuring home ranges.

Wild and wooded country full of white-tailed deer and other prey, precisely what the cougar needs to survive, is widely available in the eastern United States. Yet years of associating the cougar with the wilderness of the West leaves many to skeptically pre-judge the claim of the cougar in places such as New England. Surveys using informal questioning have shown that lack of habitat or wilderness is the primary reason that outdoor recreation enthusiasts give for denying the existence of cougars in the East. Setting aside all other aspects of the debate, a sound argument cannot be made to deny the cougar a chance in the East based on whether there is enough habitat.

Arguments can be made about whether the eastern forests offer enough protection from human persecution and conflict. While the Black Hills cougar population in South Dakota represents proof that the cougars tolerate higher road densities than those found in much of the eastern public lands, it has not offered them total protection from human conflict. It is safe to say then that if cougars were surviving in a similar habitat such as the Black Hills in the East, we would probably know about them. For some time, from roughly 2001 to 2005, the region experienced one road kill a year.[37] Brocke's findings in the Adirondacks support this, but contradict the Davis findings on the suitability of the Allegheny National Forest region. Brocke compares unique habitats, Florida and the West vs. the East, with convincing mathematics. The Adirondacks has been considered a release site for reintroducing wolves; but many wolf studies support Brocke's worries, and although it is enticing, the Adirondacks may not be the wildest site in the Northeast. Instead, central Appalachia and parts of Maine seem to offer excellent habitat as well as buffer habitat connectivity.

Cougars do not need wilderness to exist. In fact, true wilderness, a place completely unaltered by humans, is virtually non-existent in the lower forty-eight states. Cougars do need access to large blocks of land and established populations to supply recruitments or replacements from natural or unnatural deaths. Cougars could survive in the East because there is enough habitat to establish and sustain small populations. Though widely accepted, lack of habitat in the East is not a reason to argue for their nonexistence or deny their future. Given favorable political and social habitat, a few released pairs could survive in the right forest and eventually repopulate less wild regions.

PART FOUR:

THE FUTURE

CHAPTER THIRTEEN

RESTORATION:
BRINGING BACK THE COUGAR

Speculation on whether cougars exist has dominated the thoughts of citizens, sportsmen and women, nature enthusiasts, and others, for the better part of the past century. But the ultimate question is not about what has happened to the cougar. The important question is -- do we want to return the animal to its former haunts in order to take advantage of the available ecological niche? For while the debates, controversies, and accusations continue to cloud the issue of whether the elusive big cat has survived, the rich verdant hills of the Northeast continue to produce tremendous deer herds without the presence of a significant predator. Since most biologists agree that there is enough habitat available for the cougar, we can begin to wonder where an animal of this size and power might be appropriately repatriated. If the public truly wants cougars, will they accept the potentially dangerous predator in their own neighborhoods? Should we actively support the return of the cougar to the East?

Restoring an animal to its former range is never an easy task; the amount of necessary planning and painstaking dedication often goes unappreciated. Tragically, nearly every wild thing in the eastern United States had been reduced to scarcity or extirpation prior to 1900. Deer, bear, fisher, wolf, and beaver had all been decimated. If not for the deliberate translocation of some of these species from remnant population clusters, we would not have witnessed their eventual comeback. The daunting task of returning the cougar back to the eastern forests would pose an even greater challenge.

The first step would be to determine which areas are suitable for cougar repatriation.[1] Most wildlife experts agree that there are several places from which to choose.[2] Secondly, an evaluation of public attitudes regarding cougars is necessary. Few restoration efforts ever succeed without strong public support. A public opinion survey is most useful if it establishes a baseline of attitudes toward cougars prior to any efforts at public education. Once a suitable habitat is found within a region where there is an interest and acceptance of the cougar, then the educational, sociological, economic, and other components of the restoration could be addressed.

Today, wolves have returned to Yellowstone and the elk to Kentucky. Fisher scout the New England hills again, and bald eagles soar over more lakes and rivers each year. These revitalized species have been largely successful, free from persecution and in some cases from the threat of habitat loss. Restored wildlife are a part of our world because people wanted certain species. The huge number of people claiming to see cougars may reflect a conscientious desire to have them back; however, these ideas may fade when confronted with the reality of a large carnivore. A firm rationale is required to defend the act of inviting cougars back home into eastern woodlands. Now that so many species have returned and are doing well, the need for one more might not inspire as much enthusiasm.[3]

There are, however, several benefits to having the cougar back in the East. To many people, the most obvious benefit is the reduction of the over-abundant white-tailed deer. Deer have become so numerous in the East that a close inspection of almost any highway shoulder is almost certain to reveal a mangled mess of vehicle-killed venison. Browse lines along most hiking trails also reveal signs of high deer densities. Once nearly absent from the East, the white-tailed deer has rebounded to historic numbers. For example, in Kentucky, some deer held out during European settlement in the Jones-Keeney Refuge in Cadwell County and the old Woodlands Refuge, where deer increased from a remnant 1,000 animals in 1920 to today's herd of 690,000 statewide.[4] But when the deer returned, they came back to a different ecosystem - one without the wolf or the cougar. With the abandonment of agricultural land and the consequent availability of endless acres of browse, their numbers have grown to plague-like proportions.

The return of the cougar would once again put tension on these herbivores and activate the age-old forces of evolution. If the wolf and the cougar were both re-established, even more significant changes would be realized in those regions, as the enormously abundant white-tailed deer would decrease to an optimum population . Songbirds would return to greater number and vigor, as forest understory plants would be allowed to grow and provide nesting cover. There would be better water absorption from the increase of shrubs and other ground cover, an increase in small herbaceous mammals, and a decrease in automobile-deer collisions. There might be health benefits as well; Lyme Disease is dispersed by deer via the deer tick and is one of the fastest spreading vector-born diseases in the country.[5] Large predators such as cougar are also effective at reducing the number of so-called mesocarnivores or mid-sized predators such as raccoons, foxes, and feral cats. These smaller carnivores are often implicated in the spread of diseases that can affect domestic pets and man, including rabies. Thus, there are plenty of reasons to have the cougar back. It would therefore seem an easy sell to return predators and reduce the deer.

Unfortunately deer problems are old issues, and resident eastern cougars would be new -- human nature is such that we prefer to tolerate old yet familiar problems, rather than embrace new solutions. The talk of releasing pumas will cause immediate safety concerns, fears of depredations, and misconceptions regarding lions and their threat to deer hunting.[6] Many experts do not think the cougar restoration movement will make it past the issues of fear and liability.[7] Fear of cougars is widespread in the wake of human fatalities reported by the sensation-promoting media.[8]

One segment of the population likely to see through the sensationalization of cougar attacks by the media are consumptive users of wildlife, or hunters. Contrary to popular belief, the existence of wild turkey and countless other wildlife is directly due to efforts and contributions from hunters. This was especially true prior to the 1960s and the active environmental advocacy of today. Hunters support the conservation of wildlife, and in survey after survey, they demonstrate more knowledge of predators than any other population segment.

Cougar-caused human fatality is exceptionally rare, and hunters know this.[9]

Polls conducted in the West indicated that hunters and trappers expressed encouragement and gave support for the wolf and the puma. The general public failed to demonstrate the same degree of understanding toward these predators and their role in state forests and parks. Public opinion about predators and cougar restoration in the Northeast is unknown. Finding out what the attitudes are toward large carnivores is essential before embarking on the restoration process.[10]

As mentioned, the careful construction of a short survey is critical. To be more specific, a cross sample of citizens and their feelings about wildlife, cougars, and restoration is needed from a statistically analyzed, unbiased survey. It would have to be carefully crafted to get the right kind of information. For example, should the sample come from the general public, hunters, or rural residents? Additional surveys can follow up after a good understanding of attitudes, fears, concerns, and desires has been firmly established. Follow-up surveys will determine the best release site, as that is not based solely on habitat. The greatest obstacles in the successful return of cougars are human persecution, fear, and cougar-human conflict.[11]

In Kentucky, the majority of surveyed citizens were in favor of restoring the elk to their state. Public opinion surveys were extremely important in Kentucky because of its livestock and agricultural economy. Concerns ranged from trampling and consumption of row crops to the spread of disease from wild elk to domestic stocks. Meetings were held with stakeholders, and the concerns regarding agriculture were addressed. From the meetings it was decided that the first set of animals released would be radio-collared in order to appease the Kentucky Cattlemen's Association, and that they would not be released near any row crop areas, only in remote non-agricultural zones. Eventually, after many meetings, surveys were completed and surprisingly 90% of respondents favored the restoration.[12]

In Virginia, similar surveys were also conducted, and the response showed a majority of the people were in favor of bringing back the elk there, too. But other interesting attitudes were brought to light, namely that when respondents had an informed level of understanding about the elk restoration issue, they were in favor of the project, while those not confident in their knowledge of the animal and its restoration were against it. People that were undecided could be easily persuaded into voting against restoration, and were among those with a limited understanding of the species and the natural world.[13]The restoration of large carnivores requires additional public education because it is always controversial. In actuality, the herbivores such as deer can create a great deal of damage, and because of their population potentials unchecked by predators, herbivores can bring about a greater change to the character of an area than carnivores.[14]

In North Florida there has been hot debate over Florida panthers. The Florida Advisory Council of Environmental Education gained insight on public attitudes and knowledge regarding panthers and their reintroduction through some intense survey questioning.[15] Since Florida already has panthers within its southern counties, respondents had some knowledge and acceptance of living with panthers. The majority (83%) were supportive of the species return to northern Florida. Only 7% objected to the attempt of returning the large predator, and an optimistic 6% strongly supported the endeavor. Furthermore, an estimated 91% strongly favored the continued efforts to save the endangered Florida panther.[16]

But in 1993, after an experimental release of eighteen cats, there was a strong opposition from a growing minority. According to local newspapers, panthers frightened several suburban residents who sighted them near their homes. Many others claimed that panthers had killed pets and livestock. According to biologists, the complaints were exaggerated, but they expanded into concerns over human safety. As expected, there were concerns about livestock predation -- but the surveys did not predict the extreme fears.[17]

One Lake City resident was under the impression that cougars regularly feed on cattle, but had the public been properly prepared and educated, they would have known that cases of cattle kills by panthers in south Florida are so exceedingly rare as to be almost nonexistent. There were even concerns from hunters, who usually have a good grasp of wildlife issues. Had the assimilation process of panther education and appreciation taken place, these fears might have been lessened.[18]

Misunderstanding and ignorance is plentiful when it comes to wildlife. Lately, the hunter and the trapper are under attack by non-consumptive special interest groups. The public's unattractive view of the hunter exists in part because one or two individuals with guns can demonstrate irresponsible behavior. It is those few out of the many that can destroy an entire recovery program and damage the image of sportsmen and women, who generally support the restoration of wildlife.

To this end, wildlife managers must reach out and enlighten the potential offenders beforehand. Hunters and trappers will need to be involved, because they are out there in the creature's habitat, and one frightened individual acting in ignorance can take down a cougar and dismantle an entire recovery program. Thus, involvement rather than isolation of the hunting population will prove paramount to any recovery program.[19]

This kind of approach was successfully employed in the Adirondacks, where a small lynx population was released. This policy of involvement worked nicely in New York, and won over the support of previously ill-informed hunters and trappers who had unfounded concerns over the repopulating of lynx in the Adirondacks. Mathew Black, a wildlife student from Yale University, noted the success of the lynx program's policy of involvement in the following statement:

> The potential of a cooperative approach has been demonstrated in the Adirondacks, where a statewide trappers organization, which at first opposed the lynx reintroduction for fear of restrictions on their activities, eventually came to support it enthusiastically. Wildlife personnel supervising the reintroduction invited trappers to express their concerns during open meetings, and created an educational program which outlined identification characteristics of lynx and protocols for release of any that might be accidentally captured. The trappers were persuaded to donate funds and adopt the lynx as their symbol, despite a clear statement that lynx would not become available for trapping in the future.[20]

Similarly, hunters would have to be convinced that cougars would not deplete the deer herds. Because cougars can impact deer, the entire cougar ecology will inevitably present itself. Proponents will use the cougar's killing of deer as a beneficial outcome of restoration, but in doing so they will cause hunters concern that cougars will negatively impact their sport. Open meetings addressing this concern will prove to be most important. An honest, direct approach that conveys the statistics will be most effective. The truth is, with the exception of a mother with kittens, individual cougars do not take that many deer, and the number of cougars likely to exist even after years of success in the restoration will not pose a threat to deer hunting.[21] Besides, cougars often prey on sick deer and therefore act as agents of natural selection. They are drivers of evolution and modifiers of behavior much more than population controllers. What hunters ought to be more concerned with are the behavioral changes that deer will experience in places where the cougars inhabit. Cougars force deer to be alert, to expend more energy on being vigilant, and to shift their use of habitat. They create an ecology of fear, so to speak. In these places it is likely that deer will become more wary and therefore a more difficult quarry. Some hunters may welcome the greater challenge for their stalking skills, but others may not.

It is also possible that deer would evolve from their current trend of unwariness and become elusive toward all possible threats. This in itself may reduce the number of roadkills and deer damage complaints. Presently, white-tailed deer are found virtually everywhere, even in highly developed states such as Connecticut and Rhode Island. Many of these deer show little fear of humans, and they are often small. It is possible that the presence of the cougar could correct this and increase the value of the deer as a game species.

The acceptance of wolf restoration by hunters is a strong indication that cougars could likewise find acceptance. The importance of education cannot be over-emphasized, as it had a strong hand in guiding the introduction of wolves into Yellowstone. Protests were anything but mild, and they extended from the Yellowstone region clear across the country. Equally strong were voices praising the idea of returning wolves to Yellowstone. During a time when wolf education has been made widely available, there were still ancient misconceptions, as documented by Senator Conrad Burns of Montana, who confidently stated, "There will be a dead child within a year if wolves are taken to Yellowstone." It is interesting to note that in over one hundred years, there has been only four documented cases of a non-rabid wolf killing a human being.[22]

Speculations are incomplete as to whether panther restoration could raise such strong opposition, but should concerns escalate, the ignorance would surely be much more profound. Matthew Black has studied the eastern cougar situation and found that alternative methods of education are needed in order to elicit positive attitudes about cougars. Black states that "understanding and educating the human population is indispensable to any successful predator recovery effort. Education attempting to foster attitudes towards predators by increasing the public's factual knowledge about them proved ineffective, often reinforcing negative attitudes among those who already harbor them."[23] In other words, an approach targeting the negative beliefs held about cougars is likely to fail. While this approach has been successful for other wildlife, each species is different. Black suggests a more cognitive and practical approach for cougars. He recommends this over an attitudinal or valuation focus. This is critical, because people are likely to accept information that supports things they already believe, and further enlightenment can only go so far in raising awareness. It will be better to not try and change peoples minds about certain things regarding predators -- but rather to focus on the positives or validate feelings. Instead, look for opportunity, build upon the present response to cougar sightings that often focus on giving kind explanations for misidentification and thereby tactfully correcting witnesses, because the opinions of and relations with state biologists are as important, if not more so, than the attitude people hold toward the cougar.

Black concludes that the ambiguity over the species' presence in the wild affects attitudes toward wildlife officials and that relations with these officials affect the way people view wildlife. In this case, it would directly affect attitudes about their panther release efforts. The general feeling would be that, if the authorities are unwilling to accept the public's cougar sightings, then how good can their word be about the cougar restoration project? Likewise, if the only contact that hunters and anglers have with wildlife officials occurs during a citation, then how positive will their attitudes be towards these officials? Wildlife agencies need to reach out and allow for more public assistance and exposure. "Local resistance to predator recovery often has its roots in mistrust of agencies charged with managing the recovery, rather than in the dislike of the animal itself," says Black.[24] One interesting point about acknowledging the cougar's current presence is that policy makers are then able to ease tensions over releasing more cougars on the basis that the existing animals, such as in Florida, have rarely caused trouble. A strong argument must be prepared beforehand to justify additional animals. For example, the release of additional animals would safeguard the population.

The most important task of any predator release education project is the elimination of fear. North Florida is an excellent example of how fear based on misunderstandings can escalate. The truth is that an attack from an eastern cougar on a human is extremely unlikely. Cougars have been responsible for less than twenty five deaths during the 20th century, while serious dog bites exceed 800,000 annually.[25] Some dog bites are fatal, and others seriously injure the unsuspecting victim. Nevertheless, the issue of fear is significant, and statistics such as those comparing cougar attacks to dog bites and dog killings must be addressed. Of course, the public will still have to be warned of an unlikely attack and informed as to what should be done in an encounter with a cougar.[26]

The success or failure of Florida panthers in north Florida and southern Georgia will have a direct impact on efforts to restore predators in the Central Appalachians and the Northeast. One way to prepare is focusing on the positive findings about Florida panthers. As in the case of returning elk to Kentucky and Virginia, there will likewise be concerns about economic loss regarding cougars. While cougars are not going to raid orchards or row crops, they may prey on livestock. The near absence of cattle kills and other livestock kills in Florida may help settle fears further north. Cougars are known to occasionally take domestic animals; these are usually smaller stock such as goats, sheep, and even pets.[27] Most of this depredation has occurred in the West where cougar populations are high, and livestock are not fenced in. Furthermore, depredations by any predator pale in comparison to livestock lost to lightening, disease or poor husbandry.

Other economic considerations include the cost of reintroduction in relation to the benefits yielded from having cougars back in the eastern forests. When considering any release program, a cost-benefit analysis study is usually set up to determine the worth of the project.[28] If the economic and intrinsic values surpass the expense of the re-introduction, the project is deemed valid. Two of the best examples of translocated wildlife are the repopulating of the beaver and the wild turkey. Both were once extirpated from many eastern states, but are now thriving and expanding into every available habitat. Both species were trapped, transported, and released to start new core populations.[29]

The species that returned the most in benefits was the turkey. The return of the turkey restored some of the finest sport hunting that the Northeast has to offer.[30] It also generated much interest from birders and hikers. Bringing beaver back has improved water conservation and increased wetland productivity for waterfowl. Beaver are now plentiful enough to be trapped and could generate some extra revenue for die-hard trappers protective of their way of life, but the return they offer is of an intrinsic value.[31] In contrast, the wild turkey generates billions of dollars in hunting sales each decade. This kind of benefit is the easiest to quantify and therefore justify for implementation. The consumptive value usually offers a species a better chance at finding a re-introduction program. Similarly, anything that has been assigned a market value is better protected.[32] The air we breathe does not have a market value and has not been well-protected in the past. This concept is great defense for consumptive uses of resources such as hunting.

A re-introduction of cougars would have both consumptive and intrinsic value. Initially, the intrinsic value is all we could appreciate, as the cats would be too rare to allow sport hunting.[33] Intrinsic value is generated by the animal's existence, and it is commonly referred to as the existence value that people derive just by knowing the animal lives wild and free.[34] Nature enthusiasts would certainly gravitate toward those publicly announced release sights in hopes of spotting a cougar, but until populations grew and recolonized wild regions of the East, there wouldn't be much chance of purposefully locating and enjoying cougars for film or photo. Sightings of the elusive cats would be largely by chance for many years, if not indefinitely.

Studies of ecotourism for cougars do not show any measurable interest. The shy and cryptic nature of the animal prevents this from developing the way it does for species like bald eagles, which draw large crowds at reservoirs where they often flock during winter. The moose is another popular species, bringing in thousands of visitors to places like Moosehead Lake in Maine and Moose Alley on Route 3 in New Hampshire.[35] Unlike the cougar, the moose is highly visible and very much unafraid of humans. They are perhaps the most photogenic of all the northwoods creatures. Conversely, people may give false hope that cougars can be seen in hopes to entice ecotourists to their establishments. Matt Black concludes that the great majority who aren't lucky enough to spot an eastern cougar should be left "never knowing what they are missing."[36]

Still, the countless number of cougar followers who are interested in the mystery that has surrounded the animal for decades will discover their whereabouts and will popularize these regions. This has occurred at the Quabbin Reservoir in Massachusetts, which became a much more popular hiking place after cougars were reported there.[37] In the eyes of the public, such sighting locales can suddenly become viable wilderness habitat where any rare species can be seen and perhaps photographed. Following the reports of cougar sightings, the Quabbin instantly became an attractive place for nature and wildlife enthusiasts in Massachusetts, and many more sightings followed. The 81,000-acre forest gained respect. Attendants at the volunteer-run visitor center rate questions about wildlife reasonably high, even thirty years after the first widely publicized cougar sighting. Is it coincidental that the organization Friends of the Quabbin Reservoir was created after the reservoir gained its wild image -- in part as a result of the sightings?

Clearly the spin-off effects of a creature as wild as the cougar can do great things for a particular region's image. People actively pursuing wildlife to observe and enjoy will also derive significant satisfaction from knowing that a particular species does exist in a certain area, and they will be willing to pay for that enjoyment and chance sighting. The cougar can be sustained economically through the intrinsic value it offers. The question is does it generate benefits beyond the costs of reintroduction in far greater ways than other species of the same type of value, and would this make its reappearance economically attractive?[38]

To answer this, proponents will have to bolster economic justifications and shed light on the other reasons for reintroducing eastern cougars. Cougar recovery will have to be justified in part on the ecological and moral reasons - that it is proper to make redemption on a mistake and to bring the animal back after its persecution. The absence of a predator halts the evolution of its prey and hinders the health of the ecological balance. Its return is in good keeping with non-game natural heritage philosophies. These are sound reasons that have allowed for the success of so many restoration programs, but fiscal issues may be more difficult to overcome. The return of the cougar will be much more feasible and attractive if the methods of reintroduction are inexpensive. Some lessons have already been learned from the relocation efforts in north Florida, and that may help lower costs. The radio telemetry monitoring of collared cougars will be on the list of procedures driving up expenses.

The use of telemetry is often a part of wildlife reintroduction.
Photo by Jay Tischendorf

Biologists would have to give careful consideration to all methods of translocation, including capture, housing, transportation, and release. One valuable lesson learned in north Florida was that cougars taken from the wild and directly released were the ones who did the best in terms of survival.[39] Those who were translocated and held in captivity for short periods of time may have assimilated to humans and consequently gotten into human-related conflicts. A quick and coordinated joint effort must occur between the site of capture and the site of release. The

Kentucky elk restoration lost hundreds of animals while they were being trucked in from the West because of a snowstorm that immobilized traffic and left the herd trapped for hours.[40] Biologists do not want their animals becoming stressed during the transportation process because this can result in weakness and eventual death.

Each cougar would have to be checked over for good health and absence of disease. When wild turkeys were being restored to Massachusetts, biologists released semi-domesticated birds, which could not endure the harsh New England winters. Later, native wild turkeys were set free, and with the cooperation of Mother Nature and a series of mild winters the flocks survived. The purists may not like it, but after a species has been lost to a particular region, the genetic similarity of the replacement population is not always a perfect match. Vermont's restored population of peregrine falcons are actually originated from captive stock derived from the West.

The success of translocated panthers in Florida is going to have a great influence on restoration planning further north. Since it is a mandate within the Florida panther recovery program to establish populations outside of south Florida, pushing that agenda is likely to be the wisest way to prompt recovery in the central Appalachians and the Northeast. If those Florida panthers are successful, then reintroduction may follow northward. Focusing on this effort is wise because initial studies have shown that there is sufficient habitat for the panthers in north Florida and south Georgia, more than expected. This would suggest that released panthers ought to do well and clear the way for additional releases outside of Florida. David Maehr wrote in his, *The Florida Panther: A Flagship for Regional Restoration*: "Some of the cougars settled to the west of the release site in the Suwannee River basin - an area of abundant prey and cover. Several other individuals engaged in long-distance dispersal, including several that entered southeastern and south central Georgia - suggesting that additional habitat existed beyond the state line. Limited space was not a problem."[41]

Studies on wolf restoration have focused on the Adirondacks and have found that "the current ecological and social conditions in the Adirondack Park are probably unsuitable for timber wolves."[42] However, preliminary studies point to western Maine as a good wolf restoration site. This region may also be a good site for the cougar because, unlike the Adirondacks, it is contiguous to New Brunswick, northern New Hampshire and even the more remote portions of Vermont. It is estimated that northern New England could support as many as 1,500 wolves.[43]

Habitat and prey are available for the cougar in the East. The concern is what happens after the crate is opened and a flash of tawny fur races past the biologist on its way into the forests. Will they proliferate and create problems? Will people become afraid as they did in north Florida when the long-tailed felines happen to pass by, or will the public be exhilarated and invigorated, knowing that now what they are seeing is real?[44]

The likelihood of a cougar restoration commencing any time soon is remote. That first baseline attitude survey has yet to be completed, and more definitive assessments of suitable habitat sites are needed for formality. It is important to assure that local economies living with the cougars are not unfairly saddled with costs, and that they are able to reap the benefits in exchange for accommodating the predators.

The reasons for restoring the cougar are all strong and valid. Since the cougar is in many ways truly "the wildest of all," it stands to reason that it is also a creature whose preservation encompasses all others, including birds, bears, deer, and countless other rare and/or desirable species. The cougar is considered an umbrella species; its presence is an indication of the health of the forest and its wilderness values.[45] As Aldo Leopold once said, "A thing is right when it tends to preserve the integrity, stability, and beauty of the biotic community. It is wrong when it tends otherwise."[46] People have chosen conservation in recent times because creatures such as the formidable cougar enhance our world according to our present values.[47]

Nevertheless, with the fear of cougars perceived as high, it appears that a broad campaign would have to occur over a period of time. The concerns and speculations, as necessary as they are to express and consider, will generate more public anxiety than will the actual presence of the predator itself. The recolonization of the cougar and the possible presence of the wolf in Yellowstone went unnoticed, but when the public was told of such predators being released there was instant trouble. Yet they had been living with them all along.

CHAPTER FOURTEEN

BIOLOGY OF A PREDATOR

In an attempt to explain the lack of evidence for the cougar in the East, many have claimed that the cats in the East might behave differently because of the East's unique environment. Thus rendering knowledge of western tracking and spoor identification of limited use. There is no way of proving that cougars do not behave differently in the East, since their presence cannot be confirmed. However, there is very little difference observed in Florida panthers as compared to western pumas. Therefore, it is very unlikely that cougars north of Florida would exhibit any different behavior or biology. Scientists agree that the cougar's natural history is largely uniform across its North American range except for some variations in home ranges.

Because of this, the cougar's territory requirement is of great interest when speculating about their existence in the East. This requirement is variable throughout regions in the West, and is the most likely gross difference, if there were to be any, between eastern and western cougars. This is because of the high prey density and immense biomass found in the East. It was mentioned previously, but can be quickly elaborated on here.[1]

Territory or home range can be defined as the well-established area of land that a cougar routinely occupies. These are fixed areas that individual cats stay within as residents. The home range should not be confused with geographic range or the areas where the species occur. The home range consists of the cougar's favorite hunting sites, denning shelters, and water sources.[2] Scientists know that the sizes of these ranges reflect the richness of the land they occupy.

In a desert region, the cougar is more likely to establish a larger territory than in an area of greater precipitation. In general, a lush forest typically supports more cougar prey per square mile than an arid land. Since the East is humid and densely foliated with abundant water supplies and prey species, it can be assumed the cougar's average home range in a place such as the Northeast is considerably smaller than that of their western counterpart.

But what about the difference between male and female home ranges? The ranges of male cougars are set up so that they overlap the ranges of one or more females. In a small, marginally viable population, such as what is alleged to exist in the East, the male might have trouble locating or overlapping with a female. Therefore, in a compromised population the availability of females might influence the size of a male's home range, even if the male's range has a high prey density. It is thus possible that the male cougar's home ranges in the East are larger than western cougar's ranges. This is all speculation, but it could explain the eastern cougar's lack of detection. It is worth guessing that male cougars roam about basically as transients, and females remain in inaccessible, heavily concealed, unusually small home ranges, that are full of prey and other necessities.

Putting all speculations aside, the average home range for a western male cougar is from 25 to 500 square miles. A female can range from 8 to 400 square miles.[3] One thing scientists know for sure about ranges is that this aspect of a cougar's natural history is widely variable. Whether the home range is large or small, the task of locating a female is always easier when a male has an established home range.[4] Transients must travel in an undefined and vast area while also continuously seeking prey in an unfamiliar setting. If a transient is able to meet its basic survival needs while on the move, he will continue to search the landscape indefinitely for a female to mate with.

Biologists may never know when the cougars in the East mated, gave birth, and raised their young; but this aspect of their lifecycle seems much less likely to have been any different from other cougar populations across North America. Studies have failed to show that cougars choose any particular time of year for mating Yet it seems logical that mating may occur more frequently at specific times for certain populations in well-defined geographic areas. During a recent study, Florida panthers were not found to mate at any given specific time during the year, and the same findings seem to hold true for other populations in the warmer climates. Cougars in the northern United States often give birth anytime from early spring until the end of summer.[5]

Cougars have notable mating habits, as they are known to copulate up to seventy times in twenty-four hours and continue to do so for eight days. The female goes into heat quickly and may stay receptive for nine days.[6] They often remain together for a few days after mating.[7] It is amazing how these solitary, wide-ranging animals, can find each other to complete the act. Scientists believe that the cougar uses its keen sense of smell to locate a mate. Although the scream of the cat is thought to be a way that males and females find one another, the scientific evidence is not conclusive.[8] Somehow the cats do come together at the right time, perhaps using some vocalization, scent, and extensive travel combined.

Cougars leave their mothers after the first year.

About ninety-six days after mating, the female retires to a heavily covered and sheltered site, where she gives birth to one to four kittens.[9]

The young can be called cubs or kittens. Kitten is preferred over cub whenever larger cats are mentioned because the term cub may be associated with the roaring-cats, such as lions and tigers. The mother only has six functional nipples out of eight. The young compete for the nipples of their choice. After two weeks the kittens open their eyes, but it takes more time before the kittens are independent. In seven to eight weeks the mother is able to leave them for up to thirty-six hours while they are occupied at a kill site. Naturalists are able to identify the presence of kittens at a kill site by the disruption of vegetation. The matted down area of vegetation will often spread out to fifty feet. This is because the site is a favorite play area.[10]

The den site is often moved several times before they abandon the use of a regular den altogether. Eventually after about twelve to eighteen months the disbanding process begins, and the mother deliberately pushes her young aside, discouraging them from their strong attachment to her.[11] Sometimes when they fail to heed her requests, and she is entering the heat, curious males responding to the mother will often kill the defenseless kittens. Ordinarily, the female will give birth every two to three years. The kittens retain their spots and leg stripes for about six months, but sometimes longer. The legs and flanks are the last area to lose stripe marks.[12] Anyone familiar with the cougar cannot mistake the kittens for the domesticated cat, as the kittens are distinctly wild and stockier in appearance.

The cougar is the largest of the purring cats. In North America it is the largest of the wild felines, with only one exception -- that being the jaguar of Central America, which is occasionally found north of the Mexican border.[13] The cougar is far more slender and of smaller bone than the robust jaguar.[14]

Mountain lions are usually a tawny light brown color. The mustache or black face markings are distinct across its geographic range. However, the overall coloration of the cougar can change slightly from region to region. Those in the more northern regions are sometimes a dull gray. While underbelly is creamy white, the cat's coloration is uniform on the upper sides and back. A cougar's tail can sometimes measure the same length as its body; the tail is topped off with a touch of black or burnt sienna. At the shoulder these cats are typically two feet tall and a female will measure about six feet on average from nose to tip of the tail.[15] The male is larger and heavier, averaging about seven feet long, with extreme cases measuring nine feet. In The Puma: Mysterious American Cat, authors Goldman and Young provide a wonderful photograph taken of a male cougar in Colorado that weighed in excess of 217 pounds. It was nine feet long and had a paw radius of six inches.[16] The average full-grown adult male weighs 100 to 170 pounds, while the female weighs from 80 to 110 pounds.[17]

Most everyone has had the eerie experience of hearing the blood curdling screams of domesticated cats late at night. The human-like quality to this caterwauling can best be described as a shrill screech. Magnify this spine-chilling experience ten times, and you can imagine the terror experienced by witnesses who have heard the cougar.

The most common analogy of the puma's vocalization is that of an adult woman screaming in terror for her life. Tischendorf described the most common report people give of a cougar vocalization is one sounding like a woman shrieking in extreme distress. Imagine the fear such a call might inflict upon a lone traveler deep in the forest. Surprisingly, Tischendorf does not believe this reported call is really the most common vocalization. Tischendorf explains, "the cougar has been associated with this scream for so long, but it is rarely ever heard."[18] Undoubtedly, it is such an experience, or the exaggeration of one, that has added to the mystery and legend of this elusive species. Downing observed that fox calls were often misidentified as cougar cries, while Maehr noted that he never heard any such vocalization in all his years of study within south Florida's panther habitat.[19]

In The Puma: Mysterious American Cat, co-author Young details the notes of Maynard, an earlier American naturalist who experienced another form of the Florida panther's vocalization: "It is very inquisitive when its dominions are invaded during the day, and will often follow the intruder for some distance, uttering a low moaning cry, but is always careful to keep concealed."[20]

Other sounds made by the cougar have been described as low soft grunts, coughs, loud meowing, and even bird-like whistles. Occasionally, the cougar is known to produce loud calls, especially during the time when the female is coming into heat. In fact, many naturalists have observed that most vocalizations are probably related to mating.[21] Certainly some of these screams may be produced during confrontations between males over their respective ranges. However, this would account for a very low number of their cries, because the dynamics of their ranges tend to limit such violent and deadly confrontations.

In many accounts, the call of the puma is recorded as indistinct and unusual. Wendell Taber of Somerset County in Maine described the sounds an eastern cougar made one night in the mid 1800s, where tracks were found the next morning:

> I listened for quite some time in the middle of the night to what seemed to me an almost melodious series of loud continuous calls covering quite a range in pitch. Being acquainted with most sounds of the Maine forest nightlife, I was puzzled. I tried to associate the sound with some member of the cat family, but there seemed to be no association I could distinguish. The following morning I found in the mud, perhaps 200 yards distant, one foot print of a large mammal, a footprint as large or larger than that of a moose. This print matched perfectly the drawing Ralph S. Palmer supplied in his Mammal Guide for the mountain lion or panther.[22]

Young describes the experience of a Florida panther's call as "unearthly":

> "At times the cougar utters a peculiar shriek; and I once heard this in the dead of night, when encamped on the St. John's River in Florida. The animal seemed to be directly over my tent; and the unearthly yell made my flesh creep, and brought me out to the fire, that was burning brightly before the tent."[23]

Theodore Roosevelt, well known for his love of the outdoors, said that "certainly, no man could well listen to a stranger and more wild sound."[24] Another outdoorsman, Mead (1899), described the cry of the eastern cougar and swore that the "unearthly scream of a panther close at hand will almost freeze the blood in one's veins, and for an instant paralyze any form of man or beast."[25]

While the purpose of the cougar's scream is the subject of continued debate, it has been recently determined that the so called "whistle" of a cougar acts to bring cubs back to the mother.[26] Also, captive cougars have been known to "whistle" when greeting their caretakers. According to Maehr, an experienced biologist who has worked intensively on Florida panther programs and research, the most common vocalization of the cat is a bird-like chirp.[27] Even so, there are still many unanswered questions regarding the range of calls emitted by the cat. The animal's secretive nature continues to foil the attempts of even the most patient and persistent of naturalists.

The consensus among biologists is that the animal is capable of a wide variety of vocalizations, but that it prefers to remain silent. Other sounds of the forest are often confused with that of the cougar, and at times, the reverse is true. This is just one more factor contributing to the difficulty in locating the cat. In the daily life of the cougar, the use of screams, purrs, and other vocalizations is extremely rare. On any given night in the forest, a variety of wild sounds can be heard, but determining which ones are that of the cougar and which are not, is a tough proposition.

As for its choice of prey, the cougar eats deer because deer usually provide the best return for unit of energy expended. The cougar's anatomy is a perfect design for killing deer. Although the puma will take an occasional bird or squirrel, it is the deer that sustains it. Apparently, other prey species require more effort to hunt and must be caught more often. The average adult cougar will take one deer every seven to fourteen days. This period shortens to once every three days for females who are nursing or providing food for growing kittens.[28]

The cougar's anatomy is a perfect design for killing deer.
Photo by Jay Tischendorf

After a cougar has consumed a deer, it lays low in a secluded site where it is free to recline and rest. Cougars remain hidden in the site for a day or two, digesting and gaining strength, before setting out on the next hunt.[29] The cougar is known for covering its prey after it has consumed all that it can.[30] Surprisingly, the cougar sometimes leaves a deer half-eaten and moves on in search of another. This occurs when the meat becomes spoiled or putrid; cougars rarely respond to carrion or bait in the easy way that canines do.[31] They strongly prefer fresh meat and are extremely fond of organs rich in blood. As nothing is wasted in nature, coyotes and foxes will eventually take advantage of the easy meal left behind, but most of the time the lion returns to its cache and will do so repeatedly until every last bit of meat has been consumed. The deer and the cougar are interlocked in an ongoing predator-prey relationship.[32] In fact, many habits of the white-tailed deer have evolved in order to survive specifically against cougar attacks. The excessively high deer populations seen today throughout the East are evidence of the missing half of this relationship, and of the important ecological and evolutionary work that cougars and other large carnivores perform.

The average adult cougar will take one deer every seven to fourteen days.

The alternative prey of the cougar consists of a wide variety of birds and mid-sized mammals. The habitat that the cougar uses as its range obviously determines the alternative species available for food. In certain areas where there is agricultural activity, domesticated cattle can be added to the list, but damage to livestock is minimal under normal conditions.[33]

Wild turkey, ruffed grouse, snowshoe hare, mice, beaver, wild pig, and porcupine complete the list of secondary food items for the cougar. There are documented cases of cougar enduring on these meager prey items, and history records cougar that have suffered ill fate due to the ingestion of porcupine quills.[34] The porcupine, slow in its defense, is rendered helpless when flipped on its back, exposing its soft underbelly that is free of quills. In their ravenous hunger, wolves, coyotes, and cougar alike sometimes stab themselves and end up with a mouthful of quills. If the quills don't work free they can interfere with swallowing; and eventually, after weeks of aggravation and an inability to eat, kill the predator.

Documentation of cougar surviving on these secondary prey items suggests that the eastern cougar could survive through a period of low deer populations. Those who deny the species' existence believe such a period of low deer numbers can account for the animal's extirpation, but it is apparent that cougar can survive to some extent on non-deer prey. Kevin Hansen states in his book <u>Cougar</u> that the Colombian ground squirrel frequently becomes a main course item in Idaho.[35] He also displays a chart conveying the percentage of prey items. This chart clearly proves the puma's willingness to take alternative prey. A high percent of the Peruvian puma's diet consists of rodents. Hansen's book, states that, "when the abundance of their primary prey declines, cougars have been known to switch their diet."[36] Some researchers, however, stress that breeding females could probably not make it without deer to feed their young with, because of the energy factor and inefficiency of utilizing other food. Interestingly, these alternative prey species are hunted in the same manner that deer are taken.

The cougar hunts in solitude and captures its prey by using ambushing and stalking techniques. It will use its keen sense of smell to locate a likely wildlife travel corridor or an established deer trail. Next, it seeks a site in concealment where it may have enough open space to visually locate its prey, stalk it, chase it down and then leap upon it. At other times, it may lay hidden completely out of sight, and from this strategically selected site it pounces on its prey, catching it completely by surprise. This method is used less often than the stalking technique, but juveniles may find the ambush method more efficient.[37]

Once the prey is secured, the cougar delivers a swift and powerful bite to the neck. Usually, the neck is broken, but ultimately the predator kills its prey quickly. Deer can often give a significant fight, and cougar have been known to receive great injury from flailing hooves and driving antlers. Moose pose an even greater threat to the cougar, though several eyewitness accounts have described the strength of the cougar in such encounters as incredible. The predators have been seen carrying deer up steep cliffs, and even dragging moose, a rare event. Cougar can run fast for short distances and have been known to take the pronghorn antelope. The cougar is one of nature's finest hunters because of its strength, stealth, and accuracy.[38]

There are documented cases of a cougar attacking or killing a human. Such attacks are exceedingly rare, especially considering the number of people and the time they spend living or recreating in cougar habitat. Pumas that attack and kill humans are hunted and destroyed to prevent reoccurrence. This response also gives the public peace of mind and allows for game officials to target one abnormal cougar instead of the entire species. Regardless of these precautions, humans who travel into known cougar territory are advised to be wary.

As noted, a cougar attack on a human is an extremely rare event. Nevertheless, there are a few pointers that will help abort the unwelcome advances of a bold cougar. First, don't travel alone in cougar country. Keep in mind that movement such as jogging or bicycling, or the crying voice of a child may attract a curious or hungry cat. In the rare event a cougar is encountered, it is best to talk softly and to maintain eye contact. Try to keep a few trees or bushes between you and the cat. Do not make sudden movements or crouch down. Always resist running away in panic, as this may trigger the predatory response in the animal and initiate a chase.[39] Because cougar are fond of following humans and are inquisitive by nature, never assume that a cougar that has seen you is going to attack if it seems unafraid. They are prone to staring before fleeing, but they are usually afraid of humans and will avoid any further contact with you. Theodore Roosevelt once said it best: "It would be no more dangerous to sleep in woods with mountain lions than if there were ordinary housecats."[40] While it gets the point across, this is obviously an overstatement.

The cougar has many interesting and peculiar habits besides its fondness of following humans. Its swimming ability and extreme patience are just a few notable traits. It is these habits that lure those of us who love the wild into cougar habitat. Each of us hopes to observe one of these known traits, and there is always the chance of learning something new about this mysterious predator. It is the dream of every hunter and naturalist to sight a wild creature as elusive as the cougar and to remain undetected long enough to witness some unusual behavior. Ironically, it is usually the cougar that is watching us.

Generally, we can summarize the knowledge gained about cougar's habits and biology by saying that they are shy, reclusive creatures that usually depend on deer for food. Experienced cougars stalk, leap, bound, and tackle prey with crushing bites and well developed claws. They travel a great distance over enormous home ranges and usually leave nothing but tracks as proof of their whereabouts. Normally silent but capable of a variety of vocalizations, they come together only to mate; the cougar that begins life with its siblings playing and chasing each other, grows up to lead one of the most solitary lives of any mammal.[41] *Puma concolor* is a perfect deer killing design, a capable and agile hunter, and its vast presence from the Canadian north to the far southern reaches in Pantagonia have given it a significant place in American cultures. It is proof of the evolutionary success that allows this cat to continue to carry its genes on into the future. It is this same adaptability that may allow for the cougar's successful reintroduction to the East.

CHAPTER FIFTEEN

RECOMMENDING A FUTURE

There is no reason to think that the controversy of whether cougars exist or not will ever be solved without trying a few things that have never been tested. People will continue to have sightings of cougars, and journalists will continue to report them. The cycle will continue, and the tiny bits of evidence picked up over the decades will keep the wheel rolling and thus the cycle going. In this book several searches have been mentioned but none have really advanced each other. Aside from Van Dyke's and Brocke's studies, there have been no advances in our knowledge of how to look for cougars in the East. Yet everything about the East makes finding cougars difficult. The lack of tracking surfaces, the lack of any prior knowledge on where to look, and the short life span of existing tracks in southern Appalachian winter snows -- all make detection difficult.

Some new tools, however, have been introduced into the scene. The use of remote cameras and scent posts equipped with hair snares and video equipment has given the searcher a great advantage over previous investigators. The ability to test DNA origins and their specifics has also prepared the way for some specific answers in the near future. All that is needed now, it seems, is a widespread, scientifically orchestrated, well-organized search. But the lack of any substantial evidence of a breeding population after several decades seems proof enough that the time has now come to think towards the future.

Nevertheless, die-hard believers will continue to call for cooperatively funded investigations. Probably an investigation utilizing volunteers specifically trained and linked together is best. Each volunteer representing an area in which they could respond to sightings upon short notice. The best way to train such persons is for them to study in areas currently known to have cougars and which resemble the habitat in the East. Such areas should be studied for frequency of sign and the change in that frequency according to terrain, season, life cycle of cougars present, and weather conditions. From that experience, certain expectations can be concluded and appropriate methods adopted. Since efficiency is important from a financial point of view, intensive searches will have to be chosen carefully. Locating historical clusters or places that have revealed sign/sightings over long periods of time may provide a link to cougar populations prior to human proliferation. Old growth forests, inaccessible mountains, or swampy areas void of constant human visitation may make good choices, but the cougars which have been seen or suspected in populated areas ought to be given consideration, too.

Since nothing can stop people from " seeing" cougars it is worthwhile to continue mentioning some methods to at least improve the integrity of reports and to help eliminate the ridiculous ones from wasting patient state biologist's time. In regards to active searching, there are a number of impractical methods that have never been employed and that may be useful in high suspect areas of limited space. Instead of placing cameras rigidly within quadrants and systematically covering space, cameras should be placed in funnels or passes. In other words, it would be worth monitoring places where cougars would have to travel or would probably choose to travel, such as well-concealed streambeds or miniature valleys, old logging roads with cover on both sides, and the tops of ridges. Cougars may avoid areas where human disturbance has occurred, so detour areas ought to be chosen. Detours could even be created, running through such disturbances as clear cuts. It is also important to remember that cougars may not be found exclusively in remote regions. In a place such as the Quabbin, it might be worthwhile for die-hard believers to organize an old-fashioned game drive, where evenly spaced volunteers hike toward each other in straight lines from several miles apart or in an enclosing circle. Another method might utilize a motor vehicle at night or dawn/dusk along paved roads at low speeds within suspected regions. A sighting could then be followed up immediately for physical proof.

Van Dyke's and Brocke's methods have never had a debut because the substrate for such tracking has not and may not be found. Dry dusty roads with light sand are rare in the East, and when they do exist, they last only briefly before the weather alters the conditions. Still, it would not be impossible to gain the cooperation of local towns and have such conditions created or "raked over" for considerable distances. It may be true, as Robert Downing reported in his search, that snowfalls in the warm central Appalachians offered little for tracking; however, snow is not a bad medium in the colder Northeast.

One thing that is really lacking and might account for the difficulty in locating cougars, if they exist, has already been mentioned, but could be remedied by active recruiting. The East and its many cougar searches have typically involved people with limited or no experience in cougar tracking. If an expert could be borrowed and sent into a high activity area, results might be quickly accomplished. Jim Halfpenny and others like him need to be invited for several days worth of tracking and looking for mounds or scratch hills and deer kills.

Cougar hounds have been used, as they were for Downing's investigative work, but seldom have they been set to run an active track set. It would not cost too much to have an experienced cougar hunter travel to the East and run his/her dogs. A number of professional houndsmen - Jack Childs, Bob Wiesner, Chuck Anderson, Sr., and Scott Theilman, for instance, who have utilized their remarkable hounds and talents not only for sport hunting, but also research settings, could be available. And some puma researchers such as Kerry Murphy are accomplished houndsmen in their own right. It might be better to have trained dogs permanently available with a capable handler ready upon short notice to respond to a sighting.

When a cougar, is seen, or thought to have been seen, it obviously should be photographed and video-taped. Afterwards, the area should be filmed again with some size references put in place. This is a strong recommendation for any unusual wildlife sighting documented by photo or video. Sightings alone do not hold up as evidence, and photos are basically useless without size references. State wildlife biologists need to be reminded that when people call in a sighting, tracks or photographs will be much more useful to them when they are size referenced. This would eliminate much wasted effort and speculation over housecats.

Cardoza, of the Massachusetts Fish and Game Department, suggested that standards be established for the documentation of sightings and accompanying evidence. These standards would describe the proper methods for determining sizes in film and photo. The standards would also apply to the way in which witnesses were questioned and the information taken from them. Undoubtedly, a standard Sighting Report Form should be adopted all across the East.

Cardoza called for standard protocols in the securing, examining, and shipping of evidence. In his paper for the Wildlife Society Bulletin of 2002, he urged that a "signed chain of custody" be accepted and used each time evidence was sent to a laboratory. Red strip envelopes to ensure security and avoid tampering with, as well as other security containers used within many federal agencies, could be incorporated in the system.

Cardoza also thought that workshops would be useful, and he looked to The Northeast and Southeast Association of Fish and Wildlife Resource Agencies to consider holding periodic meetings. The success of the Eastern Cougar Conferences of 1994 and 2004 prove the point. From these meetings, strategies can be shared and new methods can be developed for learning or information-gathering about cougars in the East. The Eastern Cougar Network is an example of gaining reliable knowledge by providing "the big picture" and sharing information across borders.

Although media coverage is a likely source for the phenomena, it may be that more coverage is necessary. Except, now, the coverage needs to be responsible. If more people are aware of the issue, it becomes reported more often, and then becomes discussed as a controversy. Studies show that controversial issues, when allowed to be discussed, progress to more constructive dialogues. People are more likely to come forward if they feel it is acceptable to do so. It is also likely that some people are encountering cougars or their spoor and not recognizing the event for what it is. With more media coverage, this situation might improve. Unfortunately, the integrity of the articles on cougars has been very poor. The media mention a sighting and sensationalize it, but rarely offer professional advice on tracking or collection of evidence.

They ought to mention how to recognize scratch hills, deer kills, and tracks. What is not needed are irresponsible articles, discussing the irrational fear of the cougar and the bashing of wildlife agencies. The winds need to shift from the speculative to the future. Articles, ought to discuss the need to restore cougars now that the United States Fish and Wildlife Service has declared them extinct in the East. The ability to do so would now fall out of federal hands and into the individual state responsibilities. And what about the possibility that western cougars may repopulate the eastern woodlands? Why not some media attention on these future issues?

Since a good part of what we know regarding cougars in the East has come from individuals and small non-scientific investigations comprised of enthusiasts and sportsmen or women, public participation is critical. The deer season is a golden opportunity to gather information. Literally millions of hunters venture into the woods armed and ready for big bucks. If they could be given some basic information on recognizing cougar sign, it would constitute an investigation unparalleled, and more importantly eliminate false reports. This information could be in the form of flyers or even small drawings and diagrams located in annual hunting and fishing regulations pamphlets. It would help reduce the false reports because the talk of hidden cougars would also decline as hunters discern false sign, tracks, from potentially interesting or possible cougar sign. Public participation is an available and inexpensive tool that is critically important now that talk of reintroduction is at hand. Ideally, some discussion or written information about the need to reintroduce cougars ought to begin appearing where the hunting population will find it.

Finally, there is one suggestion that would be highly effective in locating cougars. This is the release of a radio-collared male cougar that is expected to follow and secure the home range of a female. Liability concerns and expense have prevented serious discussion about this for the simple sake of research work. It would be feasible in the context of a complete cougar recovery program to establish a new population.

And while all of this stimulates the nature enthusiast with the challenge of a good treasure hunt, activity aimed at locating cougars may falsely give the impression that they are extant. Such a notion, and it seems to be the unofficial agreement among the interested public, could hinder the progress of reintroducing cougars. Zealots may exaggerate evidence and try further to convince biologists that cougars have survived. Purists could take this a step further, and try to foil reintroduction efforts, claiming that genetic contamination will occur by supplanting relic cougars with genetically different western cougars. The result of which could indefinitely, perpetuate the status quo and leave the eastern ecosystem without its top umbrella predator species for another ten decades or at least until those advancing western cougars establish themselves.

Therefore, since no one can stop the sightings, the cougar hunt will remain a pursuit; however, this pursuit ought not to keep reintroduction efforts from maturing and gaining momentum. In fact, let there be more publicity, but let now the publicity be constructive, educational, not sensationalized and let it appear with the twin goal of acknowledging sightings as offering little proof, and the need to support the already in place Natural Heritage efforts and philosophies, that have embraced the successful return of so many other wildlife species. If some proof of cougars is to follow, then let it not foil this ambition, but rather support it by quieting the fears and concerns, with the apparent concession that cougars can live quietly among us, peacefully living within their niche, without incident, human attacks or depredation; the reintroduction of cougars is of utmost importance and the time is ripe for it now.

CHAPTER SIXTEEN

ANSWERS HIDDEN WITHIN

Man is fascinated by the unknown, the improbable, and enamored with the impossible. Humans like to hold onto beliefs without justification. Biologists know this and struggle against it, as scientists are obligated to do; anthropologists suggest this intrigue has a survival advantage. We love to probe the mysterious, demonstrating a tendency to create myths that reflect the times and trends of the current day. If there is one explanation that fits with the cougar mystery, it is our current need to perpetuate the wild and primitive past, to have panacea for contemporary guilt in the age of mass extinction.[1] But why has this myth of surviving eastern cougars remained unchanged since 1890? Why would people in the late-1800s have this need? Were they not the ones killing the cougars for bounties? How could cougar sightings in the early 1900s be explained this way? There was little concern for imperiled species at that time.

In fact, the cougar story does not meet this myth and folklore criterion. It is a certainty that *Puma concolor* once existed throughout the eastern United States. The question is does it still exist or is this a case of suggestion, legend, and rumor? With some evidence that cougars have walked freely through the eastern woodlands in recent years, the question really needed is whether there is a breeding population of these so called "Ghost Cats." Because even if a cougar was taken, carcass and all, laid on the desk of a state biologist and proven to be of North American origin, it would not end the debate or solve the question.[2] We still do not know if the evidence collected thus far suggests a continually existing species surviving through the nadir of low deer numbers, or one supplanted from other populations, or a transient species, whose members -- never breeding nor establishing territories - arrive from great distance, wander through an area, and vanish like foxfire in the woodland mist.

Evidence from other cougar populations show that the species can survive tremendous adversity and remain undetected for long periods of time, roaming widely or hidden in isolation, perpetuating in scant numbers, bottle necked by genetics.[3] Downing conveyed the possibility that cougars in the East could have survived low deer densities within specific places, and current studies have shown the species' ability to supplement its deer diet, subsisting almost completely with alternative prey.[4] Historical records documenting the habitat devastation from settlement and agriculture suggest that some places may have held refuge for the cougar. Northern Maine, for instance, was never completely cleared, and logging was not the clear-cut kind that we see today. Unlikely as it may be, there is reason to believe that the cougar could have survived.

This is an unconventional thought, believed by a few and denied by most in the professional wildlife arena. There are no substantial accounts of roadkills, recurring depredations, or accidental shootings. Wherever cougars live, even in low numbers, scat, tracks, scrapes and signature spoor that they leave at kills predictably give their presence away. These are all indications of cougar populations, and they have not been found consistently in the activity zones where eastern sightings are prevalent. This includes the Great Smoky Mountain National Park and Shenandoah National Parks, western Maine, north central Vermont, Pennsylvania, Adirondack Park or in the Quabbin Reservoir.[5] Many of these places, mined with modern camera traps and hair-snares baited with attractants, have been closely monitored. Additionally, places such as the Quabbin have been combed intensively by wildlife trackers - nothing additional has been discovered.

This is precisely why almost every contemporary wildlife biologist will confidently state that the eastern cougar known to our forefathers is gone for good, even though long lists of reputable biologists have believed otherwise. Indeed, the United States Fish and Wildlife service, in 2011, declared the eastern cougar extinct. But a phenomena such as this typically defies the consensus.[6] The sightings continue and the evidence, though sporadic, has continued to be obtained. Initially, circus train wrecks were thought to explain the sightings, but in time the high number of alleged observations documented by the individual researcher proved this an invalid presumption. Finally, the escaped pet theory took root, despite the fact that the number of released captive cougars does not seem to equal the number of sightings.

In fact, controversial phenomena tend to be under-represented by reports.[7] Since the official agreement or mutual understanding is that cougars do not exist, many people are likely to avoid announcing their encounter with one. Fear of ridicule or concerns over credibility may keep some of the best sightings unknown. Credibility is important here, and biologists, being scientists, must pay close attention to it. How many outdoorspeople believe there may be cougars, or seemed reasonably sure about a track, but for fear of unconventionality and incredulity if proven wrong, decided to deny a piece of evidence? How many biologists feel that they would know if these animals existed - relying on the evidence to have come forward from some other field office?[8]

Science is full of analogous experiences of similarly hidden phenomena that reached a point of controversy, continued unexplained, and then were either acknowledged or refuted. Each case overlaps into the sociological or psychological realm; the case of the eastern cougar is as much a cultural and sociological consideration as any wildlife topic may be. For instance, there are several weather conditions, physiological disorders, and psychological disorders which began as observable but unorganizable phenomena.[9] Frequency estimates of these events and disorders were initially low but later proved significantly higher.

Likewise, agency biologists, some of whom never check out the cougar reports, may be preventing further discovery. Thus, it seems likely that there are more people experiencing an alleged cougar sighting than there are documented reports. Some may even fail to recognize that what they have seen is eventful or substantial. If mistaken identity were not accountable for the majority of perceived eastern cougars, the number of escaped pets would have to be high, and the number of people owning a cougar would have to be astounding. This is in light of the modern popular explanation for eastern cougars, which is that they are released or escaped captives.

With thousands of sightings stacking up over the recent decades, it is only logical to think that other species such as domestic cats and coyotes could account for them. Wildlife authorities are not fully trained for recognizing cougars, as known cougar populations live in Florida and the West. Eastern biologists are never prepared for the inundation of mistaken identity calls they receive each year. Veteran biologists admit the cougar phenomena reminds them of the days when the coyote first made its appearance in the Northeast. Citizens were calling in reporting large wolf-like animals, and the biologists were telling them that they were crazy. After checking out the scene and finding what merely looked like dog tracks, biologists returned irritated to their offices. In many cases, it wasn't until trappers started showing up with coyote or coy-dog carcasses, that the agency's party line finally, and necessarily, changed.

Any good biologist will readily admit that distinguishing cougar tracks from dog and coyote tracks is not always a straightforward, easy kind of thing in the real-life outdoor world of snow, mud, and sand. Tracks are sometimes so difficult to verify that even renowned cougar author and biologist Stanley Young misidentified them for Bruce Wright, who subsequently let a well-casted but misidentified track stand as prima facie evidence of eastern cougars - they were canine tracks. Most people, inclined to blame feral dogs or the notorious coyote, may walk right over a cougar-cached deer. But the dozens of reasons for not finding the cougar east of the Mississippi may not be as strong as the reasons widely accepted for its extirpation.

In the end, tracks and evidence of all kinds have been found, but none of it very convincing of a real resident population. Instead it suggests that an occasional cougar can be found in the East; some tracks may create a cluster of evidence, others generate more media attention, but then the media attention passes and typically nothing consistent turns up. Such scenarios strongly suggest that the cougars producing the evidence are transients, and as Van Dyke showed in his studies, transients are nearly impossible to detect. Many believe that these are males looking far and wide for females, or pet animals that have been released when grown out of the cute and cuddly stage. These are the most prevalent explanations. Does the quest thus end with the conclusion that all of the excitement is based on false identifications of other more common creatures, sensationalized by the media, and perpetuated with momentum by the occasional escapee and or transient? If not, then it seems that in order to make this something more than a mere phenomena, there would have to be simultaneous explanations or an unlikely combination of events falling into place in just the right way.

For example, cougars would have to be largely avoiding collisions with automobiles, and those that are hit would have to have avoided recognition, report, or discovery. Those people fortunate enough to see a cougar must fail to capture the event on film. When investigated, the site of the encounter or observation fails to relinquish demonstrable proof. Biologists conducting the investigations are doing so with bias against their existence, and they inadvertently overlook or fail to recognize their tracks. Finally, when the topic is debated among professionals and interest groups or activists, personal inclinations must be transposed between believers and nonbelievers so as to cloud the facts and perpetuate misconceptions.

How likely is it that all of these things are taking place? It is possible, but not very. The truth is that events do occur, accidents happen out of unforeseen circumstances, and living organisms must engineer millions of dynamic events without error in order to exist. A combination of simultaneous events can come together to create an unlikely reality.

So, at either end of the spectrum, whether the fact that common events are more likely to occur than rare ones, or that every once in awhile a nearly impossible event occurs, you can find believers and an argument to support it. In short, is it wiser to think these events are occurring and the cougar remains undiscovered -- or that it has become extirpated and replaced by escapees and transients?

The documentation of roadkills throughout the Midwest and in Florida support the latter conclusion. With the exception of the Floyd County, Kentucky specimen and the Wilbur Cross Parkway kill in Connecticut, there have been no roadkills in the East. That Kentucky cougar had South American and North American genes - it may well have been a mix of captive and wild born - making both believer and nonbeliever correct. The truth is, even if it really existed, a cougar population could not be proven to be a relic population anyhow.[11] A breeding population could be documented, but it would take time to complete the research.

Perhaps the reason so many people think they see a cougar is because they want to see one, and maybe with the introduction or natural recolonization of western cougars into eastern forests it would appear as if what the Native Americans called Pi Twal, "the long tailed one," had never left us. Imagine the chance sighting of this large tawny cat slipping across the trail ahead of you in the dappled light of evening.

APPENDIX I

FIELD STUDY:
CAN ANYONE TRACK A COUGAR ?

This is a contributing chapter from the notes of Jay Tischendorf DVM. Let it be known that Tischendorf does not believe there are relic breeding populations of cougars in the East. Instead, Dr. Tischendorf and the CRF would like to see efforts go toward securing a reintroduction program. The following section is offered in hopes to document the presence of individual cougars from any source and those that may one day find their way east from distant known populations.

*****

The mountain lion was a female and her trail, an ephemeral record of her quiet passing in the moist snow, was extremely fresh. Following her pugmarks through the Yellowstone National Park backcountry as part of a long-term study into mountain lion ecology, I hoped to discover if this secretive cat might be returning to kittens at a hidden den. The tracks, winding along the steep, rugged slope led me to a small field of talus. Here, the slope barren of all but a few dead Douglas fir snags standing in venerable majesty, the early spring sun had loosened the Wyoming winter's white-knuckle grip, leaving the ground bare. Tracking the cat across the rocks would be difficult, but I knew her purposeful trail would resume in the tell-tale snow beckoning me onward at the far side of the rocky zone.

Carefully crossing the lichen-covered scree, where a misstep would surely mean a sprained or broken ankle, I reached the distant border of the talus field and confidently began searching for the cat's trail. Hiking first up and then down along the interface of rock and snow, my confidence gave way to perplexity as I realized ... there were no tracks!

A sudden awareness hit me and I knew the chill it brought with it was not from the Yellowstone cold. As I turned toward my backtrail across the treacherous talus, my mind was already alert to what it knew had to be the answer. In a lifetime spent in the woods and working with wildlife, I had never been so unnerved. She was here! Seemingly without conscious command, in an instant my eyes took in the standing trees on the barren rockfield. A shiver traversed my spine as just as suddenly I locked in on the intense, penetrating gaze of the seven-foot long cat. Utterly silent, lying across a branch twenty feet up in the largest fir standing on the talus -- a tree under which I had just walked -- she seemed to be looking right through me.

*****

While not all tracking experiences are quite so exhilarating, tracking wildlife provides outdoor enthusiasts with some of the most rewarding and satisfying moments afield. This is especially true when tracking predators such as mountain lions. Predators are usually fewer in number and more difficult to locate than other animals, which makes opportunities to follow their spoor even more special. Also, predators, especially the large ones like mountain lions, wolverines, wolves, and bears, are seemingly enshrouded in intangible mystique. Identifying the sign and following the trails of such animals imparts one with a keen sense of sharing in the hidden magic of the natural world.

The objective of this chapter is to share some information on mountain lion sign -- tracks, trails, scat, and such -- and how to identify it. But, as noted by Harley Shaw, one of the world's most prominent mountain lion biologists, trying to write about identifying tracks and sign is like trying to tell someone how to play the piano. Basically it just doesn't work as well as simply getting out there day after day and doing it with a knowledgeable teacher. With that in mind, I will say from the very start that there are some exceptional field guides available in print to aid in your noble quest. A brief list of some of these is provided at the end of this chapter. I've also included the names and addresses of several tracking and nature observation programs that should be of interest to outdoorspeople at any level of expertise. I will also acknowledge here that my own knowledge of tracks and tracking comes from spending many wonderful years of trail time across North America, from city parks and sandlots to mountain summits, and learning from many wonderful people, beginning with my late grandfather, Elbert Tischendorf. Regarding the challenge of tracking pumas specifically, or mountain lions as they are most often known in the American West, Gary Koehler, Kerry Murphy, Bob Wiesner, Harley Shaw, and Jim Halfpenny stand out as special mentors.

In the absence of appreciable numbers of mountain lions to track, the next best thing for many people will be none other than the feral house cat. While I am deeply opposed to letting house cats roam freely outdoors -- they are notorious and indiscriminate killers of our natural fauna -- the tracks, trails, and scat of the wandering house or farm cat provide a miniaturized but reasonable and indeed fascinating facsimile of that of its much larger cousin. House cats also provide a readily available living model of overall feline anatomy, behavior, movement patterns and gaits, foot structure, and toe and heel pad configuration. Bobcats -- populations of which are fortunately substantial throughout much of North America, including the East -- are another suitable surrogate for sign and spoor for mountain lion tracking.

Still, there is no better teacher than the real deal. In the West or in Florida, with a little bit of homework and perhaps the right outfitter, guide, or naturalist to help lead the way, it is relatively easy to locate puma sign. Everyone's situation related to time, money, and travel is different, but if it is ever possible for you to spend time tracking America's great cat in its native haunts, I hope you will immerse yourself in the singular experience.

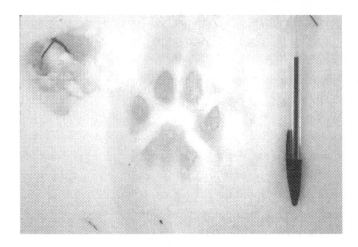

Figure 1
Cougar track in snow. The Bic pen is used as a size reference.
Track measured 3.5 inches long by 3.5 inches wide. Note the bi-
lobing of the leading edge of the heal pad and the tri-lobing of
trailing edge. The print made by a mature female in Yellowstone
National Park, is unusually symmetric for a cougar.

With these foregoing caveats and suggestions in mind, let's talk about puma sign. Puma tracks, like those of most cats, typically appear as a composite impression of four toes and a distinctive plantar or palmar pad (FIGURE 1). This pad is usually referred to as the 'heel' pad, but anatomically it is actually comparable to the ball of our foot or the callous area of our hand. Nonetheless for simplicity, I'll use the more general term 'heel pad' here. The leading edge of this pad is bi-lobed and the trailing edge is tri-lobed (FIGURE 1). A close look at the feet of a friendly house cat will demonstrate these and other similar features discussed in this chapter.

A thorough understanding of the features of the feline foot is necessary, as is an appreciation of how the actual anatomic features translate into the major characteristics or subtle nuances of tracks. This knowledge is critical because in most parts of the country, particularly where there is snow, dust, or mud, pugmarks will be the most common form of sign left by pumas. It is also imperative to have a solid understanding of the key features of the feet and other characteristics of dogs or their wild canid brethren, such as coyotes and wolves, as it is these animals' spoor that are most often confused with those of the puma. The elusive and little-known fisher is another potential source of mistaken track identity throughout much of North America, but space here precludes a full discussion of this fascinating creature's tracks, trails, and sign.

Some additional characteristics of feline tracks are as follows. At its widest point, measured across the outer toes, a puma track will range from about three to 4.5 inches in width. Regarding length -- since cat tracks are often almost round, the length, measured from the tip of the longest toe back to the trailing edge of the heel pad, is about the same. In actuality, a puma's forefeet may actually be slightly wider than they are long. Conversely, a puma's hind feet may be slightly longer than wide. In this regard, the hind print of a puma may somewhat resemble the track of a dog or other canid, which in general, whether hind or front foot imprints, tend to be oval or oblong in overall shape.

Width of the heel pad is also a useful guide because, unlike measuring across the widest width of the toes, which can splay markedly outward, its dimensions vary little from track to track. In pumas, the maximum pad width typically measures anywhere from 1.25 to 2.5 inches. A pad over two and a half inches across is almost certainly -- but not necessarily always! -- that of an adult male. Incidentally, even the track of the smallest puma kitten will likely exceed the size of a large adult male bobcat, if not in actual dimensions then certainly in its robustness. Furthermore, under most circumstances, the tracks of a small puma kitten will usually be accompanied by those of its mother, so here again it should be relatively easy to distinguish between the tracks of a bobcat and a young puma.

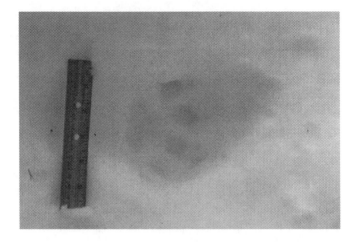

Figure 2
Cougar track in snow. This is the track of an adult male that
unsheathed its claws to gain traction descending a steep, icy hill
in Yellowstone National Park. The lack of bi-lobing and tri-lobing
suggests this individual was relatively old. Tracks from this individual
measured approximately 4-4.5 inches in length and width, which
is about as large as one will ever see. Note the asymmetry as well
as the general robustness of this print compared to Figure 1.

Another characteristic of felid feet relates to their claws. Cats have
retractable claws, so their tracks typically don't show claw marks. Tracks
of dogs or other canids usually do, but ...beware, this is not always the
case. It was Robert L. "Bob" Downing who pointed out to me, in fact,
that contrary to what common sense would dictate, when walking in
mud, dogs may actually be less likely to leave claw marks. And in fact,
cats may unsheath their claws anytime and anyplace, so it is always a
possibility that a given cat track may clearly show claw marks. Such
marks, however, tend to be round and very precise, as if a needle or a
small diameter nail (as in hammer and nail, not toenail) was carefully
poked into the ground or substrate (FIGURE 2) . In general, the toenail
marks of dogs tend to be larger, more robust, and less fine, defined and
precise, than those of felids.

As an aside, please note I use the words 'typically' and 'usually'
quite regularly in this chapter because there are really no one hundred
percent hard and fast guarantees about tracks or other sign, nor for that
matter any other aspect of life in general. Nothing is certain -- except

that nothing is certain -- but some things are more typical, or expected, than others. For instance, as noted above, some cat tracks may show claws (FIGURE 2). Others may show five toes, for instance a polydactyl (i.e., extra-toed) house cat, or in the case of a puma or bobcat, more likely a case where the track of the hind foot has indirectly registered atop that of the forefoot, creating the visual impression of a fifth toe. Other cat tracks may reveal only a rough hint of bi- or tri-lobing of the heel pad, increasing the likelihood that the track may be misidentified (see FIGURE 2).

Cat tracks are also usually asymmetric, especially those of the forefeet. Imagine that you were somehow able to fold a cat track in half after drawing a line lengthwise through it, right down the middle, separating the two middle toes and continuing back through the heel pad, dividing it in two as well. If you could do this, the two halves of the track -- if it is like almost all cat tracks -- would not match up. Try this, using your imagination with FIGURE 2. Or better yet, make an impression of your friendly neighborhood cat's paws or your own hand in moist sand or mud and then pretend to divide it in two, comparing the respective halves. Your thumb equates roughly with the dewclaw on the forefoot of cats and most dogs, and since this appendage rarely shows up in these animals' tracks, you will have to disregard its impression to do justice to this comparison. In any case, human hands are also asymmetric. Indeed, the human hand is a reasonable model for the asymmetric foot of a cat, with the respective digits of both species all being of slightly different lengths (the 3rd digit, or so-called 'middle finger' being longest in both man and cat).

Figure 3
Track of dog. Film canister measures 2 inches. Note the symmetry
of this print, and the triangular heel pad lacking bi-lobing at
its leading edge. Note the arrangement of the toes around the
heel pad, and the distinct star shaped "ridge" resulting from
dirt being compressed between the toes and heel pad.

Unlike cat tracks, canid tracks are symmetric. In other words, the two halves of a dog track are mirror images and match up if you were somehow able to fold them together (FIGURE 3). This is almost always true for both front and hind canid prints. Symmetry can also be demonstrated in other respects with dog tracks. Figure 4 shows a stylized dog track overlaid with five parallel, or mostly parallel, horizontal lines. These lines connect various features of the track -- for instance the tips and trailing edges of the middle and outer toes, respectively. Note how these paired toes, respectively, are the same length and width, thus contributing to the symmetrical, mirror image effect of the two halves of the track. The benchmark or baseline against which the other horizontal lines are compared is that along the base of the heel pad, a line which essentially lies perpendicular to the animal's direction of travel.

There are also several diagonal lines drawn atop the track in FIGURE 4. These lines run the length of the outer toes and demonstrate the angle of the toes relative to the trailing edge of the heel pad. California puma researchers Shawn Smallwood and Lee Fitzhugh demonstrated that in most canid tracks, typically, the outside toes (i.e., the toes positioned furthest laterally) point outward at a pronounced angle (typically approximately 45-75 degrees) relative to a baseline across the trailing edge of the heel pad. The outer toes in cat tracks, conversely, typically point more or less straight ahead when evaluated from the baseline (see FIGURES 1 and 2).

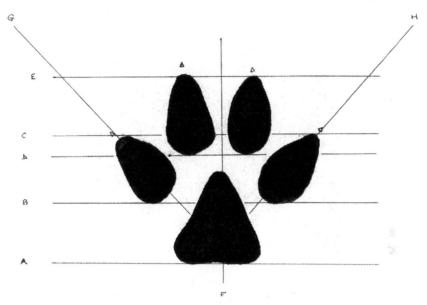

Figure 4

Stylized diagram of canid track overlaid with lines to demonstrate symmetry. Line A denoting trailing edge of the heel pad, lies perpendicular to the animal's direction of travel, and forms the baseline against which lines B,C,D and E are compared. Lines B and C connect the trailing, and leading tips, respectively, of the two outer toes. Lines D and E do the same for the two middle toes. Track symmetry is evident because all of these lines are essentially parallel with each other and the base, Line A. Line F divides the track in half and demonstrates the symmetry. Lines G and H transect the long axis of each outer toe, illustrating the angle at which the toes project from the baseline. In this case roughly 50-60 degrees. The same toes in a cougar track would point more or less straight ahead.

A full discussion of puma tracks alone could fill an entire volume, but let me share one other feature that may help one discriminate a cat track from a canid track. This feature was elucidated by Bob Downing and Virginia Fifield, the early eastern cougar investigators who spent many hours studying animal tracks, especially those of felids and canids, in an effort to find ways to clearly differentiate one species' track from another. In cats, the imprint of the heel pad is typically deepest toward the front. In other words, if you were able to look at a cat track in cross section (i.e., from the side), the impression of the pad would slope from the rear aspect of the print downward toward the front. In wild canids the pattern is reversed, with the pad imprint deepest at the trailing edge. Here, in cross section, the pad's impression would slope from the shallow front down and back toward the rear. In domestic dogs there is much variability with regard to the slope of the heel pad, so use this feature with caution with domestic breeds.

Before leaving the subject of tracks, let me say that track I.D. and tracking is not true tracking unless it is accompanied by a solid understanding of animal movement patterns, including how and where the feet are placed under a given gait. A slow walk, fast walk, trot, gallop, or bound all leave a different signature, so to speak, of track imprints. Again, a thorough coverage of this topic is beyond the scope of this chapter, but noted naturalist-biologist James Halfpenny does an excellent job of clarifying this material in his landmark tracking guide cited at the end of this chapter. Time spent observing domestic dogs and cats move in their different gaits is also very useful.

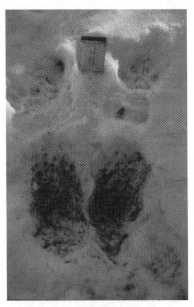

Figure 5

So-called scrape, scratch or urine mark of a male cougar

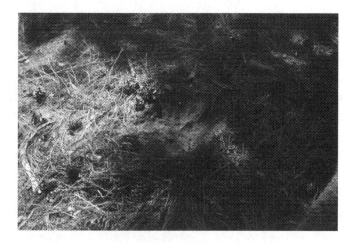

Figure 6
Cougar scrape in pine duff, southern Colorado. Note the two
distinctive "trenches" and the characteristic pile of duff deposited at
the rear of the scrape. A Swiss army knife is used as a size reference.

True tracking also entails an understanding of other forms of wildlife
sign. For instance, FIGURE 5 and FIGURE 6 depict mountain lion
'scrapes' -- one in snow and one in the dirt and duff lying at the base of
an evergreen tree. Scrapes (or 'scratches' as they may sometimes be called)
are territorial marks usually attributed to resident adult male pumas.
Adult females may possibly also make these peculiar marks which play
an important communication role in cat populations. I prefer the term
'scrape' because to me it implies a more deliberate, controlled movement
than a 'scratch,' which seems to imply a haphazard, random action.

Scrapes are probably made most typically by the hind feet, which the
cat methodically pushes down and backward, scraping it deliberately and
apparently carefully through the substrate. The result is a neat, orderly,
three-component structure characterized by two shallow trenches, four
to five inches wide (comparable to the width of a slightly splayed adult
puma foot) and nine to twelve inches long, and a pile of duff, dirt,
leaves, or other substrate. The pile is the result of the scraping movement
and thus lies at the rear of the feature. Cats may urinate, defecate or
otherwise scent-mark the pile, but do not always do so.

Scrapes are often made by pumas at saddles along ridges, at the
bases of prominent trees or rock outcroppings along their preferred

trails, and at other key landmarks around their ranges. Under the right circumstances, which admittedly are not altogether understood, it is not unheard of to find five to ten fresh scrapes along a mile stretch of trail. Scrapes are a reliable indicator of the presence of a resident puma, and likely suggest the presence of other pumas against which the maker is marking or protecting his territory, or with which the maker is hoping to breed. Interestingly, one of Yellowstone's most accomplished trackers, Gerry Green, a grizzly bear researcher and keen observer of nature, was sure he had found a puma scrape during a visit to the Missouri hills of his youth in the mid-1980s. Such sign is exciting to find, and in eastern North America a definitive scrape would surely be an important discovery.

Scat, or excrement, is another important form of animal spoor or sign. Puma scat, like that of house cats, can take several forms depending on diet and other internal and external variables. The blood and protein-rich defecations occurring immediately after a puma has fed on fresh prey are wet, runny, and formless. Formed scat appears later, and is typically blunt-ended, multi-segmented, and roughly 1 to 1.75 inches in diameter. A full length scat, including all segments, may extend four to six inches in length or more and its color may vary from black to gray, brown, or even ivory, depending on its content, weathering, and other factors. An excellent series of comparative photographs of wildlife scat, including that of the mountain lion, can be found in the tracking guide authored by James Halfpenny and listed at the end of this chapter. Scat is deposited upon or within territorial scrapes, at kill sites, along trails, at traditional latrine sites -- where one can find months' or years' worth of scat -- perhaps under an overhanging rock nearby to a well-used puma pathway -- and in other locations. Keep in mind that cats also have a proclivity to bury their droppings, so any evidence of scat burial should impart one with a high degree of suspicion that a felid was involved.

Where there are pumas, there will be animals killed by pumas. Puma spoor is typically richest at such kill sites, and where a puma has killed and fed on a large ungulate such as a deer, its primary prey, there is almost invariably a cornucopia of evidence to indicate the identity of the predator. This includes tracks, scat, possibly day beds and hair samples, urine marks in snow, the kill itself, of course, and in the case of the puma perhaps also dung heaps, latrines, and territorial scrapes as well as scratchings on trees or logs. The latter sign (tree scratchings) may reflect hygenic behavior (i.e., cleaning and/or sharpening the claws) or possibly a territorial behavior. These marks will be much more fine, reflecting the pinpointed, needle-like quality of cat claws, than those made by the thick, blunt claws of bears.

Figure 7
Cow elk killed by a cougar, Yellowstone National Park. The elk is positioned on its back, with its head flexed and twisted ventrally, such that it lies atop the chest, between the forelegs. The bright reddish -pink tongue makes a good reference point. The cougar covered this kill with a scant collection of debris including sagebrush, hair, and a stick.

Regarding predation behavior -- remember, pumas hunt by stealth and surprise. Their kills, and the location of their kills, reflect this. FIGURE 7 shows a cow elk killed by a puma. This kill occurred in a dense patch of sagebrush. Note that the head and neck are twisted at an improbable angle, the cervical spine (i.e., the neck) having been broken by the cat during the attack. In a typical attack sequence, a puma, using available cover, will stalk within close range of its prey, perhaps twenty to fifty feet or less, then make a fast final charge. This charge is almost invariably directed at the head and neck of the prey. In long-necked ungulates this site is an incredibly vulnerable point -- both in terms of anatomy and physics, or what I call anato-mechanics. A combination of the impact and the puma's great momentum, coupled with a simultaneous bite to the neck and/or a powerful twist of the prey's head and neck with its paw and grappling hook-like claws, is usually enough to abruptly sever the spine of the prey. A well-executed attack will often drop a deer or elk literally where it stands. Prey that continue to struggle once taken to the ground are met with a terminal bite to the trachea, or so-called windpipe.

Careful skinning and dissection of the neck and facial areas of the prey might thus reveal claw marks whose arrangement and spacing is consistent with those of a puma. One might also observe a bite mark or two, and related pre-mortem hemorrhage, with obvious fang puncture marks at either the dorsal (i.e., the back of the neck) or ventral (i.e., the throat) areas. Signs of a struggle are usually minimal, but not all puma attacks go smoothly, so there may be evidence of a short chase. Again, keep in mind that pumas use stealth and need cover to hunt, so one would expect to find most puma kills where there are ample places for the puma to remain concealed and to stalk within striking distance of its prey.

Having made a kill, a puma will drag or carry the animal to a protected, secluded site nearby, and begin the process of feeding. As predator biologist and lifelong woodsman Gary Koehler pointed out to me in Yellowstone in the mid-1980s, pumas, using their teeth or rasp-like tongue, will literally clip or lick away the fur of the prey, starting around the junction of the ribs and abdomen or flank. At such sites the skin looks as though it were shaved. The characteristic resulting bundles or tufts of clipped hair, as they are spit, coughed, hacked, and pawed out of the cat's mouth, often form a neat and orderly fan-like ring around the prey. Having made a clean access point, the mountain lion will rip or bite into the animal and remove the spoilage-prone stomach and intestines, known collectively as the paunch, and drag them well away from the kill. Typically these gastrointestinal (GI) structures, whose strong odor and rapid decay might tend to attract scavengers or spoil the remaining meat, are then covered by the cat with whatever debris, duff, leaves, or other ground cover is immediately available.

The puma eats the blood-rich lungs and heart first, it seems, then begins eating from the major muscle groups of the prey item -- the shoulders, neck, thighs, and back. During the feeding process, which may last several days, the puma may periodically move the carcass to fresh locations, often -- but not always! -- covering the kill, as it did the GI structures, with whatever dirt, duff, or debris is handy. The elk in FIGURE 7 has been covered, for instance, with a sparse collection of sagebrush debris, including, most prominently, a single stick. In this case there was little available for the puma to use. This suggests that even when the result is ineffectual, the puma's innate motivation to cover and protect its kill is well entrenched in their genetic makeup. Other kills might literally be buried under a thick covering of light brush or leaves.

When not actually feeding, a puma will usually remain close to the kill, ever vigilant for scavengers or other predators, which may be attracted to the carcass and which the puma may kill if given the opportunity. A female puma with kittens may remain at a kill until basically nothing remains but a few bones. Typically, though, a puma utilizes its hard-won kill until the caloric return on the investment is merely minimized, not necessarily non-existent, and then moves on to fully digest its recent meals and continue patrolling its home range.

As noted earlier in this chapter, comprehensive coverage of puma sign, gathered over the lifetimes of many hunters, houndsmen, biologists, and trackers, would fill a huge volume. All of us are in fact still learning, as the timeless secrets of Nature are slowly revealed and interpreted. Hopefully, though, the brief, foregoing discussion of puma sign and behavior will aid readers as they keep an eye out for puma sign and try their own hand at the rewarding pastime of tracking.

Three final comments: One, whether tracking pumas or pack rats, it makes good safety sense to always work and travel in pairs. Two, animal kills, carcasses, and scat are excellent sources of pathogens such as bacteria and parasites. Always handle such materials with extreme caution and care, and always with protective gloves. A face mask and safety eyewear isn't a bad idea either when one considers that infection with a tapeworm such as *Echinococcus multilocularis*, common in wild canids, or hantavirus, carried by many rodents, can be fatal. Be alert for ticks and fleas, too, which are often vectors for other debilitating or terminal diseases like bubonic plague, tularemia, Lyme disease or Ehrlichiosis. Finally, given the rarity of puma sign in the East and Midwest, it is imperative that any suspicious evidence be carefully preserved via photographs, illustrations, or other means, preferably after having been corroborated in its natural, original condition by one or more authorities.

SUGGESTED READINGS
AND CONTACTS

R. W. Brown, M. J. Lawrence, and J. Pope. 1984. The Larousse guide to animal tracks, trails, and sign. Larousse and Company, Inc. New York, New York.

Jack L. Childs. 1998. Tracking the felids of the borderland. Printing Corner Press. El Paso, Texas.

James Halfpenny. 1986. A field guide to mammal tracking in western North America. Johnson Publishing Company. Boulder, Colorado.

Olaus J. Murie. 1954. A field guide to animal tracks. Houghton Mifflin Company. Boston, Massachusetts.

Paul Rezendes. Tracking and the art of seeing -- how to read animal tracks and sign. 1999. HarperCollins Publishers, Inc. New York, New York.

K. Shawn Smallwood and F. Lee Fitzhugh. 1989. Differentiating mountain lion and dog tracks. Pages 58-63 in Ronald H. Smith, editor, Proceedings of the Third Mountain Lion Workshop. Arizona Game and Fish Department, Phoenix.

TRACKING COURSES:

American Ecological Research Institute (AERIE)
Jay W. Tischendorf
Post Office Box 1826
Great Falls, Montana 59403 USA
406 453-7233
TischendorfJ@Hotmail.com

A Naturalist's World
Jim Halfpenny and Diann Thompson
Post Office Box 989
Gardiner, Montana 59030 USA
406 848-9458
www.tracknature.org
trackdoctor@tracknature.com

Keeping Track, Inc.
Susan C. Morse
Post Office Box 444
Huntingdon, Vermont 05462 USA
802 434-7000
www.keepingtrack.org

Walnut Hill Tracking & Nature Center
Nick Wisniewski and Valerie Major
325 Walnut Hill Road
Orange, Massachusetts 01364 USA
978 544-6083
www.walnuthilltracking.com

End Notes

INTRODUCTION

1. Tougias, R. 1994. The Return of the Mountain Lion. *Appalachian Trailway News Magazine.* October: pp. 21-24.
2. Hansen, K . 1992. *Cougar: The American Lion.* Flagstaff, AZ: Northland. pp. 2, 6.
3. Grenwell, R. "The Place of the Puma in the Natural History of the Larger Felids," in J.W. Tischendorf and S.J. Ropski, eds. *Proceedings of the Eastern Cougar Conference*, 3-5 June 1994, Erie, Pennsylvania. Fort Collins, CO: American Ecological Research Institute. pp. 9-15.
4. Busch, R. 2004. *The Cougar Almanac: Natural History of the Mountain Lion.* NY, NY: The Lyons Press. pp. 1-88.

CHAPTER 1

1. Cardoza, J. 1976. The Black Bear in Massachusetts. *Research Bulletin* Vol. 18, pp. 1-9.
2. Tyrrell, L. 1996. "National Forests in the Eastern Region: Land Allocation and Planning for Old Growth," in Mary Davis-Byrd, ed. *Eastern Old-Growth Forests.* Washington, DC: Island Press. pp. 245-273.
3. Extinct Vertebrates of U.S.A. Territories and Canada Since 1492. *http://www.dwave.net/~tony/mars/extinct.htm*
4. D. Orwig to R. Tougias, email correspondence, December 19, 2009.

5. T. Gola to R. Tougias, email correspondence, January 12, 2004.

6. Outwater, Alice. Water: A Natural History.N.Y: Basic Books, Chapters 1and 2.

7. Morrell, A. 1986. *Beaver Behavior,* Happy Camp, CA: Naturgraph. p.10.

8. Morrell, A. 1986. *Beaver Behavior,* Happy Camp, CA: Naturgraph. pp. 21-25.

9. Tischendorf, J. 1993. Panther Prints, *Friends of the Eastern Panther (FOTEP) Newsletter.* Fall issue.

10. T. Gola to R. Tougias, email correspondence, March 20, 2004.

11. Herz, K. 2001. *Connecticut Wildlife Magazine, Annual Reports-Fish and Wildlife Board* – Archives.

12. Young, S.P. and E.A. Goldman. 1946. *The Puma: Mysterious American Cat.* Washington, DC: American Wildlife Inst., p. 7.

13. *Ibid.,* p. 6.

14. Hansen, K . 1992. *Cougar: The American Lion.* Flagstaff, AZ: Northland. p. 55.

15. Altherr, T. 1996. "The Catamount in Vermont Folklore and Culurture, 1760-1900," in J.W. Tischendorf and S.J. Ropski, eds. *Proceedings of the Eastern Cougar Conference,* 3-5 June 1994, Erie, Pennsylvania. Fort Collins, CO: American Ecological Research Institute, pp. 50-97

16. Williams, S. 1793. *Natural and Civil History of Vermont.* Walpole, N.H.

17. Altherr, T. 1996. "The Catamount in Vermont Folklore and Culurture, 1760-1900," in J.W. Tischendorf and S.J. Ropski, eds. *Proceedings of the Eastern Cougar Conference,* 3-5 June 1994, Erie, Pennsylvania. Fort Collins, CO: American Ecological Research Institute, p. 57.

18. *Ibid.,* pp. 58-59.

19. *Ibid.,* pp. 70-73.

20. *Ibid.,* pp. 70-71.

21. *Ibid.,* p. 69.

22. *Ibid.,* pp. 75-76.

23. Bolgiano, C. 1995. *Mountain Lion: An Unnatural History of Puma and People.* Mechanicburg, PA: pp.180-191.

24. Young, S.P. and E.A. Goldman. 1946. *The Puma: Mysterious American Cat.* Washington, DC: American Wildlife Inst., p. 23.

25. Young, S.P. and E.A. Goldman. 1946. *The Puma: Mysterious American Cat.* Washington, DC: American Wildlife Inst., p.10.

26. Young, S.P. and E.A. Goldman. 1946. *The Puma: Mysterious American Cat.* Washington, DC: American Wildlife Inst., p.11.

27. *Ibid.*, pp.15-40.

28. *Ibid.*, p. 24.

29. M. Shanley to R. Tougias, telephone interview by author, March 2, 2006.

30. Young, S.P. and E.A. Goldman. 1946. *The Puma: Mysterious American Cat.* Washington, DC: American Wildlife Inst., pp. 24-25.

31. J. Cardoza to R. Tougias, telephone interview by author, January 23, 2004.

32. Wright, B.S. 1972. *The Eastern Panther: A Question of Survival.* Toronto, Canada: Clark and Irwin, pp. 155-164.

33. Davis-Byrd, Mary. 1996. "Extent and Location of National Forests in the Eastern Region: Land Allocation and Planning for Old Growth," in Mary Davis-Byrd, ed. *Eastern Old-Growth Forests.* Washington, DC: Island Press. p. 22.

CHAPTER 2

1. Tougias, R. 1994. The Return of the Mountain Lion. *Appalachian Trailway News Magazine.* October: pp. 21-24.

2. Wright, B. 1948. Survival of the Northeast Panther *Felis concolor* in New Brunswick. *Journal of Mammology,* p. 29.

3. "Hitchcock Panther Talks, 1958-1984." Hitchcock Collection, Vermont Historical Society, Doc. 290, Folder 10.

4. Tougias, R. 1994. The Return of the Mountain Lion. *Appalachian Trailway News Magazine.* October: pp 21-24.

5. Allardyce, G. 2001. *On the Track of the New Brunswick Panther*. Fredericton, New Brunswick: GraphXperts.

6. Wright, B.S. 1972. *The Eastern Panther: A Question of Survival*. Toronto, Canada: Clark and Irwin, p. 3.

7. Allardyce, G. 2001. *On the Track of the New Brunswick Panther*. Fredericton, New Brunswick: GraphXperts. pp. 55-63.

8. Wright, B.S. 1972. *The Eastern Panther: A Question of Survival*. Toronto, Canada: Clark and Irwin, pp. 3-4.

9. *Ibid.,* p. 3

10. *Ibid.,* p. 3.

11. Wright, B. 1959. *The Ghost of North America: The Story of the Eastern Panther*. NY, NY: Vantage, pp. 1-20.

12. Allardyce, G. 2001. *On the Track of the New Brunswick Panther*. Fredericton, New Brunswick: GraphXperts.

13. Wright, B.S. 1972. *The Eastern Panther: A Question of Survival*. Toronto, Canada: Clark and Irwin, p.23.

14. *Ibid.,* pp. 35-37.

15. *Ibid.,* p. 38.

16. *Ibid.,* p. 39.

17. Hitchcock, 1983. "The Vermont Panther," speech before the Vermont Institute of Natural Sciences, Woodstock, April 14, 1983, in Hitchcock Collection, Vermont Historical Society, Doc. 290, Folder 10, "Hitchcock Panther Talks, 1958-1984," p. 5

18. "Hitchcock Biography," Hitchcock Collection, Vermont Historical Society, Doc. 280, Folder 7.

19. *Ibid.,* p. 10

20. *Ibid.,* p. 30.

21. Allardyce, G. 2001. *On the Track of the New Brunswick Panther*. Fredericton, New Brunswick: GraphXperts. pp. 59-63.

22. "Early Notes and Letters," Hitchcock Collection, Vermont Historical Society, Doc. 250, Folder 1

23. *Ibid.*

24. "Hitchcock Panther Talks, 1958-1984." Hitchcock Collection, Vermont Historical Society, Doc. 290, Folder 10.

25. Tougias, R. 1992. Cougar Expert Departs. *Daily Hampshire Gazette.* November 17, 1992.

26. V. Fifield to R. Tougias, telephone interview by author, February 10, 1991.

27. Tougias, R. 1992. Cougar Expert Departs. *Daily Hampshire Gazette.* November 17, 1992.

28. Downing, R.L. and V.L. Fifield. 1978. *Differences Between Tracks of Dogs and Cougars.* Worcester, MA: Worcester Science Center, pp. 1-2.

29. V. Fifield to R. Tougias, telephone interview by author, February 10, 1991

30. T. French to R. Tougias, telephone interview by author, September 12, 2002.

31. V. Fifield to R. Tougias, telephone interview by author, February 11, 1991

32. V. Fifield to R. Tougias, telephone interview by author, February 10, 1991.

33. Wright, B. 1973. The Cougar is Alive and Well in Massachusetts. *Massachusetts Wildlife* Vol. 24, pp. 2-19.

34. T. French to R. Tougias, telephone interview by author, September 12, 2002.

35. J. Cardoza to R. Tougias, telephone interview, March 22, 2005.

36. J. Cardoza to R. Tougias, telephone interview, May 24, 2005.

37. T. French to R. Tougias, telephone interview by author, September 12, 2002.

38. Tougias, R. 1992. Cougar Expert Departs. *Daily Hampshire Gazette.* November 17, 1992.

39. Culbertson, N. 1976. *Status and History of the Mountain Lion in the Great Smoky National Park.* Great Smoky Mountains National Park, Management Report No. 15, pp.1-4.

40. Bolgiano, C. 1995. *Mountain Lion: An Unnatural History of Puma and People.* Mechanicburg, PA: p.164

41. Downing, R. 1984. The Search for Cougars in the Eastern United States. *Cryptozoology* Vol. 3, p. 31.

42. Downing, R. 2004. *Changes in the Habitat of Cougars in the East.* Lecture, Eastern Cougar Conference. April 29, 2004. Morgantown, WV.

43. Downing, R.L. 1981. "The Current Status of the Cougar in the Southern Appalachian," in *Proceedings of Nongame and Endangered Wildlife Symposium*, Athens, GA. pp.142-151.

44. Downing, R.L. and V.L. Fifield. 1978. *Differences Between Tracks of Dogs and Cougars.* Worcester, MA: Worcester Science Center, p. 2.

45. Downing, R. 1996. "Investigation to Determine the Status of the Cougar in the East" in J.W. Tischendorf and S.J. Ropski, eds. *Proceedings of the Eastern Cougar Conference,* 3-5 June 1994, Erie, Pennsylvania. Fort Collins, CO: American Ecological Research Institute, pp. 47-48.

46. Downing, R.L. 1979. *Eastern Cougar Newsletter.* USDI, Fish and Wildlife Service, Dept. Forestry, Clemson University, Clemson, SC. May: pp.1-6.

47. Downing, R. 1984. The Search for Cougars in the Eastern United States. *Cryptozoology* Vol. 3, p. 41.

48. Bush, R. 2004. *The Cougar Almanac: Natural History of the Mountain Lion.* NY, NY: The Lyons Press. pp. 50-88.

49. Wisnieski, N. and V. Major. 2004. *Wildlife and Puma Tracking Workshop.* Lecture. Eastern Cougar Conference, Morgantown, West Virginia. May 1, 2004.

50. Downing, R. 1984. The Search for Cougars in the Eastern United States. *Cryptozoology* Vol. 3, p. 42.

51. Downing, R.L. 1979. Status of the Eastern Cougar in the Southern Appalachians. *Eastern Cougar Newsletter,* USDI, Fish and Wildlife Service, Department of Forestry, Clemson University. Clemson, SC. January: p. 3.

52. Downing, R.L. 1981. "The Current Status of the Cougar in the Southern Appalachian," in *Proceedings of Nongame and Endangered Wildlife Symposium*, Athens, GA. pp. 142-151.

53. R. Downing to R. Tougias, email correspondence, August 29, 2004.

54. Downing, R. 2004. *Changes in the Habitat of Cougars in the East.* Lecture, Eastern Cougar Conference. April 29, 2004. Morgantown, WV.

55. R. Downing to R. Tougias, email correspondence, August 29, 2004

56. Downing, R.L. 1982. *Eastern Cougar Newsletter.* USDI, Fish and Wildlife Service, Department. Forestry, Clemson Univ., Clemson, SC. February: pp.1-6.

57. Downing, R. 2004. *Changes in the Habitat of Cougars in the East.* Lecture, Eastern Cougar Conference. April 29, 2004. Morgantown, WV.

58. R. Downing to R. Tougias, telephone interview by author, December 9, 1997.

59. Downing, R. 1984. The Search for Cougars in the Eastern United States. *Cryptozoology* Vol. 3, p. 32.

60. *Ibid.,* pp. 32-34.

61. United States Fish and Wildlife Service. 1982. *Eastern Cougar Recovery Plan.* United States Fish and Wildlife Service. Atlanta, Georgia.

CHAPTER 3

1. Reed, T. "Friends of the Eastern Panther: Activities to Date," in J.W. Tischendorf and S.J. Ropski, eds. *Proceedings of the Eastern Cougar Conference,* 3-5 June 1994, Erie, Pennsylvania. Fort Collins, CO: American Ecological Research Institute, pp. 139-140.

2. T. Reed to R. Tougias, telephone interview by author, February 18, 1993.

3. *Ibid.*

4. Reed, T. Panther Prints. *Friends of the Eastern Panther (FOTEP) Newsletter.* Summer, 1991.

5. Tischendorf, J. Panther Prints. *Friends of the Eastern Panther (FOTEP) Newsletter.* Fall 1990.

6. Reed, T. Panther Prints. *Friends of the Eastern Panther (FOTEP) Newsletter.* Spring1990.

7. Tischendorf, J. Letter to State and Provincial Authorities. Vermont Historical Society. Hitchcock Collection (miscellaneous folder).

8. S. Morse to R. Tougias, telephone interview by author, October 19, 1996.

9. *Ibid.*

10. 10. Reed, T. "Thoughts of an Amateur," in J.W. Tischendorf and S.J. Ropski, eds. *Proceedings of the Eastern Cougar Conference*, 3-5 June 1994, Erie, Pennsylvania. Fort Collins, CO: American Ecological Research Institute, p 144.

11. *Ibid.*, p. 145.

12. *Ibid.*, p. 145.

13. *Ibid.*, p. 146.

14. C. Alexander to R. Tougias, telephone interview by author, September, 1997.

15. Kirk, J. 2004. Aslan Resurrected: Searching for Wild Panthers in a Domesticated World. *Harper's.* Vol. 308, April, p. 54.

16. Tischendorf, J. to R. Tougias, live interview, May 1, 2004.

17. Tougias, R. 1994. The Return of the Mountain Lion. *Appalachian Trailway News Magazine.* October: pp 22-24

18. Lutz, J. *Eastern Puma Research Network (EPRN) Newsletter.* Summer 2004.

19. J. Lutz to R. Tougias, email correspondence, June 7, 2010.

20. J. Lutz to R. Tougias, telephone interview by author, July 28, 2004.

21. J. Tischendorf to R. Tougias, telephone interview by author, August 29, 2009.

22. Culbertson, N. 1976. *Status and History of the Mountain Lion in the Great Smoky National Park.* Great Smoky Mountains National Park, Management Report No. 15.

23. Cardoza, J. 2002. The Eastern Cougar: A Management Failure? *Wildlife Society Bulletin.* Vol. 30(1), pp. 267, 269.

24. M. Dowling to R. Tougias, live interview, May 1, 2004.

25. T. Lester to R. Tougias, email correspondence, September 5, 2004.

26. T. Lester to R. Tougias, email correspondence, June 1, 2004

27. M. Dowling to R. Tougias, email correspondence, April 10, 2004.

28. M. Dowling to R. Tougias, live interview, May 1, 2004.

29. T. Lester to R. Tougias, telephone interview by author, February 26, 2008.

30. M. Dowling to R. Tougias, email correspondence, August 15, 2004.

31. H. McGinnis to R. Tougias, live interview, May 2, 2004.

32. T. Lester to R. Tougias, email correspondence, July 9, 2008.

33. A. Wydeven to R. Tougias, personal letter, June, 1998.

CHAPTER 4

1. Young, S.P. and E.A. Goldman. 1946. *The Puma: Mysterious American Cat*. Washington, DC: American Wildlife Inst., p. 17.

2. R. Hussler to R. Tougias, telephone interview by author, August 27, 2004.

3. R. Hussler to R. Tougias, telephone interview by author, August 28, 2004.

4. R. Hussler to R. Tougias, telephone interview by author, August 27, 2004.

5. Goodwin, G. 1932. New Records and Some Observations on Connecticut Mammals. *Journal of Mammalogy* Vol. 13 (1), pp. 36-40.

6. *Ibid.*

7. Swift, Debora. 2003. The Wildest Of All. *Hartford Courant Newspaper: Northeast Magazine*, April.

8. Sampson, B. 2004. Outdoors. *Norwich Bulletin Newspaper*, January 17, 2004.

9. P. Rego to R. Tougias telephone interview by author, April 20, 2004.

10. *Ibid.*

11. Hitchcock Collection. Vermont Historical Society, (loose folder).

12. Osgood F. 1938. The Mammals of Vermont. *Journal of Mammalogy* Vol. 19 (4), pp. 435-441, 438.

13. Spargo. 1950. *The Catamount in Vermont.* Vermont Historical Museum.

14. Hitchcock, 1983. "The Vermont Panther," speech before the Vermont Institute of Natural Sciences, Woodstock, Vermont. April 14, 1983, typescript in Doc. 290, Folder 10, "Hitchcock Panther Talks, 1958-1984" Hitchcock Collection, Vermont Historical Society, p. 5.

15. Tougias, R. 1994. The Return of the Mountain Lion. *Appalachian Trailway News Magazine.* October: pp. 22-24.

16. H. McGinnis to R. Tougias live interview, May 1, 2004.

17. State of Vermont Sighting Report Form. 2004.

18. State of Vermont Sighting Report Form. 2004.

19. S. Morse to R. Tougias, live interview, April 28, 2004.

20. Young, S.P. and E.A. Goldman. 1946. *The Puma: Mysterious American Cat.* Washington, DC: American Wildlife Inst., p.33.

21. Tome, P. 1854. *Pioneer Life, Or Thirty Years a Hunter.* Harrisburg: Aurand Press, (reprint, originally published for the author in Buffalo), p. 20.

22. Browning, M. 1942. *Forty-Four Years of the life of a Hunter, Being Reminiscences of Meshach Browning, a Maryland Hunter.* (roughly written down by himself). Revised and illustrated by E. Stabler. Winston-Salem, NC: Winston Printing Co., pp. 389-399.

23. Shoemaker, H.W. 1917. *Extinct Pennsylvania Animals: Part I, the Pennsylvania Lion or Panther* (rev. ed.) Altoona, PA: Altoona Tribune Co.

24. McGinnis, H.J. 1982. On the Trail of a Pennsylvania Cougar. *Pennsylvania Game News* Vol. 53(2), pp. 2-8.

25. Dearborn, N. 1927. An Old Record of the Mountain Lion in New Hampshire. *Journal of Mammalogy.*

26. McGinnis, H.J. 1982. On the Trail of a Pennsylvania Cougar. *Pennsylvania Game News* Vol. 53(2), pp. 2-8.

27. *Ibid.,* pp. 2-5.

28. Dearborn, N. 1927. <u>An Old Record of the Mountain Lion in New Hampshire</u>. Journal of Mammalogy.

29. McGinnis, H.J. 1982. On the Trail of a Pennsylvania Cougar. *Pennsylvania Game News* Vol. 53(2), pp. 2-8.

30. 30.Shoemaker, H.W. 1917. *Extinct Pennsylvania Animals: Part I, the Pennsylvania Lion or Panther* (rev. ed.) Altoona, PA: Altoona Tribune Co.

31. McGinnis, H.J. 1982. On the Trail of a Pennsylvania Cougar. *Pennsylvania Game News* Vol. 53(2), pp. 2-8.

32. Dearborn, N. 1927. <u>An Old Record of the Mountain Lion in New Hampshire</u>. Journal of Mammalogy.

33. McGinnis, H. 1994. "Reports of Pumas in Pennsylvania, 1890-1981," in J.W. Tischendorf and S.J. Ropski, eds. *Proceedings of the Eastern Cougar Conference*, 3-5 June 1994, Erie, Pennsylvania. Fort Collins, CO: American Ecological Research Institute, p. 115.

34. *Ibid.,* pp. 98-125.

35. C. Raithel to R. Tougias, telephone interview by author, February 22, 1997.

36. C. Brown to R. Tougias, telephone interview by author, July 13, 2009.

37. Dearborn, N. 1927. <u>An Old Record of the Mountain Lion in New Hampshire</u>. Journal of Mammalogy.

38. Cram, G. 1901. Panthers in Maine.*Forest and Stream*. Vol. 156: (3), Feb., p. 16.

39. Wright, B.S. 1972. *The Eastern Panther: A Question of Survival*. Toronto, Canada: Clark and Irwin, p. 27.

40. E. Orff to R. Tougias, email correspondence, June 17, 2005.

41. *Ibid.*

42. *Ibid.*

43. Young, S.P. and E.A. Goldman. 1946. *The Puma: Mysterious American Cat*. Washington, DC: American Wildlife Inst., p. 24.

44. *Ibid.*

45. Wright, B.S. 1972. *The Eastern Panther: A Question of Survival*. Toronto, Canada: Clark and Irwin, p.105.

46. *Ibid.*, p. 105.

47. J. Cardoza to R. Tougias, telephone interview by author, January 25, 2006.

48. Wright, B. 1973. The Cougar is Alive and Well in Massachusetts. *Massachusetts Wildlife* Vol. 24, pp. 2-8, 18-19.

49. Freeman, S. 1997. Cougars. *Springfield Republican*, March 14, 1997.

50. V. Otis to R. Tougias, telephone interview by author, May 5, 1992.

51. S. Ciberowski to R. Tougias, telephone interview by author, April 5, 1994.

52. Chupasko, J. 2004. *Pamphlet and Data*. Harvard Museum of Comparitive Zoology.

53. Chupasko, J. 2004. *The Importance of Collections for Voucher Specimens*. Poster Session, Eastern Cougar Conference, Morgantown, West Virginia, April 29, 2004.

54. Chupasko, J. 2004. *Pamphlet and Data*. Harvard Museum of Comparitive Zoology.

55. *Ibid.*

56. J. Tischendorf to R. Tougias, telephone interview by author, October 24, 2009.

57. Freeman, S. 1997. Mountain Lion Sightings Reported by Readers. *Sunday Republican*, March 23, 1997.

58. Sousa, F. All Outdoors. *Springfield Republican*, July 22, 2004.

59. R. Doiron to R. Tougias, telephone interview by author, September 16, 2004.

60. F. Sousa to R. Tougias, telephone interview by author, December 18, 2001.

61. F. Becklowski to R. Tougias, telephone interview by author, May 24, 2009.

62. Wright, B.S. 1972. *The Eastern Panther: A Question of Survival*. Toronto, Canada: Clark and Irwin, pp. 31-40.

63. Norton, A. H. 1930. *Mammals of Portland, Maine and Vicinity*. Port Society Natural History.

64. Wright, B.S. 1972. *The Eastern Panther: A Question of Survival.* Toronto, Canada: Clark and Irwin, insert.

65. Dowling, M. et al. Eastern Cougar Network. 2004. *www. easterncougarnet.org.*

66. *Ibid.*

67. *Ibid.*(actual original photo at Vermont Historical Society-Hitchcock Files)

68. Jackubus, W. 2004. Wildife Biologist, Maine Fish and Wildlife Agency. *Cougar Reports* (Jackubus' attached notes reporting incidents).

69. Kemper, K. 2004. Wildlife Biologist, Maine Fish and Wildlife Agency. *Cougars Reports.*

70. W. Jackubus to R. Tougias, telephone interview by author, September 8, 2007.

71. Young, S.P. and E.A. Goldman. 1946. *The Puma: Mysterious American Cat.* Washington, DC: American Wildlife Inst., p. 27-28.

72. *Ibid.*

73. *Ibid*

74. A. Hicks to R. Tougias, telephone interview by author, July 14, 2004.

75. A. Hicks to R. Tougias, telephone interview by author, July 16, 2004.

76. J. Close to R. Tougias, telephone interview by author, July 16, 2009.

77. Reed, 2004. Wildlife Biologist. New York department of Conservation.

78. State of New York Sighting Report Form. Attached letters and files (2003-2004).

79. *Ibid.*

80. *Ibid.*

81. *Newsletter.* 2003. Eastern Puma Research Network News.

WESTERN FRONT (CHAPTER 4)

1. Young, S.P. and E.A. Goldman. 1946. *The Puma: Mysterious American Cat.* Washington, DC: American Wildlife Inst., p. 30.

2. Reichling W. 2004. *Animal Tracker's Puma Research Group.* Lecture. Eastern Cougar Conference. Morgantown, West Virginia. April 29, 2004.

3. Young, S.P. and E.A. Goldman. 1946. *The Puma: Mysterious American Cat.* Washington, DC: American Wildlife Inst., pp. 29-30.

4. (staff writer). 1998. *Lexington Herald Newspaper.* June.

5. Nowak, R.M. 1976. *The Cougar in the United States and Canada. unpublished manuscript,* p. 190.

6. Brown, Travis. 2006. A Search for Cougars in Western Kentucky. *Journal of Service Learning In Conservation Biology. 2:12-15.*

7. Kellogg, R. 1939. Annoted List of Tennessee Mammals. *Proc. United States National Museum, Smithsonian Institute.* Vol. 86. (3051), pp. 245-303; 268.

8. Rhoades S. 1896. Contributions Zoology of Tennessee. Acadamy Natural Sciences. Philadelphia. Vol. 48, pp. 175-205; 201.

9. R. Hatcher to R. Tougias, telephone interview by author, November 21, 1994.

10. Biology Department, Union University, Jackson, Tennessee.

11. Biology Department, Union University, Jackson, Tennessee.

12. Alan Ricks, fish and game

EASTERN CANADA (CHAPTER 4)

1. Young, S.P. and E.A. Goldman. 1946. *The Puma: Mysterious American Cat.* Washington, DC: American Wildlife Inst.

2. American Wildlife Institute, Washington, D.C., pp. 40-43

3. Culver, M. 1999. *Molecular Genetic Variation, Population Structure, and Natural History of Free-Ranging Pumas (**Puma concolor**).* Ph.D. Dissertation, University of Maryland, College Park.

4. Gauthier, M. 2004. *Eastern Cougar Sightings: Myth or Reality?* Poster Session. Eastern Cougar Conference. Morgantown, West Virginia. April 28, 2004.

5. Bertrand, A. 2004. *Eastern Cougar Sightings: Myth or Reality?* Poster Session. Eastern Cougar Conference. Morgantown, West Virginia. April 28, 2004.

6. Cade, L. 2004. *Report On Panthers*. New Brunswick, Canada: Department of Natural Resources and Energy.

7. Tischendorf, J. 2004. *Wildlife and Puma Tracking Workshop*, Lecture. Eastern Cougar Conference. Morgantown, West Virginia. May 1, 2004.

8. Tischendorf, J. *Evaluating Puma Reports: art, science, objectivity, and diplomacy*. Lecture. Eastern Cougar Conference. Morgantown, West Virginia. May 1, 2004.

9. P. Mills to R. Tougias, email correspondence, September 2, 2002.

10. Andersen, L. *Cougar Report*. unpublished manuscript.

11. S. Kenn to R. Tougias, email correspondence, December 16, 2008

CHAPTER 5

1. Downing, R. 1996. "The Cougar in The East," in J.W. Tischendorf and S.J. Ropski, eds. *Proceedings of the Eastern Cougar Conference*, 3-5 June 1994, Erie, Pennsylvania. Fort Collins, CO: American Ecological Research Institute, pp. 163-166.

2. Lawson, J. 1959. "History of North Carolina," in S.P.Young and E.A. Goldman, *The Puma: Mysterious American Cat*. NY, NY: Dover Publications (reprint), p. 37.

3. Audubon, J. 1851. *Viviparous Quadrupeds of North America*, NY, NY, Vols. 1 and 2.

4. Bolgiano, C. 1995. *Mountain Lion: An Unnatural History of Puma and People*. Mechanicburg, PA, p. 175.

5. Downing, R. 1984. The Search for Cougars in the Eastern United States. *Cryptozoology* Vol. 3, pp. 31-49.

6. Humphreys, C. 1996. *Panthers of the Coastal Plains*. Fig Tree Press, pp. 1- 40.

7. D. Rabon to R. Tougias, email correspondence, January 15, 2004.

8. Young, S.P. and E.A. Goldman. 1946. *The Puma: Mysterious American Cat.* Washington, DC: American Wildlife Inst., pp. 23-24.

9. Young, S.P. 1959. "The Puma, Mysterious American Cat. Part I: Its History, Life Habits, Economic Status, and Control," in S.P.Young and E.A. Goldman, *The Puma: Mysterious American Cat.* NY, NY: Dover Publications (reprint), p. 24.

10. G. Therres to R. Tougias, telephone interview by the author, September 13, 2004.

11. *Ibid..*

12. G. Therres to R. Tougias, email correspondence, September 20, 2004.

13. (2004 Maryland Cougar Report File Attachment)

14. G. Therres to R. Tougias, email correspondence, September 23, 2004.

15. 2001 Maryland Cougar Report File Attachment

16. McGinnis, H. 1992. *Unpublished Manuscript.*

17. D. Linzey to R. Tougias, telephone interview by author, September 16, 2009.

18. D. Linzey to R. Tougias, telephone interview by author, October 1, 2005.

19. Harvey, C. 2004. National Park Employee. (unpublished information forwarded from McGinnis)

20. R. Reynolds to R. Tougias. Telephone interview by author, November 12, 2008.

21. D. Linzey to R. Tougias, telephone interview by author, October 1, 2004.

22. D. Linzey to R. Tougias, telephone interview by author, October 1, 2004.

23. Reynolds, R. 2004. Wildlife Biologist, Virginia Department of Game and Inland Fisheries. (information prepared for Helen McGinnis of ECF)

24. McGinnis, H. 1992. *Unpublished Manuscript.*

25. *http://groups.yahoo.com/groups/easterncougar*

26. McGinnis, H. 1992. *Unpublished Manuscript.*

27. Nowak, R.M. 1976. *The Cougar in the United States and Canada.* unpublished, p. 97.

28. *Ibid.,* p. 190.

29. *Ibid.*

30. McGinnis, H. 1992. *Unpublished Manuscript.*

31. D. Linzey to R. Tougias, telephone interview by author, October 1, 2005.

32. Nowak, R.M. 1976. *The Cougar in the United States and Canada.* unpublished, p. 190.

33. Highlands Voice. Cougars Stage Comeback? *West Virginia Highlands Conservancy,* Nov. 1980, Vol. 12(9).

34. Lester, T. 2003. *Unpublished Notes.*

35. T. Lester to H. McGinnis, forwarded email to author, December 11, 2004.

36. McGinnis, H. 1990. *Unpublished Manuscript.*

37. T. Lester to R. Tougias, telephone interview by author, March 7, 2004.

38. *Ibid.*

39. *Ibid*

40. D. Maehr to R. Tougias, live interview, April 29, 2004.

41. Audubon, J. 1851. *Viviparous Quadrupeds of North America,* NY, NY, Vols. 1 and 2.

42. *Ibid.*

43. Young, S.P. and E.A. Goldman. 1946. *The Puma: Mysterious American Cat.* Washington, DC: American Wildlife Inst., p. 37.

44. Nowak, R.M. 1976. *The Cougar in the United States and Canada.* unpublished, p. 98.

45. McGinnis, H. 2007. *Unpublished Manuscript.*

46. Boyanoski, J. 2003. Panther Reports Put Maudlin On Watch. *The Greenville News,* October 18, 2003.

47. *Ibid.*

48. M. Culver to R. Tougias, telephone interview by author, April, 2004.

THE SOUTHERN STATES (CHAPTER 5)

1. Young, S.P. and E.A. Goldman. 1946. *The Puma: Mysterious American Cat*. Washington, DC: American Wildlife Inst., p. 18.
2. *Ibid.*, p.19.
3. The listserv address is > *http://groups.yahoo.com/group/ easterncougar/*>
4. Young, S.P. and E.A. Goldman. 1946. *The Puma: Mysterious American Cat*. Washington, DC: American Wildlife Inst., p. 25.
5. *Ibid.*
6. Howell. A 1921. *A Biological Survey of Alabama. North American Fauna. Biological Survey* Washington, DC: United States Department of Agriculture, Vol. 45, pp. 41-42.
7. Young, S.P. and E.A. Goldman. 1946. *The Puma: Mysterious American Cat*. Washington, DC: American Wildlife Inst., p. 12.
8. H. McGinnis to R. Tougias, live interview, May 1, 2004.
9. McGinnis, H. 1988. *Search for Puma Tracks on Dirt Roads in the National Space Technology Laboratories and Mississippi Army Ammunition Plant Sites and the Surrounding Easement Area in Hancock County, Mississippi*. Final Report to the Mississippi Wildlife Heritage Fund, pp. 12-15.
10. *Ibid.*, pp.12-17.
11. Carter, C. and R. Rummel. 1980. *Status of the Florida Panther in Mississippi: Preliminary Report*. Jackson, MS: Mississippi Museum of Natural History, unpublished, pp. 1-11.

CHAPTER 6

1. S. Paren to R. Tougias, personal letter, March 12, 2001.
2. G. Warren to R. Tougias, telephone interview by author, July 1, 1996.
3. Vermont Fish and Wildlife Agency Cougar Report Forms, 1993-1995.
4. Vermont Fish and Wildlife Agency Cougar Report Forms, 1993-1995.

5. Vermont Fish and Wildlife Agency Cougar Report Forms, 1993-1995.
6. Vermont Fish and Wildlife Agency Cougar Report Forms, 1993-1995.
7. Vermont Fish and Wildlife Agency Cougar Report Forms, 1993-1995.
8. Vermont Fish and Wildlife Agency Cougar Report Forms, 1993-1995.
9. C. Alexander to R. Tougias, telephone interview by author, September, 1994.
10. C. Alexander to R. Tougias, telephone interview by author, September, 1994.
11. S. Paren to R. Tougias, telephone interview by author, November 5, 2001.
12. Altherr, T. 1996. "The Catamount in Vermont Folklore and Culurture, 1760-1900," in J.W. Tischendorf and S.J. Ropski, eds. *Proceedings of the Eastern Cougar Conference*, 3-5 June 1994, Erie, Pennsylvania. Fort Collins, CO: American Ecological Research Institute, pp. 50-91.
13. *Ibid.*, p. 60.
14. H. Ernest to R. Tougias, telephone interview by author, July 11, 2004.
15. (There is a misconception that the specimen tested as canine.)
16. J. McCarter to R. Tougias, telephone interview by author, April 27, 2001.
17. *Ibid.*
18. *Ibid.*
19. Ernest, H. 2000. DNA Sampling and Research Techniques. *Outdoor California*. May-June. Vol. 61(3), pp. 20-21.
20. M. Culver to R. Tougias, telephone interview by author, April, 2001.
21. Boyce, W., and H. Ernest, "DNA Identification of Mountain Lions Involved in Livestock Predation and Public Safety Incidents," in T.P. Salmon and A.C. Crabb, Eds. *Proceedings of the 19th Vertebrate Pest Conference*. Davis, CA: University of California. pp. 290-294.

22. H. Ernest to R. Tougias, telephone interview by author, January 23, 2002.

23. Ernest, H. 2000. DNA Sampling and Research Techniques. *Outdoor California.* May-June. Vol. 61(3), pp. 16-19.

24. H. Ernest to R. Tougias, telephone interview by author, January 23, 2002.

25. Young, S.P. and E.A. Goldman. 1946. *The Puma: Mysterious American Cat.* Washington, DC: American Wildlife Inst., p. 39.

26. Culver, M. et al. 2000. Genomic Ancestry of the American Puma (*Puma concolor*). *Genetics.* Vol. 91, pp. 186-197.

27. Culver, M. 2004. *Puma Phylogeography and How Genetics Is Applied to Identifying Eastern Pumas.* Lecture, Eastern Cougar Conference, Morgantown, West Virginia. April 29, 2004.

28. Chupasko, J. 2004. *The Importance of Collections for Voucher Specimens.* Poster Session, Eastern Cougar Conference, Morgantown, West Virginia. April 28, 2004.

29. M. Culver to R. Tougias, live interview, April 29, 2004.

30. Culver, M. et al. 2000. Genomic Ancestry of the American Puma (*Puma concolor*). *Genetics.* Vol. 91, pp. 186-197.

31. D. Maehr to R. Tougias, personal letter, January 9, 2001.

32. With the passing of time, certain rumors have clouded the understanding of the Craftsbury scat testing. In recent articles some authors have mistakenly reported that the scat was tested for DNA and was shown to be canine. It is the author's understanding (and personal memory) that this is not true. The scat that was tested was the wrong sample, and the proper sample had been discarded. It is also the opinion of the author that initially authorities show excitement over evidence, but almost always back-peddle on it with the absence of subsequent news.

33. Cardoza, J. 2002. The Eastern Cougar: A Management Failure? *Wildlife Society Bulletin.* Vol. 30(1), p. 268.

CHAPTER 7

1. Dowling, M. *et al.* 2004. Eastern Cougar Network. *www. easterncougarnet.org*
2. *Ibid.*
3. R. Bischof to R. Tougias, telephone interview by author, December 20, 2004.
4. Dowling, M. *et al.* 2004. Eastern Cougar Network. *www. easterncougarnet.org*
5. M. Heck to R. Tougias, telephone interview by author, December 20, 2003.
6. J. Tischendorf to R. Tougias, email correspondence, March 12, 2004.
7. J. Tischendorf to R. Tougias, email correspondence, March 15, 2004
8. D. Maehr to R. Tougias, personal letter, February 10, 2002.
9. Lowery, G.H. Jr. 1974 *The Mammals of Louisiana and its Adjacent Waters.* Baton Rouge: Louisiana State University.
10. R. Staffon to R. Tougias, telephone interview by author, February 6, 2004.
11. D. Litchfield to R. Tougias, telephone interview by author, October 22, 2003.
12. E. Borgess to R. Tougias, telephone interview by author, October 23, 2003.
13. Thompson, S. 1974. Sight Record of a Cougar in Ontario, *Canadian Field Naturalist*, pp. 88-87.
14. Bowles, J. E. Heist, and A. Woolf. 2001. Transactions of the State Academy of Science Record of a North American *Puma concolor* from Southern Illinois. Vol 4, pp. 227-229.
15. A. Woolf to R. Tougias, telephone interview by author, March 14, 2004.
16. D. Hamilton to R. Tougias, telephone interview by author, February 7, 2004.
17. M. Dowling to R. Tougias, live interview, May 1, 2004.
18. W. Heatherly to R. Tougias, telephone interview by author, April 17, 2004.

19. Dowling, M. et al. 2004. Eastern Cougar Network. *www. easterncougarnet.org*

20. T. Lester to R. Tougias, telephone interview by author, September 16, 1998.

21. M. Culver to R. Tougias, telephone interview by author, November 12, 2004.

22. Dowling, et al. 2004. Eastern Cougar Network. *www. easterncougarnet.org*

23. R. Andrews to R. Tougias, telephone interview by author, January 5, 2004.

24. Clayton, Chris. 2003. *World-Herald Bureau Newspaper.* September 30, 2003.

25. R. Andrews to R. Tougias, telephone interview by author, January 5, 2004.

26. H. McGinnes to R. Tougias, email correspondence, November 9, 2009.

27. T. Lester to R. Tougias, telephone interview by author, November 12, 1998.

28. T. Lester to R. Tougias, telephone interview by author, November 12, 1998.

29. S. Blanchard to R. Tougias, telephone interview by author, June 11,1998.

30. Scottish Big Cat Trust. http://www.bigcats.org/abc/realcats/index.html

31. A. Wydeven to R. Tougias, personal letter, March 12, 1995.

32. Bolgiano, C. 1995. *Mountain Lion: An Unnatural History of Puma and People.* Mechanicburg, PA: p. 175-187.

33. Greenwell, R. 1996. "The Place of the Puma in the Natural History of the Larger Felids," in J.W. Tischendorf and S.J. Ropski, eds. *Proceedings of the Eastern Cougar Conference*, 3-5 June 1994, Erie, Pennsylvania. Fort Collins, CO: American Ecological Research Institute, pp. 9-17.

34. Bolgiano, C. 1995. *Mountain Lion: An Unnatural History of Puma and People.* Mechanicburg, PA: pp. 163-187.

35. J. Cardoza to R. Tougias, telephone interview by author, December 5, 2003.

36. H. McGinnes to R. Tougias, email correspondence, Dec.1 2008

37. *Ibid.*

38. Bolgiano, C. 2001. Important Confirmation: Spotted Cougar Kitten Killed in Kentucky. (Excerpted letter from Steve Thomas, Wildlife Biologist, Kentucky Department of Fish and Game) Eastern Cougar Foundation Newsletter, Summer.

39. *Ibid.*

40. W. Stone to R. Tougias, telephone interview by author, May, 1996.

41. H. McGinnes to R. Tougias, email correspondence, October 29, 2003.

42. *Ibid.*

43. H. McGinnes to R. Tougias, live interview, April 29, 2004.

44. Dowling, M. et al. 2004. Eastern Cougar Network. *www. easterncougarnet.org*

45. M. Dowling to R Tougias, email correspondence Oct. 1 2004.

CHAPTER 8

1. J. Lutz to R. Tougias, telephone interview, April 6, 2002. (Lutz documented 37% of credible reports as melanistic in some areas.)

2. Lutz, J and l. Lutz. 1996. "The Eastern Puma," in J.W. Tischendorf and S.J. Ropski, eds. *Proceedings of the Eastern Cougar Conference*, 3-5 June 1994, Erie, Pennsylvania. Fort Collins, CO: American Ecological Research Institute, pp. 127-138.

3. *Ibid.*

4. Altherr, T. 1996. "The Catamount in Vermont Folklore and Culurture, 1760-1900," in J.W. Tischendorf and S.J. Ropski, eds. *Proceedings of the Eastern Cougar Conference*, 3-5 June 1994, Erie, Pennsylvania. Fort Collins, CO: American Ecological Research Institute, pp. 50-91.

5. Wright, B.S. 1972. *The Eastern Panther: A Question of Survival.* Toronto, Canada: Clark and Irwin, pp.121-123.

6. Foster, K. A Higher Than Expected Frequency of Melanism in Isolated Populations of Vertebrates and its Implications. *http://home.fuse.net/rschaffner/melanism.html* December 16, 2003, pp.1-3

7. Coleman, L. 1994. "Reports of Large Black Felids and Circus Train Wrecks," in J.W. Tischendorf and S.J. Ropski, eds. *Proceedings of the Eastern Cougar Conference*, 3-5 June 1994, Erie, Pennsylvania. Fort Collins, CO: American Ecological Research Institute, p. 191.

8. *Ibid.,* p. 190.

9. D. Holmes to R. Tougias. 2004. (Senior animal keeper, Glenn Oak Zoo, wishes to retract 1994 statement; thinks he may have been misquoted, saying he now believes it was a rare case of an exotic escapee.)

10. Wright, B.S. 1972. *The Eastern Panther: A Question of Survival.* Toronto, Canada: Clark and Irwin, p.124.

11. T. Gola to R. Tougias, personal letter, December 5, 2003.

12. Evland, T. 1990. *The ISC Newsletter* Vol. 9(3), pp. 9-10.

13. H. McGennis to R. Tougias, email correspondence, November 3, 2003.

14. Thompson, W.1896. *Great Cats I Have Met: Adventures in Two Hemispheres.* Alpha Publishing Co.

15. Belden, R. *et al.* "Florida Panther Distribution," in *The Florida Panther Conference*, Dennis B. Jordan, Ed. Fort. Myers, FL. November 1-3, 1994. pp. 2-3.

16. 16.Foster, K. A Higher Than Expected Frequency of Melanism in Isolated Populations of Vertebrates and its Implications. *http://home.fuse.net/rschaffner/melanism.html* December 16, 2003, pp.1-4

17. *Ibid.,* pp. 3-4.

18. Tischendorf J. and D. Mc Alpine, 1995. A Melanistic Bobcat from Outside Florida. *Florida Field Naturalist.* Vol. 23(1), pp. 13-14.

19. Foster, K. A Higher Than Expected Frequency of Melanism in Isolated Populations of Vertebrates and its Implications.

http://home.fuse.net/rschaffner/melanism.html December 16, 2003, p. 4

20. *Ibid.*
21. *Ibid.*
22. *Ibid.*
23. Barnes, C. 1960. *The Cougar or Mountain Lion.* Salt Lake City, Utah: The Ralton Co., p. 33.
24. Taylor, S. 1996. *Florida Panther Biomedical Investigation.* Annual Performance Report, July 1, 1996, p.5.
25. P. Rusz to R. Tougias, live interview, May 1,2004
26. *Ibid.*
27. Scott, F. 1996. "Updated Status Report on Eastern Populations of the Cougar or Puma, *Felis concolor couguar,*" in *Canada.* Wolfville, Nova Scotia: Acadia University, Department of Biology, p. 2.

CHAPTER 9

1. Downing, R. 1996. "Investigation to Determine the Status of Cougar in the Southern Appalachians," in J.W. Tischendorf and S.J. Ropski, eds. *Proceedings of the Eastern Cougar Conference,* 3-5 June 1994, Erie, Pennsylvania. Fort Collins, CO: American Ecological Research Institute, pp. 46-49.
2. Cardoza, J. 2002. The Eastern Cougar: A Management Failure? *Wildlife Society Bulletin.* Vol. 30(1), pp. 265-273.
3. *Ibid.*
4. Brocke, R. 1981. *Reintroduction of Cougar **Felis concolor** in Adirondack Park: A Problem Analysis and Recommendations.* Federal Aid Endangered Species Project e-1-3, Final Report. New York State Department of Environmental Conservation, Albany, New York.
5. V. Fifield to R. Tougias, telephone interview by author, December 13, 1992.
6. J. Tischendorf to R. Tougias, telephone interview by author, September 22, 2008.
7. J. Cardoza to R. Tougias, telephone interview by author, August 8, 2004.

8. *Ibid.*

9. P. Rego to R. Tougias, telephone interview by author, August 7, 2004.

10. G. Donavan to R. Tougias, telephone interview by author, November 12, 1998.

11. D. Kimbal to R. Tougias, telephone interview by author, December 11, 2003.

12. S. Van Arsdale to R. Tougias, email correspondence, April 10, 2004.

13. S.Van Arsdale to R. Tougias, personal letter, May 6, 2004.

14. S. Van Arsdale to R. Tougias, personal letter, April 11, 2004.

15. Cardoza, J. 2002. The Eastern Cougar: A Management Failure? *Wildlife Society Bulletin.* Vol. 30(1), pp. 270-273.

16. T. Gola to R. Tougias, telephone interview by author, January 5, 2004.

17. G. Parker to R. Tougias, personal letter, November 29, 2004.

18. S. Morse to R. Tougias, live interview, April 28, 2004.

19. M. Clark to R. Tougias, telephone interview by author, October 15, 1999.

20. M. Clark to R. Tougias, telephone interview by author, October 24, 1999.

21. M. Clark to R. Tougias, telephone interview by author, October 15, 1999.

22. C. Bontaites to R. Tougias, telephone interview by author, November 2, 1999.

23. C. Bontaites to R. Tougias, telephone interview by author, December 12, 1999.

24. Hoagland, E. 1973. "Hailing the Elusory Mountain Lion," in *Walking The Dead Diamond River.* NY, NY: Random House. pp. 46-67.

25. McGinnis, H. *False Reports in Pennsylvania.* Eastern Cougar Foundation (unpublished notes). 1985-2004.

26. Van Dyke, F., and R.H. Brocke. 1987. Sighting and Track Reports as Indicies of Mountain Lion Presence. *Wildlife Society Bulletin* Vol.15, pp. 251-256.

27. Pike, J.R., et al.1999. A Geographic Analysis of the Status of Mountain Lions in Oklahoma. *Wildlife Society Bulletin.* Vol. 27, pp. 4-11.

28. Tougias, R. 1992. Eastern Mountain Lion: legend or mythical beast? *Fur-Fish-Game Magazine.* November/ December. pp. 35-37.

29. "Fisher-Animal Fact Sheet." *http://www.zoo.org/educate/ fact_sheets/fisher/fisher.htm* December 15, 2004.

30. W. Jakubus to R. Tougias, telephone interview by author, June 9, 2008.

31. Hall, K. 2004. *Vermont Fish and Game Information Fact Sheet.*

32. Tougias, R. 1994. The Return of the Mountain Lion. *Appalachian Trailway News Magazine.* October: pp. 22-24.

33. Cardoza, J. 2002. The Eastern Cougar: A Management Failure? *Wildlife Society Bulletin.* Vol. 30(1), pp. 265-273.

34. T. French to R. Tougias, telephone interview by author, November 10, 2004.

35. A. Hicks to R. Tougias, telephone interview by author, August 29, 2008.

CHAPTER 10

1. The Great New England Sea Serpent, June Pusbach O Neil, Down East Publishing,Camden, Maine, August,1999.

2. http://news.mongabay.com/2007/0929-hance_vietnam. html

3. Poston, L. WWF. May, 2010.

4. Associated Press. April 17, 2008. "Extinct" Soft Shelled Turtle Found in Vietnam.

5. BBC News. September, 2006. New Rare Bird Spotted In India.

6. http://tahrcountry.blogspot.com /2009_04_01_archive. html

7. http://news.mongabay.com/2008/0312-hance_hippo.html

8. Tougias, R. 2010. *The New London Day Newspaper*, Bird's Eye View (archived)

9. *Ibid*

10. Fort Collins Research Institute, 2010. Meeting Challenges of Black-footed Ferret. Institute Research Article.

11. Hess, K. 2009. Saving the Black-footed Ferret. *The Thoreau Institute.* No32.

12. Galliger, T. 2006. The Grail Bird: The Re-discovery of the Ivory-billed Woodpecker. Houghton Mifflin.

13. *Ibid*

14. *Ibid*

15. Cornell Lab of Ornithology to Robert Tougias, telephone interview by author, September, 2009.

16. Cornell lab of Ornithology to Robert Tougias, telephone interview by author, October 3, 2009.

17. Florida Audubon Corkscrew Swamp Staff to Robert Tougias, live interview by author, November, 2009.

18. Galliger, T. 2006. The Grail Bird: The Re-discovery of the Ivory-billed Woodpecker. Houghton Mifflin.

19. Ghost Bird. National Geographic. December, 2006.

20. Cardoza, J. 2002. The Eastern Cougar: A Management Failure? *Wildlife Society Bulletin.* Vol. 30(1), pp. 265-273.

21. Lutz, J. *Eastern Puma Research Network Newsletter.* Summer 2004.

22. Cardoza, J. 2002. The Eastern Cougar: A Management Failure? *Wildlife Society Bulletin.* Vol. 30(1), pp. 265-273.

23. Lutz, J. *Eastern Puma Research Network Newsletter.* Fall 2004.

24. H. Ernest to R. Tougias, telephone interview by author, June 9, 2004.

25. Bauer, J. *et al.* 2003. "Puma Activity and Movements in Human-Dominated Landscape; Cuyamaca Rancho State Park and adjacent lands in southern California," in S. Becker, D. Bjornlie, F. Linzey, and D. Moody, eds., *Proceedings of the Seventh Mountain Lion Workshop.* 15 – 17 May 2003. Lander, Wyoming .

26. York, E., R. Sauvajot, and S. Riley. 2003. "Mountain Lion Movements and Persistence in a Fragmented, Urban Landscape in Southern California," in S. Becker, D. Bjornlie, F. Linzey, and D. Moody, eds., *Proceedings of*

the Seventh Mountain Lion Workshop. 15 – 17 May 2003. Lander, Wyoming .

27. Shaw, H. 1996. "The Cougar in the West," in J.W. Tischendorf and S.J. Ropski, eds. *Proceedings of the Eastern Cougar Conference,* 3-5 June 1994, Erie, Pennsylvania. Fort Collins, CO: American Ecological Research Institute, p. 162.

28. Belden, R. "Florida Panther Investigation – A Progress Report," in R.R. Odum and L. Landers, eds., *Proceedings of the Rare and Endangered Wildlife Symposium, Technical Bulletin WL4,* 1978. Department of Natural Resources, Athens, GA, pp. 123-133.

29. Belden, R. 1997. "If You See A Panther." *Florida Wildlife.* Vol. 31, pp. 31-34.

30. Fergus, C. 1991. "The Florida Panther Verges on Extinction." *Science.* Vol. 251, pp. 1178-1180.

31. D. Maehr to R. Tougias, email correspondence, September 12, 2004.

32. Rusz, P. 2001. *The Cougar in Michigan: Sightings and Related Information.* Technical Publication. Bath, MI: Bengal Wildlife Center, pp. 1-15.

33. Fecske, D. *et al.* 2004. *Distribution and Abundance of Cougars in the Black Hills of South Dakota and Wyoming.* Lecture. Eastern Cougar Conference. Morgantown, West Virginia. April 29, 2004.

34. Fecske, D. 2003. *Distribution and Abundance of Cougars in the Black Hills of South Dakota and Wyoming.* Ph.D. Dissertation. Dakota State University. Madison, South Dakota.

35. J. Wrede to R. Tougias, email correspondence, May 21, 2004.

36. Downing, R. 1996. "The Cougar in the East ," in J.W. Tischendorf and S.J. Ropski, eds. *Proceedings of the Eastern Cougar Conference,* 3-5 June 1994, Erie, Pennsylvania. Fort Collins, CO: American Ecological Research Institute, p. 164.

37. J. Tischendorf to R. Tougias, personal letter, February 10, 2004.

38. *Ibid.*

39. Brocke, R. 1985. Eastern Cougars: The Verifiability of the Presence of Isolated Individuals versus Populations. *Cryptozoology.* Vol. 4, pp. 31-49.

40. J. Tischendorf to R. Tougias, email correspondence, March 3, 2010.

41. D. Maehr to R. Tougias, email correspondence, September 13, 2004.

42. J. Lutz to R. Tougias, telephone interview by author, August 29, 2004.

43. *State of Vermont Sighting Report Form.* 2004.

44. Scott, F. 1996. "Updated Status Report on Eastern Populations of the Cougar or Puma, *Felis concolor couguar,* in *Canada,* Wolfville, Nova Scotia: Acadia University, Department of Biology, p. 2.

45. R. Brocke to R. Tougias, telephone interview by author, October 15, 2003.

46. Cardoza, J. 2002. The Eastern Cougar: A Management Failure? *Wildlife Society Bulletin.* Vol. 30(1), pp. 265-272.

47. R. Brocke to R. Tougias, telephone interview by author, October 15, 2003.

48. *Ibid*

49. Barnhurst, D. and F. Lindzey. 1989. Detecting Female Mountain Lions With Kittens. *Northwest Science.* Vol. 63, pp. 35-37.

50. Germaine, S. and K. Bristow. 1997. "Mountain Lion Kill Rates, Habitat Use, and Feeding Behavior," in *Southern Arizona. Final Report.* Arizona Game and Fish, pp. 2-17.

51. Hansen, K. 1992. *Cougar: The American Lion.* Flagstaff, AZ: Northland.

52. Barnhurst, D. and F. Lindzey. 1989. Detecting Female Mountain Lions With Kittens. *Northwest Science.* Vol. 63, pp. 35-37.

53. Van Dyke, F. and R. Brocke. 1986. Use of Road Track Counts as Indices of Mountain Lion Presence. *Journal of Wildlife Management.* Vol. 50, pp. 107-109.

54. *Ibid.,* pp. 102-109.

55. Brocke, R. 1996. "The Prognosis For Cougar Restoration in Northern North America: Inferences From A Feasibility Study," in J.W. Tischendorf and S.J. Ropski, eds. *Proceedings of the Eastern Cougar Conference,* 3-5 June 1994, Erie, Pennsylvania. Fort Collins, CO: American Ecological Research Institute, pp. 239-241.

56. Van Dyke, F. and R. Brocke. 1986. Use of Road Track Counts as Indices of Mountain Lion Presence. *Journal of Wildlife Management.* Vol. 50, pp. 107-109.

57. Downing, R. 1996. "Investigation to Determine the Status of the Cougar in the Southern Appalachians," in J.W. Tischendorf and S.J. Ropski, eds. *Proceedings of the Eastern Cougar Conference,* 3-5 June 1994, Erie, Pennsylvania. Fort Collins, CO: American Ecological Research Institute, pp. 46-49.

58. Bolgiano, C, *et al.* 2003. "Field Evidence of Cougars in Eastern North America," in L.A. Harveson, P.M. Harveson and R.W. Adams, eds., *Proceedings of the Sixth Mountain Lion Workshop,* Austin, Texas. pp. 34-39

59. J. Lutz to R. Tougias, telephone interview by author, August 29, 2004.

60. Van Dyke, F. and R. Brocke. 1987. Sighting and Track Reports as Indicies of Mountain Lion Presence. *Wildlife Society Bulletin.* Vol. 15, pp. 251-256.

61. Harveson, P.M. Harveson, and R.W. Adams, eds. *Proceedings of the Sixth Mountain Lion Workshop,* Austin, Texas.

62. Van Dyke, F and R. Brocke. 1987. Searching Technique for Mountain Lion Sign at Specific Locations. *Wildlife Society Bulletin.* Vol. 15, pp. 256-259.

CHAPTER 11

1. Rusz, P. 2001. *The Cougar in Michigan: Sightings and Related Information*. Technical Publication. Bath, MI: Bengal Wildlife Center, pp. 1-15.
2. Lee, J. The Task: Confirm Cougar Sightings. *Green Bay Press Gazette*. Sports section. January 12, 2003.
3. P. Rusz to R. Tougias, telephone interview by author, September 10, 2003.
4. P. Rusz to R. Tougias, live interview, April 28, 2004.
5. Rusz, P. 2004. *Evidence of Cougars in Michigan*. Lecture. Eastern Cougar Conference. April 29, 2004. Morgantown, West Virginia.
6. *Ibid*.
7. P. Rusz to R. Tougias, telephone interview by author, March 12, 2004.
8. P. Rusz to R. Tougias, telephone interview by author, March 12, 2004.
9. Cougar Management: Recommendations for the Management of the Cougar in Michigan. *The Wildlife Volunteer* May-June 2003, p. 6.
10. B. Swanson to R. Tougias, telephone interview by author, July 22, 2004.
11. Flesher, J. 2001. Cougars Living In Both Peninsulas, Tests Show. *Grand Rapids Press,* November 11, 2001.
12. Carney, T. 2004. *Michigan Cougars and Voodoo Science*. Lecture. Eastern Cougar Conference. May 1, 2004.
13. Statements from audience, Eastern Cougar Conference. May 1, 2004.
14. Carney, T. 2004. *Michigan Cougars and Voodoo Science*. Lecture. Eastern Cougar Conference. May 1, 2004.
15. *Ibid*.
16. P. Rusz to R. Tougias, telephone interview by author, March 20, 2004.
17. Swanson, B. telephone interview by author, July 22, 2004.
18. Rusz, P and Swanson, B. Detection of Cougars Using Low Copy DNA Sources. American Midland Naturalist. 155, p.363-372.

19. *Ibid*

20. *Ibid*

21. Kurta, A. *et al.* Does a Population of Cougars Exist in Michigan. American Midland Naturalist.158, p. 463-471.

22. Dittberner, D. 2004. Hunters Dispute Claim of Cougars in State. *Michigan Outdoor News.* June 6, 2004, p. 20.

23. *Ibid.,* p.19.

24. *Ibid.,* p.18.

25. M. Guntzville to R. Tougias, telephone interview by author, December 6, 2004.

26. Miller, K. *et al.* Eastern Cougar Network website *www. easterncougarnet.org.*

27. Rusz, P. 2004. *Methods for Detecting Pumas in the Great Lakes Region.* Lecture. Eastern Cougar Conference. April 29, 2004. Morgantown, West Virginia.

28. Rusz, P. 2001. *The Cougar in Michigan: Sightings and Related Information.* Technical Publication. Bath, MI: Bengal Wildlife Center, pp. 1-15.

29. Rusz, P. Evidence of Cougars in Michigan. Lecture. Eastern Cougar Conference. April 29, 2004. Morgantown, West Virginia.

30. P. Rusz to R. Tougias, telephone interview, October 14, 2004.

31. Richey, D. 2002. If Cougars Exist in Lower Peninsula USFS Consider Them Endangered. *The Detroit News* October 6, 2002.

32. *Ibid.*

33. *Ibid.*

34. *Ibid.*

35. P. Rusz to R. Tougias, telephone interview, February 4, 2004.

36. Virtual Visitor Center. Sleeping Bear Dunes National Park. www.nps.gov/slbe/home.htm

37. Carney, T. "National Park Service Posts Cougar Warning Signs in Sleeping Bear Dunes." Michigan Outdoor News. November 28, 2003.

38. Richey, D. 2002. If Cougars Exist in Lower Peninsula USFS Consider Them Endangered. *The Detroit News* October 6, 2002.

39. *Ibid.*

40. Rusz, P. 2004. *Methods for Detecting Pumas in the Great Lakes Region.* Lecture. Eastern Cougar Conference. April 29, 2004. Morgantown, West Virginia.

41. *Ibid.*

42. P. Rusz to R. Tougias, personal letter, November 12, 2003.

43. P. Rusz to R. Tougias, live interview, April 28, 2004.

44. Michigan Department of Natural Resources (anonymous biologist), telephone interview by author, June 8, 2004.

45. *Ibid*

46. M.Dowling to R. Tougias, email correspondence, May 10, 2005

47. eNature. National Wildlife Federation. *www.eNnature. com*

48. P. Rusz to R. Tougias, live interview, April 28, 2004.

49. P. Rusz to R. Tougias, live interview, April 29, 2004.

50. Rusz, P. 2001. *The Cougar in Michigan: Sightings and Related Information.* Technical Publication. Bath, MI: Bengal Wildlife Center, pp. 1-15.

51. *Ibid.*

52. *ibid*

CHAPTER 12

1. Baron, D. 1999. Wild in the Suburbs: Mountain Lion Attacks Rising. *Boston Globe Newspaper, Sunday Magazine,* August 22, 1999, p.12.

2. *Ibid.*

3. J.Halfpenny to R. Tougias, telephone interview by author, August 3, 2004.

4. M. Wethje to R. Tougias, telephone interview by author, July 15, 2004.

5. C. Dorrough to R. Tougias, telephone interview by author, January 7, 2003.

6. Torres, S. *et al.* 1996. Mountain Lion and Human Activity in California: Testing Speculations. *Wildlife Society Bulletin.* Vol. 24, pp. 451-460.

7. *Ibid.*

8. Baron, D. 2004. *The Beast in the Garden.* W.W.Norton.

9. Cullens, L., S. Reed, and C. Papouchis. 2003. "Depredation Trends," in S. Becker, D. Bjornlie, F. Lindzey and D. Moody, eds., *Proceedings of the Seventh Mountain Lion Workshop.* 15-17 May 2003. Lander, Wyoming, p. 166.

10. J.Halfpenny to R. Tougias, telephone interview by author, August 4, 2004.

11. *Ibid.*

12. Maehr, D. et al. 2003. Eastern Cougar Recovery is Linked to the Florida Panther: Cardoza and Langlois Revisited. *Wildlife Society Bulletin.* Vol. 31(3), pp. 849-853.

13. *Ibid*

14. Van Dyke, F. *et al.* 1986. Reactions of Mountain Lions to Logging and Human Activity. *Journal of Wildlife Management.* Vol. 50, pp. 95-102.

15. *Ibid.*

16. *Ibid.*

17. *Ibid.*

18. United Sates Department of Agriculture Forest Service, northern region.Treesearch,2002.

19. Davis, R. 1996. "Giving the Eastern Cougar a Second Chance: A Feasibility Study of Reintroducing the Cougar (*Puma concolor*) into Allegheny National Forest," in J.W. Tischendorf and S.J. Ropski, eds. *Proceedings of the Eastern Cougar Conference*, 3-5 June 1994, Erie, Pennsylvania. Fort Collins, CO: American Ecological Research Institute, pp. 243-245.

20. Struhsacker, P. 2004. *Securing a Future for Gray Wolf Recovery in the Northeastern United States.* Lecture. Eastern Cougar Conference. Morgantown, West Virginia. April 29, 2004.

21. Davis, R. 1996. "Giving the Eastern Cougar a Second Chance: A Feasibility Study of Reintroducing the Cougar

(*Puma concolor*) into Allegheny National Forest," in J.W. Tischendorf and S.J. Ropski, eds. *Proceedings of the Eastern Cougar Conference*, 3-5 June 1994, Erie, Pennsylvania. Fort Collins, CO: American Ecological Research Institute, pp. 243-245.

22. *Ibid.*

23. *Ibid*

24. Brocke, R. The Prognosis for Cougar Restoration in Northern North America – Inferences From A Feasibility Study," in J.W. Tischendorf and S.J. Ropski, eds. *Proceedings of the Eastern Cougar Conference*, 3-5 June 1994, Erie, Pennsylvania. Fort Collins, CO: American Ecological Research Institute, p. 241.

25. Brocke, R. 1981. *Reintroduction of Cougar **Felis concolor** in Adirondack Park: A Problem Analysis and Recommendations.* Federal Aid Endangered Species Project e-1-3, Final Report. New York State Department of Environmental Conservation, Albany, New York.

26. *Ibid.*

27. Ibid

28. Cardoza, J. 2002. The Eastern Cougar: A Management Failure? *Wildlife Society Bulletin*. Vol. 30(1), pp. 265-273.

29. J. Halfpenny to R. Tougias, live interview, August 28, 2004.

30. G. Parker to R. Tougias, email, May 12, 2010.

31. S. Morse to R. Tougias, live interview, August 28, 2004

32. McGinnis, H. 2004. *Eastern Cougar Files. unpublished.*

33. J. Tischendorf. 2004. *Discussion Panel* Moderator. Eastern Cougar Conference. April 29, 2004. Morgantown, West Virginia.

34. Van Dyke, F. *et al.* 1986. Reactions of Mountain Lions to Logging and Human Activity. *Journal of Wildlife Management*. Vol. 50, pp. 95-102.

35. J. Wrede to R. Tougias, email correspondence, May 21, 2004.

36. Rusz, P. 2001. *The Cougar in Michigan: Sightings and Related Information.* Technical Publication. Bath, MI: Bengal Wildlife Center, pp. 1-15.

37. Fecske, D. 2004. *Distribution and Abundance of Cougars in the Black Hills of South Dakota and Wyoming.* Lecture. Eastern Cougar Conference. Morgantown, West Virginia. April 29, 2004.

CHAPTER 13

1. United States Fish and Wildlife Service. 1982. *Eastern Cougar Recovery Plan.* United States Fish and Wildlife Service. Atlanta, Georgia.

2. Tischendorf, J. 2004. *The Jaguar in the Southwest: Implications for Puma Recovery in Eastern North America.* Lecture. April 29, 2004. Eastern Cougar Conference. Morgantown, West Virginia.

3. Kelly, M. et al. 2003. Eastern Cougar Recovery is Linked to the Florida Panther: Cardoza and Langlois Revisited. *Wildlife Society Bulletin.* Vol. 31(3), p. 850.

4. Larkin, J. 2001. *Large Mammal Restoration: Ecological and Sociological Considerations in the 21st Century.* Washington, DC: Island Press, pp. 42-45.

5. Tietjen, M. 2004. Lyme Disease: A Plea to Doctors. *http://weholdthesetruths.org*

6. Sheley, G. 1998. Mountain Lion: Attacks Still Rare, But Just in Case. *Backwoods Home Magazine.* March/April. p. 22.

7. Tischendorf, J. 2004. *The Jaguar in the Southwest: Implications for Puma Recovery in Eastern North America.* Lecture. April 29, 2004. Eastern Cougar Conference. Morgantown, West Virginia.

8. Baron, D. 1999. Wild in the Suburbs: Mountain Lion Attacks Rising. *Boston Globe Newspaper, Sunday Magazine,* August 22, 1999, p.12.

9. Bush, R. 2004. *The Cougar Almanac: Natural History of the Mountain Lion.* NY, NY: The Lyons Press. pp. 45-52.

10. Struhsacker, P. 2004. *Securing a Future for Gray Wolf Recovery in the Northeastern United States.* Lecture. Eastern Cougar Conference. April 29, 2004. Morgantown, West Virginia.

11. Duda, M. and K. Young. 1995. *Floridianians' Knowledge, Opinions and Attitudes toward Panther Habitat and Panther-related Issues: Public Opinion Survey Results Report.* Report for the Advisory Council on Environmental Education. Responsive Management, Mark Damian Duda and Associates, Inc., Harrison, Virginia.

12. H. McGinnis to R Tougias, live interview, May 1, 2004.

13. Larkin, J. 2001. *Large Mammal Restoration: Ecological and Sociological Considerations in the 21st Century.* Washington, DC: Island Press, pp. 293-300.

14. *Ibid.*

15. Duda, M. and K. Young. 1995. Floridians' Knowledge, Opinions and Attitudes toward Panther Habitat and Panther-related issues: public opinion survey results report. Report for the Advisory Council on Environmental Education. Responsive Management, Mark Damian Duda and Associates, Inc., Harrison, Virginia.

16. Duda, M. and K. Young. 1995. *Floridianians' Knowledge, Opinions and Attitudes toward Panther Habitat and Panther-related Issues: Public Opinion Survey Results Report.* Report for the Advisory Council on Environmental Education. Responsive Management, Mark Damian Duda and Associates, Inc., Harrison, Virginia.

17. Pittman,C. 2004. Panthers May be Moving North: Some Experts Think Female Cats Should Be Moved to Help Establish a Colony in Central Florida. *St. Petersburg Times.* January 2, 2004.

18. Lacy, R, and D. Maehr. 2002. Avoiding the Lurking Pitfalls in Florida Panther Recovery. *Wildlife Society Bulletin.* Vol. 30, pp. 971-978.

19. Black, M. 1994. "Public Attitudes Toward Mountain Lion (*Felis concolor*) and Their Implications for Education about the Eastern Panther," in J.W. Tischendorf and S.J. Ropski,

eds. *Proceedings of the Eastern Cougar Conference*, 3-5 June 1994, Erie, Pennsylvania. Fort Collins, CO: American Ecological Research Institute, pp. 222-224.

20. Brocke, R., K. Gustapson, and A. Major. 1990. Restoration of Lynx in New York: Biopolitical Lessons. *Transactions of the North American Wildlife and Natural Resources Conference* Vol. 55, pp. 590-598.

21. Hansen, K. 1992. *Cougar: The American Lion*. Flagstaff, AZ: Northland, p. 47.

22. Black, M. 1994. "Public Attitudes Toward Mountain Lion (*Felis concolor*) and Their Implications for Education about the Eastern Panther," in J.W. Tischendorf and S.J. Ropski, eds. *Proceedings of the Eastern Cougar Conference*, 3-5 June 1994, Erie, Pennsylvania. Fort Collins, CO: American Ecological Research Institute, pp. 222-223.

23. *Ibid.,* pp. 222-224.

24. *Ibid.,* pp. 222-224.

25. Danz, H. 1999. *Cougar!* Athens, GA: Ohio University, Swallow Press.

26. *Ibid.*

27. Bush, R. 2004. *The Cougar Almanac: Natural History of the Mountain Lion*. NY, NY: The Lyons Press. pp. 55-60.

28. Pelley, J. 2000.Quantifying Benefits of Biodivirsity Could Help Prevent Extinction. *Environmental Science and Technology.* Vol. 34(9), pp. 205-206.

29. Bishop, R. and M. Welsh. 1992. Existence Values in Benefit Cost Analysis and Damage Assessments. *Land Economics.* Vol. 69, p. 405.

30. J. Cardoza to R. Tougias, telephone interview by author, June 11, 2004.

31. Tietenburg, T. 1993. *Environmental and Natural Resource Economics.* NY, NY: Norton, p. 87.

32. T. Stevens to R. Tougias, personal letter (with literature), March 22, 2002.

33. Tietenburg, T. 1993. *Environmental and Natural Resource Economics.* NY, NY: Norton, pp. 45-89.

34. Glass, R., T. More, and T. Stevens. 1990. "Public Attitudes, Politics and Extramarket Values for Reintroduced Wildlife: Examples from New England," in *Transactions of the 55th North American Wildlife and Natural Resources Conference.* pp. 548-557

35. T. Stevens to R. Tougias, personal letter, February 15, 2004.

36. Black, M. 1994. "Public Attitudes Toward Mountain Lion (*Felis concolor*) and Their Implications for Education about the Eastern Panther," in J.W. Tischendorf and S.J. Ropski, eds. *Proceedings of the Eastern Cougar Conference,* 3-5 June 1994, Erie, Pennsylvania. Fort Collins, CO: American Ecological Research Institute, pp. 222-223.

37. D. Dale to R. Tougias, telephone interview, December 10, 2004.

38. Larkin, J. 2001. *Large Mammal Restoration: Ecological and Sociological Considerations in the 21st Century.* Washington, DC: Island Press, pp. 395-397.

39. *Ibid.,* pp. 293-296.

40. Cox, J. 2001. "Returning Elk to Appalachia: Foiling Murphy's Law," in Larkin, J. 2001. *Large Mammal Restoration: Ecological and Sociological Considerations in the 21st Century.* Washington, DC: Island Press, pp. 101-107.

41. Maehr, D. 2001. "The Florida Panther: A Flagship for Regional Restoration," in Larkin, J. 2001. *Large Mammal Restoration: Ecological and Sociological Considerations in the 21st Century.* Washington, DC: Island Press, p. 293.

42. Larkin, J. 2001. *Large Mammal Restoration: Ecological and Sociological Considerations in the 21st Century.* Washington, DC: Island Press, pp. 293-345.

43. Struhsacker, P. 2004. *Securing a Future for Gray Wolf Recovery in the Northeastern United States.* Lecture. Eastern Cougar Conference. April 29, 2004. Morgantown, West Virginia.

44. Morrison, M. 2002. *Wildlife Restoration: Techniques for Habitat Analysis and Animal Monitoring.* Washington DC: Island Press. pp.19, 21-22.

45. Larkin, J. 2001. *Large Mammal Restoration: Ecological and Sociological Considerations in the 21st Century.* Washington, DC: Island Press, pp. 42-52.
46. Leopold, A. 1980. *A Sand County Almanac.* NY, NY: Ballantine.
47. Pressey, R. L and J. Cowling. 2001. Reserves Selection and Algorithms and the Real World. *Conservation Biology* Vol. 15, pp. 275-277.

CHAPTER 14

1. Kitchener, A. 1991. *The Natural History of the Wildcats.* Ithaca, NY: Cornell University Press, pp. 65-99.
2. Harveson, L.A. 1997. *Ecology of a Mountain Lion Population in Southern Texas.* Ph.D. Dissertation, Texas A&M Univ., Kingsville, Texas. (Note: there are other factors besides prey density that determine range size, such as ambush and stalking sites.)
3. Hansen, K. 1992. *Cougar: The American Lion.* Flagstaff, AZ: Northland, p. 27.
4. *Ibid.*
5. Logan, K.A. 1983. *Mountain Lion Population and Habitat Characteristics in Big Horn Mountains of Wyoming.* M.S. thesis. University of Wyoming, Laramie.
6. Hansen, K. 1992. *Cougar: The American Lion.* Flagstaff, AZ: Northland, p. 12.
7. *Ibid.*
8. Danz, H. 1999. *Cougar!* Athens, GA: Ohio University, Swallow Press, pp. 51-54.
9. Bush, R. 2004. *The Cougar Almanac: Natural History of the Mountain Lion.* NY, NY: The Lyons Press, pp. 77-90.
10. Hansen, K. 1992. *Cougar: The American Lion.* Flagstaff, AZ: Northland, p. 12.
11. Hemker, T.P. *et al.* 1986. "Survival of Cougar Cubs in a Non-Hunted Population," in Pages S.D. Miller and D.D. Everett, eds., *Cats of the World: Biology Conservation and Management,* Washington, DC: National Wildlife Federation, pp. 327-332.

12. D. Maehr to R. Tougias, personal letter, February 12, 2002.

13. Greenwell, R. and J. Tischendorf. *The Jaguar in the Southwest: Implications for Puma Recovery in Eastern North America*. Lecture. Eastern Cougar Conference, April 29, 2004. Morgantown, West Virginia.

14. *Ibid.*

15. Danz, H. 1999. *Cougar!* Athens, GA: Ohio University, Swallow Press, pp. 44-46.

16. Young, S.P. and E.A. Goldman. 1946. *The Puma: Mysterious American Cat*. Washington, DC: American Wildlife Inst., p. 69.

17. Bush, R. 2004. *The Cougar Almanac: Natural History of the Mountain Lion*. NY, NY: The Lyons Press. pp. 88-140.

18. J. Tischendorf to R. Tougias, live interview, May 1, 2004.

19. D. Maehr to R. Tougias, personal letter, February 12, 2002.

20. Young, S.P. and E.A. Goldman. 1946. *The Puma: Mysterious American Cat*. Washington, DC: American Wildlife Inst., pp. 83-93.

21. *Ibid.*

22. McGinnis, H. 2004. Eastern Cougar Foundation – notes and references (unpublished).

23. Young, S.P. and E.A. Goldman. 1946. *The Puma: Mysterious American Cat*. Washington, DC: American Wildlife Inst., pp. 88-90.

24. *Ibid.*, p. 87.

25. *Ibid.*, p. 88.

26. Hansen, K. 1992. *Cougar: The American Lion*. Flagstaff, AZ: Northland, p. 45.

27. D. Maehr to R. Tougias, personal letter, February 12, 2002.

28. Bush, R. 2004. *The Cougar Almanac: Natural History of the Mountain Lion*. NY, NY: The Lyons Press. pp. 88-140.

29. D. Maehr to R. Tougias, personal letter, February 12, 2002.

30. Bush, R. 2004. *The Cougar Almanac: Natural History of the Mountain Lion*. NY, NY: The Lyons Press. pp. 88-100.

31. J. Halfpenny to R. Tougias, telephone interview, August 28, 2004.

32. Hornocker, M. 1970. An Analysis of Mountain Lion Predation Upon Mule Deer and Elk in the Idaho Primitive Area. *Wildlife Monographs*. Vol. 21, pp. 1-39.

33. H. McGinnis to R. Tougias, email correspondence, December 28, 2004.

34. Hansen, K. 1992. *Cougar: The American Lion*. Flagstaff, AZ: Northland, pp. 43-46.

35. Hansen, K. 1992. *Cougar: The American Lion*. Flagstaff, AZ: Northland, p. 44.

36. Bush, R. 2004. *The Cougar Almanac: Natural History of the Mountain Lion*. NY, NY: The Lyons Press. pp. 88-140.

37. Danz, H. 1999. *Cougar!* Athens, GA: Ohio University, Swallow Press, p. 59.

38. Torres, S. 1997. *Mountain Lion Alert: Safety for Pets, Landowners, and Outdoor Adventurers*. Falcon Guide Press, pp. 44-70.

39. There are cases where small groups of puma have been observed together.

40. Young, S.P. and E.A. Goldman. 1946. *The Puma: Mysterious American Cat*. Washington, DC: American Wildlife Inst., p. 87.

41. Laundre,J.W and L. Hernandez. 2008. The Amount of Time female Pumas Spend With Their Kittens. Wildlife Biology 14(2) pp221-227.

CHAPTER 15

No notes for this chapter.

CHAPTER 16

1. Cardoza, J. 2002. The Eastern Cougar: A Management Failure? *Wildlife Society Bulletin*. Vol. 30(1), pp. 267, 269.

2. Swift, Debora. 2003. The Wildest Of All. *Hartford Courant Newspaper: Northeast Magazine*, April.

3. Lacy, R, and D. Maehr. 2002. Avoiding the Lurking Pitfalls in Florida Panther Recovery. *Wildlife Society Bulletin.* Vol. 30, pp. 971-978.

4. Downing, R. 1984. The Search for Cougars in the Eastern United States. *Cryptozoology* Vol. 3, pp. 31-34.

5. Bolgiano, C, *et al.* 2003. "Field Evidence of Cougars in Eastern North America," in L.A. Harveson, P.M. Harveson and R.W. Adams, eds., *Proceedings of the Sixth Mountain Lion Workshop*, Austin, Texas. pp. 34-39.

6. Westrum, R. 1982. Social Intelligence About Hidden Events. *Knowledge: creation, diffusion, utilization.* Vol.3. No.3. March, pp. 381-382.

7. *Ibid.,* pp. 381-400.

8. *Ibid.,* pp. 383-395.

9. Ball Lightning, Multiple Personality Disorder, and Attention Deficit Disorder were all observable but unrecognizable phenomena. In the case of Child Abuse it was not until physicians were convinced by shared information, often from subordinates, that the discovery process began. The physicians unknowingly stifled the information in child abuse cases, as radiologists pointed out in vain repeated injuries in certain families. Estimates of these disorders were initially low but later turned out significant. They demonstrate how something can remain unproven, the process through which it does, and yet be very much present.

10. Bolgiano, C, *et al.* 2003. "Field Evidence of Cougars in Eastern North America," in L.A. Harveson, P.M. Harveson and R.W. Adams, eds., *Proceedings of the Sixth Mountain Lion Workshop*, Austin, Texas. pp. 34-39

11. Culver, M. *et al.* 2000. Genomic Ancestry of the American Puma (*Puma concolor*). *Genetics.* Vol. 91, pp. 186-197.